PELICAN BOOKS

A928

THE GRAMMAR SCHOOL

Robin Davis was born at Canterbury in 1916 and educated at Simon Langton Grammar School, Canterbury. Having won a scholarship to Sidney Sussex College, Cambridge, he gained a first in both parts of the Classical Tripos, trained for the teaching profession at the Cambridge University Department of Education and then taught for a short time at Nottingham High School. During the war he served with the Royal Artillery in North Africa, Sicily and Italy and then, as an Intelligence staff officer, in Egypt, Greece and Austria. Since 1946 he has been on the staff of Merchant Taylors' School, Northwood, where he is a day-boy housemaster and teaches classics and Russian. He is a chief examiner for London University General Certificate of Education, moderator in classics for the Associated Examining Board, and serves on the Advanced Level Sub-Committee of the Schools Council. He is author and co-author (with E. C. Kennedy) of several classical textbooks, including *Two Centuries of Roman Poetry* (Macmillan).

Robin Davis is married, with a son and a daughter. His hobbies are music, gardening and amateur psephology.

D1080728

THE GRAMMAR SCHOOL

ROBIN DAVIS

'The grammar school will be abolished
over my dead body' – The Prime Minister, in 1964

'Sheffield, Coventry and Wolverhampton
are stuck with grammar schools . . .'
Anthony Sampson, *Anatomy of Britain*

*Nosse volunt omnes, mercedem
solvere nemo* – Juvenal
('All want to learn, but none to
pay the bill')

PENGUIN BOOKS

Penguin Books Ltd, Harmondsworth, Middlesex, England
Penguin Books Inc., 3300 Clipper Mill Road, Baltimore, Md 21211, U.S.A.
Penguin Books Australia Ltd, Ringwood, Victoria, Australia

—

First published 1967
Copyright © Robin Davis, 1967

—

Made and printed in Great Britain by
C. Nicholls & Company Ltd
Set in Monotype Times

FOR KEITH

CONTENTS

CONTENTS

ACKNOWLEDGEMENTS

THE debt, in a book of this kind, to a wide variety of sources is enormous. A list of nearly two hundred references on pages 271–7 and some others in the text give only some idea of its extent, and to all there mentioned I acknowledge my indebtedness both for the use of their quotations and references and for the part they have played in shaping my ideas. Several people, in giving permission to quote from or refer to their works, have added their encouragement to me in my task. To these I owe a special word of thanks: not only have their letters cheered me through the 'doldrums periods' of writing, but they have also strengthened my belief that this book, whatever its shortcomings, needed writing. To the University of London School Examinations Department I am especially grateful for permission to quote statistics of theirs not generally available to the public, and to the Oxford and Cambridge School Examinations Board for permission to quote the specimen questions on page 185. Special thanks are also due to, among others, Mr G. W. Shield, headmaster of Mexborough Grammar School and Sixth-Form College; Mr G. R. Long, headmaster, and Mr John Perrett, senior housemaster of Tulse Hill Comprehensive School; and Mr S. W. B. Watson, headmaster, and Mr Antony Cobb, careers master of Mellow Lane Comprehensive School, Hayes, for allowing me to see their schools in action and supplying copious information about them. Then there is a more intangible debt that has no chapter and verse: to my wife, for preparing the index; to friends and colleagues and former colleagues scattered strategically over the English educational scene, for the help they have given me, not always consciously, through discussion; and to the boys of Merchant Taylors' School, who are a constant reminder, should I ever be tempted to forget, that education is primarily about people.

One final word. I well remember, as a schoolboy in the thirties, buying my first Penguin, price sixpence. Since then Penguin Books have become an international bank of information and

ACKNOWLEDGEMENTS

culture on which I have drawn heavily. This small in-payment is long overdue. In making it I am deeply grateful to the editor assigned to me by Penguin Books Ltd, whose insistence on anonymity I reluctantly respect, for always being a patient and constructive critic and in the process broadening the education of a schoolmaster and sharpening his wits. The faults of the book are nobody else's, least of all his, but entirely my own. The views expressed are personal to me, and the governors, headmaster and colleagues at the school which employs me are in no sense responsible for them.

INTRODUCTION

TEN years ago this book would probably never have been written. Grammar schools then were their own justification; if they did not exist, as one headmaster put it, they would have to be invented. Fifteen or twenty years ago it might have been, but for reasons so different as to result in a totally different book. It is essential to understand why the grammar school, in pre-war years one of the most firmly established of British institutions, has thus fluctuated in its fortunes and public esteem since the Education Act of 1944 if we are to grasp the full significance of the new challenge to its existence today, this time on grounds more fundamental and far-reaching.

One indirect effect of the 1944 Education Act, with its promise of secondary education for all, was that the grammar school suffered a partial eclipse. There were several reasons for this. The abolition of fees in all state schools had the result that people who hitherto had been content to pay the modest fees charged by grammar schools now became suspicious of what was offered free – a Victorian habit of mind lamented by Matthew Arnold a century before (see page 62). Such people preferred either to stretch their purses to afford education in the independent fee-paying schools (the emotive term 'public schools' is largely avoided in this book for reasons which will be explained later) or, if this was not possible, accepted a grammar school education with a reluctant, half-guilty attitude that did its public image little good. Meanwhile the grammar schools were receiving children of a new kind of parent who had before been precluded by the cost of the fees, but such parents were at first naturally somewhat reserved and sceptical about a form of education which they did not fully understand and had rarely experienced themselves. At the same time a determined effort was being made by the authorities to build up the reputation of the new secondary modern schools and give them 'parity of esteem' as an alternative path of secondary education. Every effort was made to remove the aura of 'failure' from them, and, though many of them had an unhappy start by being housed in the same buildings as the old senior elementary schools, local authorities strove wherever possible to give them new buildings and equipment, and much was made of the opportunity here offered to mould a form of training suited to the needs of the child and unfettered by traditional syllabuses and examinations. Beside this the grammar schools seemed, and often looked (for they came at the end of the queue for buildings) decidedly musty.

A book on the grammar schools during the late forties would thus have needed to give reassurance on two points. First, that they were now doing as well, if not better, 'free' what they had formerly done for fees, and that their aims and methods were similar to those of the independent fee-paying schools; and secondly, for the benefit of their new clientele, that the pursuit of academic learning, including apparently useless subjects like Latin and algebra, was well worthwhile, and doubly so if they would allow the potential breadwinners of sixteen or seventeen to stay on and pursue their studies to advanced or even university level.

In the event, however, the grammar schools needed no such advocate. Sheer economic necessity drove an increasing number of middle-class parents to turn to them as the fees in independent schools mounted. Time and good teaching brought their rewards in examination successes, and the universities, quick to spot a new source of talent, went more than half way to encourage applications from the brighter grammar school pupils. The increasing proportion of these who found their way to Oxford and Cambridge, often at the expense of rejected applications from independent schools, was a sign of the times in the early fifties. Latin, algebra and other academic subjects became promoted to status symbols of success and milestones on the high-road to a coveted professional career. Meanwhile all had not been well in the secondary modern schools. The child, it was discovered, is father of the man, and as reluctant to work without the stimulus of examinations as are most adults without the incentive of pay. Some of them started courses for the General Certificate of Education, and the recent development of the Certificate of Secondary Education, with a syllabus and standard better suited to the needs of secondary modern schools, is a step in the same direction. All this, however, only seemed further to vindicate the achievement of the grammar schools; and anyone who, in the mid fifties, sought a justification of the grammar schools would have received a brusque answer – *Si monumentum requiris, circumspice.*

But this very success caused misgivings. Only about a quarter of the children of secondary age in Britain find their way to grammar schools; the rest, classified as less intelligent, go to secondary modern schools. Public conscience had been stirred, in a less sensitive age, by the existence of a 'submerged tenth' of the population living in poverty and misery. Small wonder that the spectacle, in the twentieth century, of what amounted in educational terms to a 'submerged three quarters' should not go unchallenged. Protest against this situation has taken many forms, but concentrates chiefly on two lines of attack. First, it is a manifest social injustice that three quarters of all children of this age group should be rejected as inferior in any sense; and secondly, in what is now recognized as a time of technological revolution it is a gloomy prospect if only a quarter of Britain's children are intelligent enough to be educated for active participation in it. Objections have focused even more powerfully on the machinery of selection that produces such a result, the so-called Eleven Plus examination. No doubt it is true that this test was originally intended to guide children into the form of education for which they were best suited, not to grade them as passes and failures, and that parents who talk, as some still do, of 'winning a scholarship to grammar school' and 'failing the 11-plus' exaggerate the difficulty through ignorance. But this is merely to argue over a form of words. The tests, for all that has been done in the cause of fairness and objectivity, have proved fallible and been seen to be so. There is much in the argument that they take place too early. Worse still, they are subordinated to administrative feasibility. Even if it were possible to agree upon a national grade that qualifies for a grammar school place, actual grant of places varies from county to county and town to town according to the availability of such places: in Bootle 11·9 per cent of thirteen-year-old pupils get to grammar schools, in Merthyr

Tydfil 40·3 per cent.* Hence a growing objection to the whole process of selection at eleven; and inevitably much of the odium has rubbed off on its main beneficiaries, the grammar schools. The situation was thus summed up in the Crowther Report [22]† published in 1959: 'Once it is agreed, as more and more people are coming to believe, that it is wrong to label children for all time at eleven, the attempt to give mutually exclusive labels to the schools to which they go at that age will have to be abandoned.' Meanwhile the well-publicized growth of comprehensive schools, which dispense with the selection process altogether, has added to the charge that the 11-plus is unjust the further one that it is unnecessary. It is also claimed for the comprehensive school that by educating all children in its neighbourhood it is socially as well as educationally comprehensive, while the grammar school is socially exclusive, has a middle-class ethos, and forces working-class children to conform to alien values or remain outsiders. In this context, amid the claims of some politicians that comprehensive schools provide a grammar school education for all, while a group of young comprehensive schoolmasters pronounce their obituary on the grammar schools – 'an anachronism, although they had done a good job for the limited few in the past' [35] – the new challenge to the grammar schools appears formidable indeed.

The fate of the grammar schools involves the whole question of secondary school organization, and whether it should be comprehensive or on traditionally selective lines. The importance of this question is self-evident, but perhaps three points should be stressed. First, education demands a large and increasing share of the National Product, and every responsible citizen will want to know how his money is being spent, both centrally as taxes and locally as rates. In this field the secondary sector is expensive enough as it is, and to be effective reorganization on comprehensive lines demands a vast rebuilding programme: the case for it needs to be proved conclusively before such expenditure is embarked on. Secondly, most parents are anxious to give their children the best possible chance in life, and here what happens at

* *Secondary Education in Each Local Authority Area*, Ministry of Education List 69, January 1962.

†Figures in square brackets relate to the References, pages 271–7.

the secondary stage is crucial. Thoughtful parents will not be content to leave it to the experts, whoever they may be. Finally, it is an uncomfortable fact, of which we are constantly reminded, that Britain, a country of fifty million packed in a small island, must live by her brains. The vital question, closely involved with the comprehensive issue, is whether we can increase quantity of brain-power without sacrifice of quality; whether in effect we should listen to the proverbial encouragement of 'the more the merrier' or the don who warned that 'more means worse'; and whether, as yet, we have enough evidence to decide.

At this point the reader may well object that though he accepts the importance of this issue and the need for an informed and objective judgement about it he quickly gets lost among the technicalities and jargon of educationists. Here a sketch-map, as it were, of the terrain may help. By definition a grammar school is a school that teaches grammar (originally Latin grammar), but in common usage it has come to mean a secondary school providing an academic course, usually from ages 11 to 18. A brief study of the origins, character and growth of the historical grammar school will show how the one has developed from the other; while a review of modern experiments in comprehensive education in this country, with its shorter history but more varied pattern, will bring into focus the precise nature of the present challenge to it. Most people know that the comprehensive issue now divides the two major political Parties and that reorganization on comprehensive lines is Government policy. But unlike an issue such as the nationalization of steel it lacks the sharp outlines of a straight fight. When Sir Edward Boyle, the Conservative spokesman on Education, says that he is not against comprehensive schools and would not withdraw the Government Circular on reorganization [47], the reader may wonder what issue divides them, or whether they are shadow-boxing. This we shall examine in the third chapter, attempting to assess how the controversy became political, where the Parties stand, and the consequences at national and local level. Then, since the full weight of Government publicity has been thrown into the scales on the side of the comprehensives and against the grammar schools, we shall shift, so to speak, from sketch-map to court-room to cross-examine the comprehensive case and put the case for the grammar schools, thereby helping the thoughtful citizen to make a critical assessment of the educational creed of the New Establishment. Though the majority of grammar schools are maintained by the State there are others wholly or partially outside it. For them, too, the Government has plans, and these we shall examine in a chapter on the direct-grant and independent grammar schools. Finally, since many readers are or will eventually become parents, they may well be anxious to know where, in all these Government plans, the parent finds a place. The author shares that anxiety, and will have something to say on this issue in the last two chapters.

Why, it may well be asked, should this book be written by a working schoolmaster? The whole question of the organization of secondary education is extremely complex, and Lord James of Rusholme (himself a schoolmaster for most of his life) urged in the House of Lords its examination by an expert committee, 'for in this controversy many of the participants are simply not knowledgeable enough'. The data for its solution will not be provided by reporters breathing generalizations into a microphone against a televised background of happy children in a swimming bath. The *Anatomy of Britain* approach of the professional writer certainly goes deeper in ascertaining the facts. But the ancient Greeks knew a great deal about human anatomy while failing to discover the circulation of the blood or the existence of bacilli, and most of them believed the heart was the seat of the intellect. Similar misconceptions can easily arise if a study of education goes no deeper than anatomy. Educationists, experts though they are in their own specialist subjects, run the risk of having lost touch with the children, if they ever had it. Her Majesty's Inspectors might seem a more promising source, for they are all former teachers and well informed by a wide range of educational experience. But their terms of employment preclude the writing of books (except official reports) or addressing the general public; their wisdom is for official ears only, and this, however devious the channels, means eventually the Minister. But he is a politician and therefore, in the present political context, committed. Headmasters, impressive witnesses as they are, are generally too busy and somewhat predisposed to champion the kind of school in which they have chosen to serve. So the question 'Why a schoolmaster?' must be answered by another, 'Who else?'. Failing the appointment of an expert committee, a schoolmaster who is in daily contact with boys of all classes (for the school where he serves 'integrated' itself, at least to some extent, some twenty years ago, while still preserving its independence) may perhaps venture to make the attempt.

Northwood,   A.R.D.
April 1967.

CHAPTER ONE

THE GRAMMAR SCHOOL TRADITION

WHEN we say that a ballad or tune is *traditional*, we usually mean that we do not know who wrote it, or very much about its origins. The same is true, to some extent, of the grammar school: the institution existed long before the first record, in Latin or English, of its name, and we cannot say with any certainty to whom it owes its birth. All the same, it is possible to speak of a grammar school tradition, and in it we can trace three elements.

First, independence. Initiative for the foundation of these schools came not from the State, but from individuals and, later, groups of people with a common purpose. The State played no part in the affairs of the grammar school until the second half of the nineteenth century, and founded no 'county grammar schools' of its own until the twentieth. Even today many of these schools retain a measure of independence and some, misleadingly called 'public schools', retain it completely.

The second element is scholarship. Grammar schools have always served as a bridge to the university, though not all pupils crossed it. At first their curriculum was narrowly classical, but it has since broadened to embrace a wide range of advanced studies, latterly in particular in the field of mathematics and science. Always, however, their aim has been a high standard of intellectual attainment, and this has been self-perpetuating. Many who owed their education to these schools have returned to them as teachers and helped to maintain their academic excellence – many who, in other countries, might well have become university teachers. Two practical effects of this tradition of scholarship are very much in evidence today. The academic standards of these schools make possible shorter university courses in Britain than elsewhere, and their former pupils, especially in the sphere of science or technology, are much in demand through their having a head start on pupils of the same age in other countries – hence the so-called 'brain drain'. Moreover, the quality of grammar school sixth forms compels the comprehensive schools that claim to supplant them to match their distinction here, and to do this they must be large establishments. Both the 'brain drain' and the mammoth size of comprehensive schools are a direct consequence of the tradition of scholarship in the British grammar school.

Thirdly, grammar schools have always been selective. Nowadays selectivity, except when applied to a gear-box or an employment tax, is an unfashionable concept. But this should not blind us to the fact that the historical grammar school has been unashamedly selective in two respects. It selected those who were prepared to pay for the education it gave, using its endowments to help where there was need, and of this it claimed, through its statutes, to be the arbiter. But, it was not merely a question of having the money to pay the fees. The grammar schools felt that they offered a kind of education from which not everyone could profit, and they retained the right to control their intake by some form of entrance qualification, however simple, and to remove those who were unable or unwilling to profit from what they had to give.

All these elements in the grammar school tradition today are already eroded or powerfully threatened. The State has built many of its own 'county grammar schools', severely curtailed the independence of many more, and established a Public Schools Commission to integrate within itself those whose independence is still intact. Standards of scholarship are put at risk by the demand to broaden their intake in tune with the comprehensive principle. Their selective character was removed, in the matter of fees, by the abolition of fee-paying in all state secondary schools by the 1944 Education Act, and in the matter of qualitative intake they cannot satisfy the Government's demand for comprehensiveness and the abolition of selection at 11-plus. Yet we are constantly assured that all that is best in grammar school education both should be and is being preserved. It is this claim which compels a close look at the historical grammar school before considering its present predicament. Are the elements we have indicated in the grammar school tradition merely an outer shell, to be stripped away in the march of progress while the essential kernel is left none the less intact for being encapsulated within a comprehensive container? Or are they something more – the vital parts, perhaps, of an organic unity which withers as it is progressively dismembered?

It may be that the general reader, more concerned with the immediate threat to the grammar schools, will be tempted to skip this first chapter, feeling as repelled by so much history as was Lord Randolph Churchill by the 'damn dots' of the decimal system. If he does, he will find himself returning to it as questions pose themselves whose answer, at least in part, is historical; he may even become convinced of the value, before making a final judgement, of reading the whole chapter after all.

ORIGINS

The term 'grammar school' seems to have been first used in English in the form 'gramer scole' in 1387; but its Latin form, *schola grammatica*, can be found two centuries before that, and the institution itself may be said to have originated over a thousand years earlier still. When Trajan was emperor of Rome the Younger Pliny wrote (*Letters*, Book IV. 13) to his friend Tacitus, the historian, asking for his assistance in finding teachers for a school he was helping to found at his birthplace, Como:

When I was recently in my home town, the son of a fellow-townsman of mine, a lad of under sixteen, came to pay his respects. I asked him 'Are you at school?' He said he was. 'Where?' 'At Milan.' 'Why not here?' His father, who had brought the boy along himself, replied, 'Because we have no teachers here.' 'Why none? Surely it is vitally important for you fathers' (and as luck would have it several fathers were listening) 'to have your children educated here of all places. For where would they be happier to stay than at home, or kept under better control than under their parents' eyes, or more cheaply than at home? It would not be much trouble, then, to make a collection and engage teachers, adding to their pay what you now spend on lodgings, fares and expenses away from home. What's more I myself, who haven't any children yet, am ready to give a third of any sum you decide to raise. I would even promise the whole cost, but am afraid that my generosity would be abused at some time by improper use. . . . The only safeguard against this is for the parents to have the job of choosing the teachers –

they'll feel obliged to make the right choice when it touches their pockets, though they might be less bothered about other people's money.... So make up your minds, put your heads together; my encouragement should add to your spirit, and I want to be landed with the greatest possible contribution .... I hope you'll secure such distinguished teachers that neighbouring towns will look to us for their education as well.

Of the subsequent history of Pliny's school nothing is recorded; but his letter provides something like a blueprint of the grammar school as we have known it, at least up to the Education Act of 1944. Three things in particular stand out: first, the initiative in founding the school comes not from the state nor, as previously, from the teacher or teachers, but from a wealthy and public-spirited citizen. Government initiative in starting schools does not appear on any scale before the end of the nineteenth century and then reluctantly. Individuals had opened schools in Italy long before Pliny, but these were pretty ramshackle affairs. The proprietors were often enough Greek slaves or freedmen who would operate in such accommodation as they could find, commonly an open-fronted shop in a busy town centre; discipline was strict and mostly physically imposed – so Horace called his schoolmaster 'Whacker Orbilius', anticipating by nearly two thousand years the nickname 'Whacker Trench' coined for the present headmaster of Eton by his former pupils at Bradfield [1]; and the virtues of an early start, still surviving today in a few boarding schools, were insisted on, so that we read of school textbooks soiled by the soot of the tiny lamps by which pupils found their way to school through the dingy streets in the small hours, and the din of these schools from 5 a.m. onwards so disturbed the neighbours that the poet Martial, in desperation, offered to pay one such schoolmaster as much to keep quiet as the parents gave him to yell. Pliny's enterprise in starting his school at Como offered hope of better things in two ways: the third part he promised to add to the parents' contribution in fees gave some prospect of better accommodation on a less crowded site; and since he was a philanthropic citizen with wide interests as a lawyer and landowner and later as governor of a province, he could see the school in a wider context of public relations. He was in effect the first school governor, self-appointed.

The second feature of Pliny's school which foreshadows later grammar schools is the curriculum. This is not mentioned in the letter, but we know enough of other schools of those days to be sure that the main subjects of study would be linguistic and literary. The chief aim at the secondary stage in Roman education was to learn from Greek and Latin literature what lessons were there as a guide to conduct, and sufficient command of language to provide a fluent tongue for public speaking in law, politics and public life generally. Such a curriculum was narrow and limited, and one of the legitimate criticisms of the historical grammar school is that it remained thus limited for far too long, as we shall see. But the object of these studies was firmly cultural and not vocational and so, even as the curriculum broadened under the influence of men like Thring of Uppingham and Sanderson of Oundle, it has always remained and, if 'grammar school' means anything, should remain.

Thirdly, the parents were expected to pay fees. Pliny makes it quite clear that he is not offering a free school for Como; only a subsidy on a fixed proportion of the payment in fees. To the Romans there was never any doubt that education, and the cost of it, was a responsibility of the parents. Pliny could encourage and help, but to do more would be to usurp that responsibility. This attitude has always remained at the centre of the grammar school tradition, whatever the variations in the nature and extent of the subsidy, until the 1944 Education Act, when the abolition of fee-paying in all state schools made a revolutionary break, the effects and merits of which will be considered later. For the moment, however, we shall concentrate on the influence and importance of these three elements in the development of the modern grammar school.

It is no part of this book to provide a history of the grammar school from Pliny's time to the present day. Not that there is not room for one. G. M. Trevelyan has said that the Battle of Britain was won not on the playing-fields of Eton but in the grammar schools of the thirties [2] – an achievement that deserves its own historian. But a drowning man needs a lifeline, not an obituary, and believing as I do that the grammar schools are at present in that sort of peril I prefer to leave such a history to someone more scholarly and sanguine. For my purpose it is enough to distil the essence, and this I believe to lie in these three features of Pliny's school. We can then see clearly how that essence is at risk, whether it is worth preserving, and if so, how.

The three essential features of the historical grammar school, then, are foundation and subsidy by private – later too by corporate but non-state – initiative, an academic curriculum and till 1944, recognition of parental involvement and responsibility by charging fees.

'PUBLIC SCHOOLS' ARE GRAMMAR SCHOOLS

Before we consider these elements in more detail the question arises of the relationship between the grammar schools and the so-called 'public schools'. It is surprisingly little realized that the term 'public school' did not acquire its connotation of superiority until at least the beginning of the nineteenth century. The Latin form *schola publica* appears as early as the twelfth century, and in the fourteenth was commonly used of endowed grammar schools. Its English form appears first in a letter of the Privy Council in 1580: 'All such school masters as have charge of children and do instruct them either in public schools or in private houses'. The term simply distinguished grammar schools from private establishments or tuition in the home. Most of the famous schools unquestioningly thought of today as 'public schools' which were founded before the Victorian era were in origin ordinary grammar schools. Eton is described in its Foundation Statutes as a 'public and general grammar school'. Harrow was founded in 1571 as a grammar school. Thomas Sutton, founder of Charterhouse, procured in 1609 an Act of Parliament for 'the foundation of a Hospital and Free Grammar School'. Westminster began as a grammar school attached to the Collegiate Church of St Peter, Westminster – and so on. Such schools proved superior to the private institutions patronized at first by the aristocracy, and education at them had social and other advantages over upbringing at home by governess or tutor; so they started to send their sons to them much as in later times they made use of the public conveniences at Ascot and Lords when parted from their own lush loos. The reforms of Dr Arnold at Rugby altered these public grammar schools substantially in Victorian times, but as they were still called 'public schools' an increase in the popularity of boarding establishments – including many new foundations which 'from 1841 rolled off the line at the rate of about one a year for the next forty years or so' [3] – the term 'public school' acquired an aura of superiority which 'public convenience', so far denied its reforming genius, still lacks.

Moreover the expression 'public school', as well as being a historical accident, remains a semantic puzzle. To talk of attending a 'public school' before Dr Arnold is as anachronistic as 'saying that an eighteenth-century nobleman lived in the Regional Headquarters of the National Coal Board' [3]. But what does 'public school' mean since Arnold? The list of 'public schools' inquired into by the Clarendon Commission of 1861 contained only nine names: Eton, Winchester, Westminster, Charterhouse, St Paul's, Merchant Taylors', Harrow, Rugby and Shrewsbury. In 1942 Mr R. A. (now Lord) Butler, as President of the Board of Education, defined as 'public schools' those which are members of the Governing Bodies Association or Headmasters' Conference. But these comprised 218 schools, a number of which would not be readily recognized as 'public schools' in the popular sense, and in any case membership of these bodies changes from time to time. Those who wish to pursue the will-o'-the-wisp of a definition of 'public school' can do so in the first chapter of Vivian Ogilvie's book [3]. In a very tentative conclusion he finds the following characteristics:

(1) It is a class school, catering for a well-to-do clientele.

(2) It is expensive.

(3) It is non-local.

(4) It is a predominantly boarding school.

(5) It is independent of the State and local government, yet is not privately owned or run for profit.

How useful this definition is can perhaps best be seen by the fact that nothing is said anywhere about quality or efficiency as an *educational* institution, and that by changing the word 'school' to 'establishment' in (1) and (4) we have a serviceable definition of a high-class hotel. In fact the only worthwhile distinguishing characteristic in the above definition is the word 'independent' in (5). It is significant that the Headmasters' Conference, of which all acknowledged 'public schools' are members, has lately ceased to describe its member schools as 'public' and now calls them 'independent'. The plain fact is that they are all grammar schools, some good, some less good, some boarding, some day schools, and the relevant distinction between these and other grammar schools is that they have adequate funds and endowments to remain independent of the state while the others, less well endowed, have accepted state aid in one form or another and with it a government finger in their pedagogic pie.

But not only is the term 'public school' historically accidental and semantically misleading; it is also socially insidious. If the Headmasters' Conference has decided in its wisdom to let the expression die in favour of 'independent schools', there are those who are concerned to keep it alive, and for very different reasons. First there are those who cling nostalgically to it as a status-symbol, giving point to the epigram that in Britain what a man learns is less important than where he learns it. This in turn leads to an esoteric classification of 'public schools' with a bewildering built-in hierarchy. Thus a former colleague of mine, shortly after the war, heard a lady in a butcher's shop in Pinner bemoaning the fact that owing to the rise in prices and taxes she could not now send her son to a 'public school' – 'It will have to be Merchant Taylors' instead.' So too in the election of a new leader of the Conservative Party great play was made by journalists and others with the fact that neither contender came from Eton, but Mr Heath from a grammar school and Mr Maudling from a 'minor public school'. The present Minister of Education, whose job it is to know better, goes even further: he classifies Merchant Taylors', among others, as a *very* minor public school ([4] – the italics are the Minister's). By what process Merchant Taylors', an independent grammar school of some six hundred boys with a respectable position in the 'Oxford and Cambridge scholarships league table' merits the epithet 'minor' is a mystery too esoteric for a mere schoolmaster to fathom. Better perhaps the good lady of Pinner who did not rank it as a 'public school' at all.

At the other end of the scale are those who welcome this hier-archic nonsense as a vehicle of eventual destruction. Thus in a House of Commons debate early in 1965 one Labour member, while urging the Minister to hasten action to integrate the 'public schools' into the state system, hoped that such integration would involve the complete abolition of fee paying and also the public ownership of the land and all assets and buildings of the schools concerned [5]. The Minister gave a shrewdly evasive answer, but realizes that he has a considerable and vociferous 'tail' among his supporters for whom nothing short of outright abolition will do. To these the term 'public schools' is a godsend. The Chairman of the Headmasters' Conference entitled an article on the subject [6] 'Making Public Schools Public' – a ready-made slogan for abolitionists. But change this to something more semantically realistic – 'Making Independent Schools Dependent' – and the result is a much less vote-catching proposition, while at the same time being a good deal nearer the truth. The term 'public school' is thus little more than a smoke screen masking snobbery and fed by hostile action, and one that has little place in a book that aims to be factual and objective. For me these schools are independent grammar schools, or 'independent schools' for short. It is ironical that as I return to the main theme of this chapter, the essence of the grammar school tradition, the source to which I am most heavily indebted for a wide range of informa-tion is a book entitled *The English Public School*! [3]

FOUNDATION BY INDIVIDUAL AND CORPORATE BENEFACTION

Though many grammar schools owe their origin, endowments and often their names to individual enterprise like Pliny's, the foundation of the earliest of them is due mainly to religious bodies. By the later Middle Ages there were already a considerable num-ber of them: first were the cathedral schools – King's School Canterbury claims to be the oldest grammar school in England, tracing its origin to the coming of St Augustine in A.D. 597, and its historians believe a school existed in Canterbury in the period of Roman occupation [7] – then others attached to collegiate or larger parish churches, others again maintained or administered by monasteries. In the fourteenth century laymen too began to found schools, but the motive was still religious. The benefactors would endow a chantry whose priest was required, as well as saying mass for the dead man's soul, to conduct a school, grammar or elementary. Leeds and Wakefield Grammar Schools can be traced back to chantries of this kind. Craft and merchant guilds also founded song schools and Ipswich, as a municipality, founded its own grammar school before 1380. It is estimated [7] that by the end of the fifteenth century there were three hundred or more grammar schools, founded in these various ways, up and down the country. Of the curriculum and cost to parents of these early schools more will be said later; but the fact that they are generally described as *libera schola grammaticalis* ('free grammar school') implies that the endowment covered at least part of if not all the cost of the education given. Sometimes this would be modified, as with Lancaster Grammar School, founded in 1469, whose first master and chaplain was to instruct boys in grammar freely 'unless something should be voluntarily offered by their friends'. But always the cost of education was at least subsidized, if not completely met, from the founder's or founding body's endowment.

These generous and public-spirited foundations, commendable as they may seem to the modern reader, were not universally welcomed at the time. The Church, though often itself the benefactor, had some reservations when it was not, and there was some opposition from it, prophetic of future developments. For just as ecclesiastical authority was highly suspicious of the effects on the faithful of reading pagan classical literature, and would only tolerate even the innocuous Virgil when it had persuaded itself that he was *anima naturaliter Christiana* ('a soul by nature Christian'), so it sniffed at the grammar schools which it had not itself founded with a nose hypersensitive to possible heresy. The mood is well reflected in Shakespeare (*2 Henry VI*, IV, VII) where Jack Cade thus rebukes Lord Saye and Sele:

Thou hast most traitorously corrupted the youth of the realm in erecting a grammar school; and, whereas before our forefathers had no other books but the score and the tally, thou hast caused printing to be used, and contrary to the King, his crown and dignity, thou hast built a paper-mill. It will be proved to thy face that thou hast men about thee that usually talk of a noun and a verb, and such abominable words as no Christian can endure to hear.

Historians may dismiss this as a mere manifestation of the anti-Lollard prejudice of the time, but it typifies an attitude of the Church which revealed itself more powerfully when the state entered the educational field; hence the elaborate safeguards against denominational influence in state education of the Cowper–Temple Clause of the 1870 Education Act – 'No religious catechism or religious formulary of any particular denomination shall be taught in the schools' – and what has been called [8] the 'horse-trading' of the religious negotiations behind the 1944 Education Act, resulting in the denominationally neutral daily act of worship and agreed syllabus of religious teaching now obligatory in state schools. In the history of English education the Church, as its role of fairy-godmother receded in favour first of individual founders and then of the state, has remained a watchdog, ever vigilant lest the religious side of education suffer from denominational bias or neglect.

A shift of emphasis in the foundation of grammar schools from the ecclesiastical to the secular, more in tune with the spirit of the Renaissance, already showed itself in the establishment of a grammar school at St Paul's in 1518. The founder Colet, it is true, was a Dean and there was a touch of medieval piety in the fixing of the number of pupils at 153, corresponding to the number of the miraculous draught of fishes. But the school was otherwise free of ecclesiastical entanglements, and its endowments were entrusted not to the Dean and Chapter but to the Mercers' Company, who were also to supply the governing body. The High Master, whom they would appoint, could be a layman, and if a priest was not to hold a benefice. The period of the Tudors became a golden age of grammar school foundation, a time when it was fashionable for a man who had succeeded in his trade or profession to establish such a school in his birthplace. As well as new foundations there were many re-foundations of schools that had been casualties of the Dissolution and Chantries Acts.

To this period, for instance, belong the grammar schools at Aldenham, Berkhamsted, Tiverton (Blundell's School, founded in 1604 by a local clothier and endowed also with closed scholarships to Balliol College, Oxford, and Sidney Sussex College, Cambridge), Brentwood, Bristol, Harrow, Highgate, Manchester, Rugby and Uppingham. The list of foundations during this period by citizens of London alone is impressive [7]. Some followed Colet's example and vested the government of their schools in a City Livery Company, as did Judd with Tonbridge and Gresham with Holt in the Skinners' and Fishmongers' Companies respectively. City Livery Companies also themselves founded grammar schools: so Oundle owes its origin to the Grocers' Company. Merchant Taylors' owes both origin (in 1561) and name to the Merchant Taylors' Company. Although all these schools were predominantly lay foundations care was taken not to offend the Church; indeed Sir Andrew Judd, in his Statutes for Tonbridge, invented a formula ambivalent enough to satisfy a Vicar of Bray in those days of vacillation between Catholic and Protestant: the Master was to have a 'right understanding of God's true religion now set forth by public authority, whereunto he shall stir and move his scholars'. Repton's founder, Sir John Port, bowed even more respectfully to ecclesiastical tradition by having his school founded as a chantry. This is the time, too, of the proliferation of King Edward VI Grammar Schools – at Birmingham, Chelmsford, Stafford, Stourbridge, to mention but a few. Shrewsbury too, though later fame has truncated its full title, was originally the 'Free Grammar School of King Edward VI'. Some of these schools were not new foundations but recoveries from the Dissolution at the request of the local citizenry by grant of Charter from the King himself, with funds and no doubt a guilty conscience stemming from his father's depredations. So Shrewsbury, Bedford and St Albans petitioned successfully for the refoundation of their schools, and the citizens of Wakefield even levied a voluntary tax on themselves to complete the 100 marks per year allowed by their Charter, thereby anticipating by four centuries the Education Tax or Bonds some would like to see as a solution to the problem of rising rates at the present time [9]. Such local involvement was further fostered by

Edward VI, and after him Mary and Elizabeth, by placing a school under local control or direction of the Town Corporation. Thus in Lincolnshire alone the statutes of the King Edward VI Grammar Schools at Great Grimsby, Louth and Grantham specifically included the Mayor and Aldermen in their government; and in 1554 Queen Mary founded and endowed Boston Grammar School, placing the management in the hands of the Mayor and Burgesses. Here is the beginning of local responsibility for grammar schools which is an integral part of the administration of secondary education today.

The 'bulge', so to speak, in the birthrate of grammar schools under the Tudors swelled even more impressively under the Stuarts. In numerical terms the rate of growth doubled: 185 were founded between 1501 and 1601, 186 between 1601 and 1651 [7]. But numbers were not matched by importance or later reputation, for whereas many of the Tudor schools have since become household names only two of those from the Stuart period – Charterhouse and Dulwich – reached a comparable level. On the other hand the seventeenth and eighteenth centuries mark a degeneration, evident and accelerating anyway by 1660 [7], in the fortunes of grammar schools. The symptoms of this, whether in declining numbers (the roll of Bristol Grammar School, for instance, fell from eighty-one in 1716 to twenty in 1722, and in 1780 Shaftesbury Grammar School closed altogether for lack of pupils), pedagogic neglect or schoolboy profligacy, drunkenness and rebellion and the notorious floggings of Dr Keate at Eton, are matters for the historian, as are their causes although in so far as these are attributable to a restricted curriculum, we shall discuss them later. Nor is the eventual remedy, in the person of Thomas Arnold of Rugby, as important to our theme as are certain byproducts of his personality and ideas. For Arnold, for all his much-needed reforms, fostered in English education a classconsciousness from which it has yet to recover. Not that it is fair to lay all the blame at the Doctor's door; he was tilling fertile soil, in a country where railways had scarcely been invented before first, second and third class carriages were coupled to the brand new locomotives. Still Arnold played his part. Hitherto the grammar schools, at least in intention, had been for children of all classes. St Paul's was to be a day school for boys 'of all nations and countries indifferently', and precisely the same words appear in the twenty-fifth Statute of Merchant Taylors' School [10]. Many specifically gave preference to 'poor scholars', and in 1541 Archbishop Cranmer, when the King's Commissioners wished the Grammar School of King's Canterbury to be restricted to the sons or younger brothers of gentlemen, was forthright and uncompromising in his opposition:

Utterly to exclude the ploughman's son and the poor man's son from the benefits of learning is as much to say, as that Almighty God should not be at liberty to bestow His great gifts of grace upon any person, nor nowhere else, but as we and other men shall appoint them to be employed, according to our fancy.... Wherefore, if the gentleman's son be apt for learning, let him be admitted; if not apt, let the poor man's child that is apt enter in his room.

There follows a sharp reminder of the situation when Adam delved and Eve span: 'I take it that none of us here being gentlemen born (as I think) but had our beginning that way from a low and base parentage.'

Nor did the reality fall far short of the ideal. Aubrey's *Brief Lives* of men of the seventeenth century show a wide mixing of classes at the free grammar schools, and this is confirmed by school registers, where they exist. At Merchant Taylors' the 244 boys admitted between 1645 and 1646 [11] include the sons of a knight, a Fellow of Winchester College and the Secretary of the East India Company, 55 sons of Merchant Taylors, 20 sons of clothworkers, 6 sons of yeomen, 5 sons of clergy and the sons of a barber, basket-maker, blacksmith, bookseller, bricklayer, carpenter, cook, goldsmith, innkeeper, ironmonger, plumber, poulterer, shoemaker and labourer. Registers for Oundle and Westminster show a similar pattern [3].

Arnold of Rugby changed all this. The details of his reforms need not concern us, nor an assessment of his personality, which mature reflection has since come to place somewhere between the idolatry of *Tom Brown's Schooldays* and the sneers of Lytton Strachey [12]. Attention must rather be focused on something he said, and one consequence of what he did that drove a wedge through the near classlessness of English secondary education and banished it from all but a few schools. (Honourable mention must here be made of the now defunct Middlesex Education Authority who, at Merchant Taylors' and Mill Hill, have boldly co-operated with the governors of these schools to make the Fleming Report of 1942 a reality while other authorities effectively sabo-taged it. A similar arrangement has now been made between Marlborough College and Swindon whereby twenty-one boys from local schools joined the College, but this only at sixth-form level.) His words called for a systematic effort 'to provide for the middle classes something analogous to the advantages afforded to the richer classes by our great public schools'. The schools would have to be chiefly day schools, and the state would have to intervene. Prophetic words, foreshadowing the active role of government in education implicit in the 1944 Education Act; but also insidious in their effect. Some people before Arnold had indeed talked or acted as though the nature of education was determined by social class. But when the Doctor said it it seemed to come straight from Sinai. Moreover the almost mystical intimacy between the Headmaster and his Prefects that formed so vital a part of the Rugby régime could only be fully realized at a boarding school. Strangely enough Arnold does not expressly champion the boarding school – rather the contrary. 'Another system,' he said, 'may be better in itself, but I am placed in this.' Yet his deeds forced a different conclusion: education of the upper and middle classes, though analogous, must be different and the difference lies in the practice of boarding. It might seem odd that to get rid of one's children for six months of the year should be a mark of social distinction. There are cogent and educationally sound arguments for boarding schools, as we shall see, but this one hardly deserves pride of place. Yet pride of place the Doctor gave it, and with it a supercilious nuance to the term 'public school' that set the Victorian educational fashion. Whatever the weight given by Arnold to the two ingredients in his 'Christian gentlemen' there were others who had no doubts, and in the days when money talked the insistence on boarding gave a built-in financial exclusiveness. Decline in secondary education now gave place to renaissance, but also to social stratification; and of the lower classes there was no mention at all.

An immediate effect was the growth of a whole new crop of schools. Foundation was still by private initiative, but now with a significant difference. In 1841, when there was a need for a school at Cheltenham, no effort was made to resuscitate the moribund sixteenth-century grammar school as it would be open to lower-middle-class boys and the sons of those who had 'been in trade'. Instead some of the more select residents formed a private company of shareholders and opened the 'Cheltenham Proprietory College' for local boys and boarders from further afield. Within twenty years its roll was over 200. Marlborough followed in 1851, and though the well-intentioned Nathaniel Woodard began a group of schools by voluntary subscription over the country specifically designed for the middle classes – his first three schools, Lancing, Hurstpierpoint and Ardingly were graded and priced to suit three income levels – his action served only to underline the existing class divisions.

The issue came into even sharper relief at Bristol, seldom in the background in educational controversy. Bristol Grammar School, closed for twenty years, was reopened in 1848 with 200 pupils. In 1860 the Trustees, short of funds, were permitted to raise the fees, but some also wanted to admit boarders while others, feeling that thus the school would be lost to the ordinary citizens of Bristol, objected. The matter came before the Master of the Rolls, Sir John Romilly, who thus ruled: 'The existence of free grammar schools *without boarders* provides the necessary instruction for the lower classes of the community; the existence of free grammar schools like Eton, Harrow and Rugby *without or almost without free scholars* provides the necessary instruction for the sons of the higher classes of the community' [3] (italics supplied). Thus thwarted, the champions of boarding had their way two years later when a group similar to the founders of Cheltenham started Clifton College which, like it, was mainly for boarders but also had a considerable number of day boys and provided in the current phrase 'a thoroughly good and liberal education for the sons of gentlemen'. Local snobbery between Clifton and Bristol Grammar even reached the point that if two brothers happened to be at the different schools they must not speak when they met in the street. Games fixtures between the two schools were out of the question until after the Second World War, when a victory by the Grammar School in the first Rugby match perhaps proved something. Vivian Ogilvie gives some even more egregious examples of such 'fixture snobbery' [3].

Perhaps more significant than class distinction between schools was partition, followed by fission, inside some schools themselves. Harrow was a striking example. Intended by its founder, John Lyon, to be a local grammar school, it had become predominantly aristocratic and for boarders. A protest from local inhabitants about this monopoly by 'foreigners' was rejected in 1811 by the Master of the Rolls, Sir William Grant, on the grounds that the governors were merely carrying out the founder's intention to give an exclusively classical education and 'if the parish boys no longer benefited, it was not through any conspiracy to exclude them'. Harrow, like Rugby, had developed in course of time from an Elizabethan free grammar school serving a locality into a great Public School serving the nation, and such a development was not to be reversed.

Note here the comparison to Rugby as prototype and archetype, the use, probably for the first time in judicial language [3], of the term 'public school' in the modern sense and the inference of class distinction between subjects as well as people which many of humble origin and classical education will find nauseating. A solution, however, was found in 1853 by Vaughan, the Headmaster, who established in the school, or rather near it in a building that had been in turn a barn and a temporary church, a special 'English class' tailor-made for the local population. He explained its purpose, in words of Machiavellian diplomacy which mollified their wounded pride by appealing to snobbery over still lesser breeds, as being 'to meet the wants of a class of residents in Harrow who may not desire for their sons a High [sic] Classical Education, and who yet are reasonably unwilling to confound the mutual division of ranks by sending them to the National School'. This innovation later received the blessing of the Clarendon Commissioners (see page 23) who transformed it into a separate school where local residents could receive the 'good commercial education' they desired – the Lower School of John Lyon (founded 1876). Similar fissiparous situations produced Alleyn's

School as a Lower School of Dulwich, Laxton Grammar School from Oundle and Lawrence Sheriff School from Rugby. In 1873 Bedford Modern School, already in existence since 1764 as a 'writing school' at the request of local citizens because of the exclusively classical syllabus at Bedford School, became a grammar school in its own right. The Whitgift Schools at Croydon suffered even more puzzling permutations. The original foundation bifurcated into a 'Middle School' and a 'Poor School'; as both prospered the former was promoted to become Whitgift Grammar School, the latter Whitgift Middle School and finally, in 1955, the Trinity School of John Whitgift. Most of these schools have since risen to membership of the Headmasters' Conference and their pupils no doubt regard themselves as 'public school' with the best.

Other schools of Victorian vintage were mainly of two types. First new boarding schools, following the Arnold pattern, to suit the religious needs of particular denominations, chiefly Roman Catholics, Nonconformists and Quakers. The High Anglicanism of the Oxford Movement was already reflected in the religious observances of the Woodard Schools. Secondly new grammar schools appeared in large towns, signalized as middle-class in the prescribed manner by being predominantly day schools, but often enough a modest *cachet* was added by the title 'College'. Such were the City of London School (1837 – no nonsense about 'College' here for cockneys), Liverpool College (1840), Plymouth College (1878), and Hymer's College, Hull (1888). Meanwhile the government was beginning to show its hand.

STATE PARTICIPATION AND PATRONAGE

Broadly speaking government first became involved in English education in the guise of a reluctant Mrs Mop, was later encouraged to play Santa Claus, and now risks the equivocal role of Big Brother. Forced by the scandal of child labour in the nineteenth century to intervene in the elementary field, it touched the grammar schools at first only rarely and only in specific matters, such as Romilly's Act of 1812 providing for revision of charitable foundations where there was breach of trust, and in the

Act of 1840 whose main provision was the much-needed lifting of the ban on non-classical education. But by mid-century secondary schools were caught up in the vogue for Royal Commissions – first on Oxford and Cambridge (1854 and 1856) and then the Newcastle Commission inquiring into 'the education of boys and girls of the labour classes'. Grammar schools could hardly remain unscrutinized. First, between 1861 and 1864 the 'Nine Public Schools' – Eton, Westminster, Charterhouse, St Paul's, Merchant Taylors', Harrow, Rugby and Shrewsbury – were investigated. There was praise for progress in the previous twenty-five years in amenities, staff ratios, discipline and religious training, but criticism of the narrowness of the curriculum and the poor intellectual quality of many of their pupils. Though the best scholars usually came from the Public Schools they 'send also (and in this Eton has a certain pre-eminence) the idlest and most ignorant men'. The Commissioners recommended the introduction of subjects like mathematics, modern languages, science, music and art, and the Public Schools Act which followed in 1868 made governing bodies more representative and established a clearer demarcation between their responsibilities and those of the headmaster. But there the government bowed itself out; Mrs Mop had done her cleaning up and was required elsewhere.

Between 1864 and 1868 endowed grammar schools other than 'the Nine' were the subject of a Commission under Lord Taunton. Seven hundred and eighty-two grammar schools were investigated and in 1867 the resulting Endowed Schools Act set up an Endowed Schools Commission to approve new schemes for individual schools. Its powers, it was said at the time, were wide enough to convert a boys' school in Northumberland into a girls' school in Cornwall; and in fact a number of distinguished girls' schools, including those at Bedford, Birmingham, Bradford and Rochester and the sister schools at St Olave's and Dulwich owe their origin to it. But the main concern was with boys' schools, and by its multifarious operations, whether in combining charities serving no particular purpose to form a new school, using the funds of a school over-generously endowed to found a second school or in general administrative tidying up, the Commission vastly improved the country's grammar school resources. In all it produced 238 schemes and was then incorporated in the Charity Commission, which in turn was transferred to the new Board of Education when it was established in 1902. Again Mrs Mop's work of cleaning up was done, and this time she had even made some improvements by shifting the furniture around. There she would have gladly left it, with no ambitions to enter into residence.

Yet circumstances forced on government a more active role, despite the *laissez-faire* climate of the times. For the malaise of the grammar schools was too acute to be remedied merely by juggling with their endowments and articles of government. As early as 1795 Lord Chief Justice Kenyon had described them as 'empty walls without scholars, and everything neglected but the receipt of salaries and emoluments' [7]. At Whitgift School, Croydon, the master had held office for thirty years, but there were no boys [3]. Even worse than abuse was the shortage, thus reported by the Taunton Commission: 'In at least two thirds of the places in England named as towns in the census there is no public school at all above the primary schools, and in the remaining third the school is often insufficient in size or in quality.' The situation demanded not the apron and duster of Mrs Mop but the well-filled sack of Santa Claus. As with the Royal Commissions the pattern adopted for elementary education was again followed. The School Boards, set up by the Act of 1870 to develop primary schools, had only limited success and were replaced, in the Act of 1902, by education sub-committees of the County, County Borough and Urban District Councils. These operated in the secondary field in two ways. First, to supply the lack of grammar schools in the two thirds of the towns discovered by the Taunton Commission, they began to build 'County Grammar Schools' which they maintained fully, calling them 'provided schools'. Secondly, to meet the shortcomings of the endowed grammar schools, distinguished now as 'non-provided schools', they contributed from the rates to the cost of secular instruction. Progress was rapid: by the end of 1908, six years after the Act, there were 245 'provided' schools and 418 'non-provided', a total of 663 grammar schools controlled or assisted by the State [13]. By 1963 there were 1,295 grammar schools, nearly double the number, maintained by the State, taking 722,000 pupils [8]. Moreover the proportion of the cost of education met from rates in endowed grammar schools increased steadily. The relative value of the endowments, often made centuries before, dropped with the falling value of money, and excessive increases in fees were against the tide of the times, especially after state primary education was made free in 1918. The number of free places provided in grammar schools grew, and as the local authorities, who were increasingly paying the piper, demanded the right to call the tune, spirited local battles over control developed. For example in Watford in 1905 a capital grant for new buildings for the Girls' Grammar School brought with it a request from the Council that three of their members be added to the governing body, and when, in 1934, a further grant of £19,000 was sought to replace the Old Pavilion, the County Council made control of the school a condition of the grant. The governors protested, but control was made an absolute condition of any future application, and the restriction of building through the outbreak of war left the matter still unresolved [14].*

This anomalous relationship between endowed grammar schools and local authorities was largely regularized by the 1944 Education Act which classified all state-aided secondary schools, including secondary modern schools (many of which had previously been senior elementary schools) but excluding direct-grant schools, which will be considered later, as follows:

(1) *County Schools:* these, previously built and wholly maintained by the local authorities, presented no problem – they simply remained as they were.

(2) *Voluntary Controlled Schools:* these the local authority maintains inside and out and appoints two thirds of their governors. It also appoints the teachers, but the governors must be consulted over the appointment of the head-teacher and any teacher giving denominational instruction. Most of these are Church of England schools.

(3) *Voluntary Aided Schools:* here, while the cost of running and internal maintenance of the school is met by the local authority,

*The issue, as so often happens, was further complicated by the question of denominational teaching.

maintenance and improvements to the outside of the buildings are the responsibility of the governors. Religious and secular instruction (the latter only in secondary schools, not in primary) is controlled by the governors, but the local authorities must be satisfied about the qualifications of teachers giving secular instruction. Two thirds of the governors are appointed by the voluntary body, the rest by the local authority. For improvements in the buildings the governors may get a grant of up to 75 per cent of the cost; this grant comes direct from the Ministry, not the local authorities, but the latter are consulted. Nearly three fifths of these Aided Schools are Church of England, and all but two Roman Catholic schools are Aided or Special-Agreement.

(4) *Special-Agreement Schools:* these date back to an arrangement made by the 1936 Education Act for new schools built not, like the County Schools, by the local authority but by a voluntary body. By special agreement the local authority may pay between a half and three quarters of the cost of building. The composition of the governors and the responsibility for maintenance is as for Aided Schools. The governors control religious instruction and are consulted over the appointment of teachers giving denominational instruction; the local authority appoints other teachers. The majority of these schools (116 in 1963) are Roman Catholic, and of the rest (32 in 1963) all but one are Church of England [8].

By these arrangements the 1944 Act, the biggest milestone to date in government involvement in British education, achieved a statesmanlike compromise between ever-rising costs and the claims of religious – particularly Roman Catholic – sensibilities. Attractive as aided status looks under those arrangements, outside building costs, even when the permissive grant of 75 per cent was made, remained heavy, and it is a credit to the independent spirit of the voluntary bodies that over half the voluntary schools at secondary level (514 out of 910) were 'aided' in 1963 [8]. On the other hand 'controlled' status has by no means proved the 'take-over' arrangement that the term suggests. The Governors of the Watford Grammar Schools decided in 1944 that they could not meet the conditions required for aided status (their new pavilion, even allowing the 75 per cent grant, would have cost them nearly £5,000 by pre-war prices) and opted to be 'controlled'. Yet we are assured, and local experience confirms, that they have not as a result 'lost their individuality nor have they been reduced in public esteem' [14].

Though the ramifications of educational administration are outside the province of this book a reminder should perhaps be given that while the State's share of the cost of education is nominally met by the local authorities they in turn receive from the central government a grant of some 50 to 60 per cent. This grant is not made by the Ministry of Education but as part of a block grant from the Ministry of Housing and Local Government, thereby leaving the local authority free to decide the proportion to be spent on education. There is, however, a grant direct from the Ministry of Education towards the cost of school milk and meals. Those who maintain that the ever-rising burden of educational expenditure should be shifted from rates to taxes, whatever the merits of their case, should remember that the job has been half done already.

Government involvement in secondary education, in addition to direct help in financing the schools, has also come indirectly in several ways. To mention only two: the goal towards which a grammar school education strives is a university degree, and here the establishment of new universities, Birmingham in 1900, Liverpool and Wales in 1903, Leeds in 1904, Sheffield in 1905, Bristol in 1909 and the imaginative development of the 'new universities' of the post-war era, starting with Keele in 1949, is playing a vital part. Furthermore the introduction of 200 State Scholarships in 1920 made all universities more accessible to the less well-off, and by 1938 their number had been increased to 360. Indeed these scholarships were at first limited to pupils in grant-aided schools, thereby placing the otherwise favoured candidates from independent schools at a disadvantage; but in 1936 pupils in all secondary schools were made eligible. Meanwhile local authorities had introduced and steadily increased their own scholarships, and these have now entirely replaced State Scholarships as the channel of subsidy for university education. It has been said [2] of the period of the thirties that 'the ladder of learning was narrow and pitched at a steep incline' – but it was unquestionably there.

GRAMMAR SCHOOLS FOR GIRLS

One further consequence of the Taunton Commission of 1867, from which state participation in secondary education ultimately stems, must be mentioned. Before 1850 secondary education for girls, where it existed, was limited to the 'accomplishments' of Miss Pinkerton's Academy. But in that year Miss Buss founded the North London Collegiate School 'from which, it has been justly said, are really descended practically all the girls' schools of England' [15]. This school, about which more will be said later, was unique in its insistence on education of the whole personality, including academic training which aspired to rival that given in boys' grammar schools (chemistry lessons were given by Miss Buss's own father and were surprisingly popular), and its complete absence of class distinction. The school impressed Matthew Arnold, who was collecting evidence for the Commission, as no doubt did the forceful personality of its foundress. The Commissioners were persuaded to take girls' education seriously, urged the opening of schools on the Miss Buss model in every main town in the country, diverted some endowments from boys' schools to provide new schools for girls and started a movement that led to the foundation of a number of distinguished girls' schools (see page 35) rising to a total of eighty by 1900. Meanwhile further help had come with the establishment of the Girls' Public Day School Trust in 1872 to launch similar schools. Its sponsors were the Workers' Education Union – quaintly plebeian ancestors for the predominantly patrician voices to be heard these days in G.P.D.S.T. corridors – and the aim was to be self-supporting from fees, without making a profit. The Trust's first school, Notting Hill and Ealing High, was opened in 1873, and by 1891 it had thirty-six. The pattern was now set for the Girls' County High Schools and these grew rapidly after the 1902 Education Act until just before the outbreak of the last war the numbers of boys and girls at secondary grammar schools was roughly equal [15]. Meanwhile in 1858 Cheltenham Ladies' College was founded by Miss Beale to provide for girls the benefits associated with boys' boarding schools, and by 1883 it had five hundred girls and ten boarding houses. Other similar independent boarding schools for girls followed. Like the day schools they copied the curriculum of the boys' schools with feminist determination to prove they could do as well, but in the cult of games imitation was less happy and bordered on caricature. Miss Beale wanted to abolish croquet because it provided no proper exercise. Cricket was played in some schools, and Katherine Whitehorn, in waspish reminiscence of later Roedean days, recalls the tough brand of house-matron: 'no good going to her because you felt too frightful for cricket practice before breakfast' [16]. Even less exclusively boys' games were approached with masculine toughness and idiom. Thus the authors of *The English Middle Classes* [17] recall hearing, as they passed by a girls' school, 'amid the scuffle of a basket-ball game, the cool, brisk voice of feminine authority: "Now, Cynthia, they are pressing the attack. If I were you I should be cunning. I should put my men *here* ... and throw the ball *there*."' To be fair, the excesses of feminist zeal have now been largely corrected: domestic science, music, dancing and suchlike now have their proper place in most girls' grammar schools, and it would be hard to find one of which one could say, as was said of one school in 1911, that 'a few girls who are backward in intellectual work learn cookery' [15]. Witness around me as I write a prehistoric monster and other *objets d'art* in glazed pottery, miscellaneous examples of handiwork with needle and thread and a neatly written menu of a meal recently cooked for us – including, as sweet, Raspberry Mouse (*sic* – a culinary if not an orthographic triumph) – all the work of our twelve-year-old daughter from Miss Buss's own North London Collegiate School.

Whether the curriculum in girls' schools should be fundamentally different from that of boys, as some, notably Sir John Newsom [18], would argue, or whether this would be a setback to the movement that has culminated triumphantly in a woman Cabinet Minister and High Court Judge, is a thorny problem somewhat beyond our scope. So is the allied question of co-education. During my year of professional training as a teacher at Cambridge I was asked to write a long essay on the subject, for which I studied reports on differentiation of curricula and much learned writing before reaching a conclusion which now escapes me and is unimportant. I did not then realize, nor did my tutor point out to me, that coeducation in this country is mainly, and in maintained schools almost exclusively, a matter not of principle* but of administrative convenience. A few schools, like Bedales, are coeducational from conviction. For the rest whatever is, is right. If there are enough children pursuing grammar school courses to warrant single-sex schools, that is the arrangement; otherwise they are lumped together for half the cost, though from time to time changed circumstances occasion reorganizations which affront local tradition and feeling and add to the Minister's postbag. And though purists argue that truly comprehensive education should be coeducational the same system has generally been followed in the establishment of new comprehensive schools. So, I suspect, it will long remain.

THE CURRICULUM

Everybody knows that the classics, first Latin and later also Greek, dominated the grammar school curriculum for far too long; but to blame their original founders for this is like blaming the contemporary blacksmiths for making horseshoes. Education in the Middle Ages was the preserve of the Church, and Latin was its international language. The original purpose of the grammar schools was to educate boys to be ordained, and the medieval cleric, or clerk, was active in many spheres besides that of the parish priest – they were statesmen and diplomats, civil servants, lawyers, physicians, librarians – in fact the Church was 'not one profession but the gateway to all professions' [3]. And this situation gave Latin an importance which obtained in much later times. Newton's scientific works were written in Latin and Milton, in the seventeenth century, was Latin Secretary in the equivalent of the Foreign Office today.

The basis of all learning was the Seven Liberal Arts or Sciences. Of these the first three, grammar, rhetoric and dialectic, were called the *Trivium* and formed the syllabus of the grammar schools. Thus as late as 1663 Eton, Westminster and Winchester

*For a concise and objective statement of the arguments of principle on both sides see [8].

were described as 'trivial' schools. The other four Arts, called the *Quadrivium* – arithmetic, geometry, astronomy and music – were for university students, often enough in those days mere boys of fourteen or fifteen. Dialectic (formal logic) and rhetoric (the art of composing letters and documents in Latin with some practice in the art of persuasion) were for the later stage of school; grammar came first, and this meant the learning of Latin as a spoken language, a vocational training essential to the educated man. Grammar, with its alternative forms 'gramarye' and 'glomerye' was highly revered by the unlearned, who regarded it as a form of magic, a meaning that survives in our modern word 'glamour' [3].

But if we cannot fairly blame the original grammar schools for teaching the wrong subject, there is more substance in the objection that it was taught in the wrong way. Necessary as a sound grammatical foundation in the language was, far too much attention was paid to the grammarians Donatus and Lily at the expense of Virgil and Cicero, and later Erasmus and Newton, and what they had to say. In the Latin lesson in Shakespeare's *The Merry Wives of Windsor* (IV, ii) we can sympathize with the comments of the audience as William struggles through his declension of *hic, haec, hoc*:

EVANS: *Accusativo hung, hang, hog.*
MRS QUICKLY: Hang hog is Latin for bacon, I warrant you. . . .
EVANS: Remember, William, focative is *caret* [lacking].
MRS QUICKLY: And that's a good root.

These interruptions would strike a chord in the heart of re-calcitrant preparatory school boys, among them in his day Sir Winston Churchill who, when told the vocative of *mensa* objected that he had no occasion to address a table [19]. This over-emphasis on grammar for its own sake has bedevilled the teaching of classics for centuries, and though many of us in the trade shed no tears at the Grammarian's Funeral we are none too sure he is yet properly buried: Kennedy's Latin Grammar, Memorial Gender Rhymes and all, still brings in sizeable royalties.

If the method of teaching Latin was conservative the subject itself was even more firmly entrenched. Renaissance influence cautiously admitted Greek and Hebrew as respectable bedfellows, but other subjects had scant hope.* Not that men with progressive ideas were lacking. In 1593 Thomas Cranmer, whom we have already seen (page 30) as champion of the right of the poor man's son to education, drafted a scheme for a new College of Christ Church, Canterbury, with provision for teaching in physic (medicine) and civil law (each with a Reader paid £20 per year) and also for 'sciences' and French, as well, of course, as divinity and the classical languages [7]. Nothing came of it, but some fifty years later Richard Mulcaster, first headmaster (1561–86) of Merchant Taylors' School, was forthright in his championship of English: 'Our hole tung was weined long ago, as having all her tethe,' and again, 'I love Rome, but London better; I favour Italy, but England more; I honour Latin but worship English.' He believed the time had come to regulate its grammar and spelling. His words, too, were backed by deeds in that he performed pageants and plays with Merchant Taylors' boys before Queen Elizabeth on a number of occasions. The following entry in the accounts of the Office of the Revels in the time of Elizabeth is a sample of several:

1582 – 1582/3. Christmas Twelftide & Shrouetide. – A historie of Ariodante and Geneuora shewed before her maiestie on Shrove tuesdaie at night enacted by mr Mulcasters children, for which was newe prepared and Imployed, one Citty, one battlement of Canvas, vij Ells of sarcenet, and ij dozen gloves . . .†

Indeed Mulcaster can claim to be the father of the 'school play'. Music and drawing also formed part of his curriculum, and believing we should 'have a speciall care, that the body be well appointed' he included in his programme dancing, wrestling, fencing, walking, running, jumping, riding, hunting, shooting, handball and football, which 'brawneth the whole body. It helpeth weake hammes by much moving and simple shankes by thickening of the flesh no less than riding doth.' In other ways, too, for instance his advocacy of teacher training colleges at

---

*Sometimes the supremacy of Latin was even reflected in the school's name: thus Buckingham's grammar school is still called the Royal Latin School.

†Appendix II in [10].

universities and his belief, prophetic of Plowden, in cooperation between parents and school – 'Parents and maisters should be familiarly lynked in amitie and contynual conference, for their common care' – he is centuries ahead of his time. In some respects his views were traditional: he believed in corporal punishment – 'my ladie birchely', as he put it, has her place. On the matter of selection and fee-paying in grammar schools his ideas, which will be mentioned later, are out of fashion today, but practised almost to the letter in some of the best schools in Britain. They at least deserve consideration, and will receive it in a later chapter. All in all Richard Mulcaster is a figure much underrated in the history of English education.*

Mulcaster's ideas had little immediate impact, and though Francis Bacon pleaded for the introduction of other subjects – history, modern languages and above all science – little was done. In 1787 Knox, Headmaster of Tonbridge, wrote a book expressing his willingness for history, geography, mathematics, French and some forms of artistic and physical training to be introduced as additional subjects but it is not known how far these ideas were carried out. Earlier, in 1611, Oldham Grammar School had actually prescribed English, along with Latin and Greek and good manners, in its statutes. In 1796 Oundle, foreshadowing Sanderson, gave the boys 'a competent idea of the several manufactures and the metals from the rude material and the mines to their improvement' and had in use a book on 'surveying' [3]. Sherborne introduced history, geography and English literature, and about the same time Rugby included mathematics, English history and English literature. But these were straws in the wind, and in 1805 such modest attempts to broaden the curriculum suffered a devastating blow. When Leeds Grammar School attempted to introduce modern studies Lord Eldon ruled in Court of Chancery that year that no part of a school's endowment could be used to pay teachers of French or German or to create a commercial department. A grammar school, by Dr Johnson's definition, was 'a school in which the learned languages are taught grammatically' and this judgment remained law till the

*Quotations are from his *Positions* (1581) and *Elementaire* (1582). For fuller consideration of him see [10].

Grammar Schools Act of 1840. Such non-classical teaching as there was had to be done either as an extra, which made it expensive, or by classically trained masters who generally resorted to handbooks of miscellaneous information given by question and answer. One dealt with religion, logic, morality, atmospheric phenomena, sound, earthquakes and volcanoes, the tides, metaphysics, jurisprudence, medicine, chemistry, botany, architecture, painting, sculpture, mechanics, astronomy, mythology, history, geography, etc. in 340 pages [3]. As one thinks of the fat textbooks on one or even one aspect of such subjects to be seen today in schools the depth of treatment can be well imagined. A clue lies in the story of how Lord Eldon himself took his degree at Oxford in 1770. 'He was asked two questions. "What is the Hebrew for 'the place of the skull'?" He replied, "Golgotha." "Who founded University College?" He replied, "King Alfred." And thus having satisfied the examiners in Hebrew and History, he graduated' [3].

The nineteenth century was a period dominated by four great headmasters, Butler, Arnold, Thring and Sanderson, and of these only the last two made any substantial contribution towards reforming the curriculum. Butler came to Shrewsbury in 1798, succeeding a man who had left the school to look after itself while he amused himself by hanging up a flitch of bacon and seeing who could kick highest, he or his second master [20]. Butler's chief concern was academic distinction and this he achieved by holding frequent examinations and even paying 'merit money' for success in them. Indeed if Mulcaster can be called the father of the 'school play' and Arnold of the boarding school ethos, Butler is the great-grandfather of the G.C.E. He is said to have been reproached by a visiting bishop for sharpening a pencil in chapel ready to correct exercises afterwards. He rated among the qualifications of a 'public school' the ability of its pupils to obtain public honours at the universities – something which, if the term 'public school' must be used, admittedly makes more sense than some other attributes we have seen claimed for it; and it was, I suspect, his instinct as an academic pot-hunter more than anything else that led him to admit mathematics at Shrewsbury in 1817. It paid dividends, for twenty-eight of his pupils became

Wranglers at Cambridge. Perhaps he was a 'crammer', but this is a term often applied by the envious to successful teachers. The real weakness, for all his Wranglers, was that he left the predominance of the classics unchallenged. Charles Darwin wrote of his boyhood at Shrewsbury:

Nothing could have been worse for my mind than this school, as it was strictly classical, nothing else being taught, except a little ancient geography and history. The school as a means of education was to me a complete blank. During my whole life I have been singularly incapable of mastering any language. .... The sole pleasure I ever received from such (classical) studies was from some of the Odes of Horace, which I admired greatly [20].*

Darwin was publicly rebuked by his headmaster for his interest in chemistry and nicknamed 'Gas' by his friends.

Arnold, it is true, permitted modern history and mathematics to be taught at Rugby, and included French and German in the regular timetable, though only as dead languages to be read, not spoken. Perhaps more important was his humanizing of the classical curriculum, focusing greater attention on content than hitherto. He was interested enough in physical science and believed it important, but could not see how it could be fitted into a school timetable. It was too big to be treated as a sideshow and if given proper place would crowd out more important things: 'Rather than have Physical Science the principal thing in my son's mind, I would gladly have him think that the Sun went round the Earth, and that the Stars were merely spangles set in a bright blue firmament' [21].

Thring's contribution was more encouraging. He began by stressing the importance of proper buildings for a school – what he called 'the almighty wall' – and justified the new buildings at Uppingham by increasing its numbers from 25 to 320. Believing as he did that the programme of work should suit the average

*How he missed the mathematics – for he would have been only ten when it was introduced at Shrewsbury in 1817 – is puzzling. But he was 'unreceptive to mathematics' in any case and later had to abandon medical studies at Edinburgh because the operating theatre nauseated him (Sir Gavin de Beer, 'Makers of Modern Science', in The Times Educational Supplement of 23 March 1956).

boy and not, as with Butler, the future prizewinners, he operated a timetable with a far more modern pattern. In the morning, – classics, scripture, mathematics, history, geography and English composition, which he stressed; in the afternoon there were various subjects – French, German, chemistry, drawing, carpentry and turning – from which the boys could choose. Music was introduced for everyone, with regular school concerts, some given by visiting artists. He started lessons in instrumental music and in time a third of the school was taking them. He developed systematic physical training, opened the first gymnasium in an English school in 1853 and built a swimming bath. There were laboratories, workshops, an aviary and school garden, and in 1869 he started a school mission at Woolwich which later moved to Poplar. Promising though these innovations seemed, their influence outside Uppingham was limited for two reasons. First Thring's personality, though strong, was not, like Arnold's, of the kind to win dedicated converts. So Thring's liberal curriculum did not become fashionable as did Arnold's brand of boarding education. Secondly Thring, despite his progressive-looking timetable, still believed that it should have a central core, and this must be the classical languages. Dead languages, he maintains, are better than living ones 'because once you are past sentence structure the more difficulties in a language the better; because a dead language cannot be learned parrot-fashion from a governess; because being inflected they train the mind in accuracy; because the difference in word-order compels the pupil to attend to the sense' [15]. These arguments, well worth consideration today when the classics have their backs to the wall, were hardly likely to dislodge them when they were still supreme.

Sanderson of Oundle was a far more radical figure and belongs as much to the twentieth as to the nineteenth century – his régime at Oundle extended from 1892 to 1922. Unlike his predecessors he was not content to graft science and other modern subjects on to the classical curriculum. He operated the other way round, starting from the scientific method – 'finding out' as he called it: 'I began by introducing engineering into the school – applied science. . . . Then I ventured to do something daring; it is most daring to introduce the scientific method of finding out the truth –

a dangerous thing – by the process of experiment and research. We began to replace explicit teaching by finding out.' This method was applied to other subjects: he established a 'laboratory for history, full of books and other things required in abundance, so that boys in all parts of the school could, for some specific purpose (not to learn; to go to school to learn was egotistical) find out the things we required for today' [20]. Boys were made into teams in which each had his place, as important as any other boy. Sanderson built laboratories and workshops and set up a forge, foundry and experimental farm. He obtained rough castings from a marine engineering company which were fitted, finished and tested by the boys and then installed in ships. For reading Shakespeare the class would be turned into a theatrical company with three or four Othellos, Desdemonas or Iagos who would act their parts simultaneously or in succession. Even Latin became 'a means of studying the lives and thoughts of a great civilizing people' [3]. Such ideas were bound to have their influence (Gresham's School, Holt, for instance dropped Greek altogether after 1900), but this was less than we might expect. The forces of inertia were strong, and it so happened that Sanderson was made into a hero by H. G. Wells, whose book about him, in seeking to glorify its subject, overdid the venom against those who dared to differ. For the Establishment headmasters this was enough; a man who excited the admiration of such a person could be safely dismissed.

So it was not, in the end, the great headmasters who finally broke the monopoly of the classics in the grammar schools but two other developments. First the growth of science and technology. The writings of Herbert Spencer and T. H. Huxley, the former stressing the usefulness of scientific knowledge, the latter the training in scientific method and the spirit of inquiry, had their effect. Perhaps even more important were the Exhibitions of 1851 and 1862, which showed other European countries making disturbing headway in the application of the very manufacturing techniques they had learned from Britain. Science, it seemed, must be given more place in the schools. Matthew Arnold summed up the mood in words which, though written nearly a century before it, foreshadow the 'literacy' and 'numeracy' of the Crowther

Report [22]: 'He whose aptitudes carry him to the study of nature should have some notion of the humanities; he whose aptitudes carry him to the humanities should have some notion of the phenomena and laws of nature' [3].

Secondly the growing science of psychology launched a blow from another direction. Hitherto it had been believed that there were in the mind separate faculties of memory, imagination, logical reasoning and so on which could be trained, memory for instance by learning Latin vocabulary, logical reasoning by geometry and the like. Phrenologists even localized these faculties in various bumps on the head. This doctrine was first questioned by the German J. F. Herbart (1776–1841) and then proved false, in 1904, by the demonstrations of the American E. L. Thorndike. His experiments, using the statistical methods recently introduced by Sir Francis Galton, showed that 'training' the 'memory' by learning poetry or Latin vocabulary did not improve the memory generally but merely skill in learning poetry or Latin vocabulary. The belief in 'faculties' was exploded, and with it the idea of 'transfer of training' which depended on their existence. Nowadays the psychologists are less dogmatic. It is conceded that transfer does take place to some extent between two subjects which have identical factors provided that the pupil is aware of those factors. But the word 'factor' is a technical term, and differs from the old 'faculties'. 'Faculties were posited on the basis of unsystematic observation and verbalization of certain stereotypes and prejudices current at the time; factors are carefully defined in terms of experimental and statistical procedures which follow the usual dictates of scientific method' [23]. These factors, Verbal Ability (V), Verbal Fluency (W), Numerical Ability (N), Spatial Ability (S), Perceptual Ability (P), Memory (M) and Inductive Reasoning (R) are given letters to avoid confusion, arising from verbal implications or resemblances, with the discredited 'faculties' (especially Memory). I mention these later developments in psychological research because some opponents of Latin ([21] for example) quote Thorndike's claim in 1904 that transfer of training does not exist a little too glibly, as if psychology had stood still ever since. I happen to believe that Latin, properly taught, is one effective way of improving V and W and to some extent R; it is a little embarrassing to find those who disagree meeting one's modest guns with bow and arrow psychology.

In 1904, however, Thorndike's conclusion was a bombshell to the classicists. Ready to meet the claim that the content of their studies was irrelevant in a scientific age with the counter-claim that it was unrivalled as a mental discipline, they found this too challenged. Lord Eldon's ban on the teaching of non-classical subjects had been revoked by the Grammar Schools Act of 1840 and nothing now impeded the broadening of the curriculum. Some schools had taken immediate advantage of this freedom. Cheltenham, from its foundation in 1841, had a modern side called the Civil and Military embracing a wide range of subjects including engineering and Hindustani; Leeds Grammar School, original victim of the Eldon judgment, could now have its laboratories and develop chemistry. In 1869 Harrow founded a Scientific Society and soon after appointed a science master and built up a successful modern side. Meanwhile the numbers of children receiving grammar school education rose phenomenally – from fifteen thousand in 1868 to over seventy-five thousand in 1895, five times as many. Two factors still limited the growth of non-classical subjects. First, many of the Oxford and Cambridge scholarships were still earmarked for classics and not, as is largely the case today, open to a wide range of subjects. It was tempting for schools to seek prestige by shaping scientific square pegs to fit the copious supply of classical round holes, and many did so. Then again it was all very well to approve the introduction of these new subjects, but who was to teach them and how? Inevitably, to begin with, they were taught largely by classically trained schoolmasters because there were pitifully few others. The headmaster of Winchester put his finger on the difficulty when he told the Clarendon Commissioners that he would like to include more history but did not know how to teach it in set lessons [15]; and there was little use in teaching chemistry if it consisted merely of learning lists of atomic weights and formulae like tables or principal parts of verbs. There was at least a generation's backlog to be made up between the will to introduce the new subjects and the wherewithal to teach them in terms of manpower and method. Schools knew how to teach the classics – nearly two thousand years of trial and error and Butler of Shrewsbury had shown the way. Better to tread the safe well-trodden paths and make sure of the scholarships. And so, even up to the beginning of the last war, the classics clung precariously to their position in many schools. R. H. S. Crossman, Leader of the House of Commons in the present Labour Government, thus describes his Winchester days in the twenties: 'Scholarship meant mastery of two dead languages; history ended with the fall of Rome; English had to be assimilated outside the classroom; French was taught by classics masters proudly "using the English pronunciation"; and science (two hours a week for most of us) was despised as the occupation of lab-boys' [24]. The present Director of the Oxford Institute of Education confesses that between 1922 and 1926 at one of the 'better public schools' he had no lessons in drawing or music and did not enter a science laboratory except to listen to a lecture on architecture [15]. At my own local grammar school I was more fortunate: by the time I had started Greek I already had some grounding in chemistry and biology, and later achieved a 'good grade' in physics at 'O' level which I owed entirely to a dedicated science master who had a small class and gave us plenty of experimental work in electricity and magnetism. Nowadays it is biology often enough that is offered as science for all except intending science specialists (apparently biologists are in rather less short supply than physicists or chemists) and this is a pity, for physics, as a medium of training in scientific method, seems to me to have the same kind of advantages as Thring claimed for Latin for training in language. Great progress has been made in the *method* of teaching non-classical subjects, and much useful guidance on this appears, for instance, in the handbooks on these subjects published from time to time by the Incorporated Association of Assistant Masters, but in science and mathematics, for reasons which need no recital here, we lack the men. There is good reason to believe (see Chapter 4) that this situation, already critical, would be further worsened by a policy of mass comprehensivization, and this is an important if subsidiary reason why those who advocate it should use the breathing-space of economic crisis to think again.

Meanwhile Nemesis has descended upon the classics. Not only is Greek non-existent in many grammar schools, or taught to a dedicated handful sometimes in cupboards under the stairs and in one place I know in extra lessons before or after school with no overtime bonus for teachers or taught, but Latin too is threatened. There are some who would shed no tears at the superannuation of the classics from the grammar school curriculum and feel that ostracism after nearly a thousand years of tyranny would be a kind of rough historical justice. But the survival or decay of academic disciplines is not so much a matter of retribution as of the contribution they can make to education in the widest sense. Whether the classics still have something to offer here is part of the wider theme of the relevance of grammar school education to the present day. We shall return to it in a later chapter.

Amid the clatter of classic and scientist, battle-locked to no great purpose, other subjects with unexceptionable claims and no pretensions to monopoly had been unobtrusively establishing themselves. They had the advantage of not being prisoners of their principles, and could develop a more enterprising and attractive approach. Sanderson's ideas, revolutionary as they seemed at the time, have now become commonplace in many grammar schools. The technique of his 'history laboratory' is applied not only to that subject but also to geography, and language laboratories are regarded as a necessity. There is even talk of an 'English laboratory', and certainly the organized chaos of some English classrooms today, where self-expression is encouraged to the point of exhibitionism, goes well beyond Sanderson's cautious experiments in classroom play production. Mathematics is receiving a 'face-lift' – indeed it seems something much more radical as one watches mathematics colleagues doing more homework than their pupils – to adapt it to the world of statistics and the computer. There is a movement to make the group of science subjects a 'core' or centre round which the whole curriculum is clustered [25]. This should be viewed with caution. For one thing, important as science is, not all minds are science-centred, and any suggestion that those who are not are literally 'eccentric' should be avoided. Also to replace Thring's discredited linguistic core by a scientific or any other sort of core is questionable policy. Perhaps the metaphor should not be pressed; the core, after all, is the part of the apple one throws away.

Most striking of all is the growth of the grammar school Sixth Form with its proliferation of subjects and subject-matter within subjects. Herein lies the central dilemma of the modern curriculum. The old classical programme was integrated towards a narrow goal – proficiency in dead languages and an understanding in depth of the culture of the peoples who used them. This was at once their strength and their weakness, for such concentration suited too few minds. The alternative we are now seeing is a widening of the field of choice to suit a variety of intellects, but with it a diffusion or even disintegration of the arts subjects leaving no unity at the centre. Whereas language, history, literature, philosophy and much else could be studied together as a culture in the limited field of knowledge of Greece and Rome, modern languages, modern history, modern literature, modern philosophy each cover areas so vast that a comprehensive study of them can only be superficial, while study in depth becomes partial. In science the situation once looked more promising: 'The science side has developed a unity which the arts side has lost, to the regret of many, with the decline of the classics' [22]. But as science expands with new discoveries and generates new sciences as it grows the centrifugal force of progress hurries each specialism further from the unity at the centre, and further from other once-related specialisms on the periphery. The unity which the arts side has lost the science side, perceptibly even since the Crowther Report, is beginning to lose. In this context it is idle to talk of putting the clock back or of stopping it; we cannot even stop it accelerating.

The effect on the grammar schools in terms of sheer volume of study alone is all too familiar. The universities, able to dictate their conditions while places remain limited, force more and more of the syllabus on to the schools, and the schools, in eager competition for scholarships and places, meet them more than half way. So we live in a period when, to quote the High Master of St Paul's, 'the sheer weight of the curriculum flattened out curiosity, when the hungry sheep looked up and were gorged' [26]. The Crowther Report observes a downward pressure of specialization even below the sixth form and a consequent squeezing out of English subjects. It is this which lies behind Lord Snow's celebrated warning about the Two Cultures and that Report's preoccupation with 'innumerate' humanists and 'illiterate' scientists.

Various solutions have been offered to meet this difficulty. There is the proposal of Mr A. D. C. Peterson that arts students should take at least one science subject at A-level and science specialists at least one arts subject [27]. The chief objection to this is the added load on an already overloaded curriculum, for the pious hope expressed of reducing all syllabuses by about twenty-five per cent seems unlikely to be fulfilled.* Another suggestion is the inclusion of 'general studies' in the sixth form programme, and the Northern Universities Joint Matriculation Board have even introduced it as an examination subject at A-level. But the Crowther Report reminds us that 'subject-mindedness ... is one of the marks of the Sixth Form' and has doubts about the wisdom of examining 'general studies' though admitting that some kind of 'adventitious incentive' is desirable if such studies are to be taken seriously. The word 'general' is all too reminiscent of the well-known story of the schoolmaster who wrote on a boy's report 'generally satisfactory' and when asked what 'generally' meant replied 'not particularly'. General studies suffer from the danger of not being particular enough. All the same they are a welcome development and much better than letting specialization go unchecked.

Two other signs of the times are more encouraging. First the growing popularity of subjects which of their nature bridge to some extent the gap between the Two Cultures – at school geography and economics, at university level archaeology and sociology. In this respect the sociological slant of some of the courses at the new universities, Essex in particular, is to be

*There is also the fact that universities generally prefer brilliance in a recognized group of subjects, classics, natural sciences and so on, to mediocrity or even brilliance in a mixture. Students of the latter type are apt to be regarded as academic hermaphrodites and as such find it less easy to win scholarships or places, particularly at Oxford and Cambridge. I discussed this with Mr Peterson some time ago and he admitted there is no easy solution short of reforming the universities.

welcomed. I remember a boy who had taken classics at school and then changed over, late in the sixth form, to economics. He secured a university place and, eager to make a good start, wrote to his tutor to ask what books he should read in preparation for his degree course. He was told to learn the calculus and learn to type. For him the gap between the Cultures was suddenly and rudely bridged. Secondly there is growing support for the idea of 'half-subjects' at A-level, preferably those unrelated to the student's specialist studies. The case for these, aptly called Complementary Level or 'coherence' subjects, is well and cogently argued in *Educating the Intelligent* [21]. The snag is the time factor. It is suggested that syllabuses for these 'half-subjects' should be drawn up by joint panels of school and university teachers. Meanwhile existing AO- and O-level papers can be used – for instance we have found AO papers in English Literature, History and Biology useful, and O-level papers in British Constitution, Italian and Russian.

The mention of Russian brings me to my last point in this review of the grammar school curriculum. It is fashionable to draw attention to the pathetically small G.C.E. entry in Russian, and a Committee under Lord Annan, then Provost of King's College, Cambridge, recently investigated the matter [28]. Some of us are doing something about it. A few schools like Firth Park Grammar School, Sheffield, have offered it pre-O-level as a second language for some time. Others introduce it after O-level, and a striking example is Wednesbury Boys' High School, where the chief modern languages master, having given himself a conversion course late in his career, is now getting impressive results at O- and A-level and winning awards and places at Oxford and Cambridge. At both Eton and Marlborough, to mention only two schools of which I have certain knowledge, three masters are engaged in teaching it. In the Oxford and Cambridge School Examinations Board alone in summer 1964 – I choose this Board because most of its candidates come from the Independent Schools and none, so far as I know, from comprehensives – 280 took Russian at O-level, of whom 195 (about 69 per cent) passed. Yet in 1956 only 92 candidates in all the Boards took the subject [21]. In other words the number of grammar school candidates who sat the exam in *one* Examining Board alone has trebled that in *all* Boards eight years before. I mention this because the impression is growing that the big new comprehensive schools – 'glamour schools' I almost called them after their recent publicity in the press [29] and on television, but this, by derivation, would be conceding their claim to be grammar schools before it has been examined – are almost the only places where Russian is being taught. Nothing could be further from the truth.

This consideration of the development of the grammar school curriculum has been somewhat limited, and I am aware of many gaps left – for instance in my neglect of the vast progress made in recent years in arts and crafts and in physical education. The whole subject is fully and stimulatingly discussed in *Educating the Intelligent* [21], to which I would refer readers looking for more detail. For our theme is more fundamental. 'Educating the Intelligent', in the full untrammelled sense envisaged in that book, is just what many today would argue we have no right to do. Desirable as it is to discuss the design and décor of the upper storeys of the grammar school edifice we must also address ourselves to those who, generally with the best of good intentions, are busily engaged in hacking away at its foundations.

THE QUESTION OF FEES

Pliny, it will be remembered, refrained from meeting the whole cost of his school, comfortably as he could have done so, not only because he feared the funds might be misappropriated but also because he wanted the parents to be personally involved. If they were themselves paying part of the teachers' salaries they would make sure they were good. Such thinking has always played an important part in the historical growth of the English grammar school. As we examine the attitude of the founders as revealed in their statutes and endowments we observe two principles running through them: one is the inalienable right of the child to the best education he can absorb regardless of his parents' ability to pay; the other, following Pliny, is that where they can afford to contribute some of the cost they should do so not only for the financial well-being of the school but because men value most and become most involved in what they are paying for.

Concern with the first of these principles is seen in the frequent use, in medieval and Tudor foundations, of the term 'free grammar school' (*libera schola grammaticalis*) and the expression 'poor scholars' or 'poor indigent scholars' (*pauperes et indigentes*). The precise meaning of these phrases is somewhat uncertain and controversial. But it is clear that 'free grammar school' was often qualified in two ways. First there was regional discrimination, made effective either by limiting free tuition to children of local residents, or by a more elaborate hierarchy of preference as with Winchester's seventy Foundation Scholars: first came the Founder's own kin, then boys from places where either of Wykeham's Colleges (Winchester itself and New College, Oxford) held property; then from the diocese of Winchester; then from the counties of Oxford, Berkshire, Wiltshire, Somerset, Essex, Middlesex, Dorset, Kent, Sussex and Cambridge in that order; finally from the rest of England. Secondly various 'extras' were charged: entrance fees, tuition fees for boys lacking the necessary residential qualification, contributions in money or kind (fuel, candles, brooms) and unofficial offerings such as 'potation pennies', Christmas boxes and 'cockpennies' at Shrovetide. Thus at St Paul's, though tuition was free, there was an entrance fee of fourpence to pay the poor scholars who swept and cleaned; every boy must provide candles, not the cheap tallow ones but of wax, costing eight times as much; he must also give a penny to the Boy Bishop who preached the sermon in the cathedral on Holy Innocents' Day [3]. Entrance fees sometimes involved regional or social differentiation, such as sixpence for a town boy, a shilling 'if of the country or a stranger' or, according to parents' status from ten shillings for a lord's son to fourpence or even nothing 'if really poor'.

If 'free grammar school' must be qualified so must the term 'poor scholar'. In medieval grammar schools it was in theory possible for a serf's son to attend, and some did. But their numbers, and indeed the numbers of really poor who received any education at all, were comparatively small. William of Wykeham, himself of humble origin, intended by his foundation of Winchester College to provide board and maintenance as well as tuition for the poor to obtain the schooling in grammar necessary to enter the university and so serve the Church. But the limit he set to the means of an 'indigent boy' was £3 6s. 8d., and this was the salary of the usher, and exceeded the stipend at the time of sixty-seven incumbents in the diocese of Winchester. The aim was thus to create a ladder upon which poor boys could mount while not excluding those who were somewhat better off [3].

Sometimes, from a quite early period, the actual fees, where charged, were graded according to parents' income or in various other ways. We have seen that Lancaster Royal Grammar School, founded in the fifteenth century, was to instruct boys in grammar freely 'unless something shall be voluntarily offered by their friends'. Some schools are even described as 'half-free'. The Statutes of Merchant Taylors' School provide for free tuition or graded fees according to parents' means for its 250 pupils as follows:

IV. . . . [the Headmaster] shall not refuse to take, receave, and teach in the said schoole freely one hundreth schollers, parcell of the said number of two hundreth & ffyfty schollers, being poore men's sonnes and coming thether to be taught, (yf such be meete & apt to learne,) without any thing to be paid by the parents of the said one hundreth poore children for their instruction & learnyng.

V. And he shall also receave and teache in the said schoole ffyfty schollers more, being an other parcell of the said number of two hundreth and ffyfty schollers comyng thether to be taught, & being found apte and meete to learne, as aforesaid, and being poore men's children, so that their poore parents, or other their friends, will pay and give to the high m.r. for their instruction & learning after two shillings & twopence by the quarter for the peece of them.

VI. And he shall also receave & teach in the said schoole, one other hundreth more of schollers being the residue of the said number of two hundreth and ffyfty schollers coming thether to be taught, & being also found apte and meete to learne, as aforesaid, being rich or meane men's children. so that their parents or other friends will give for every of these hundreth schollers fyve shillings by the quarter for their instruction & learning [10].

A hundred free, fifty at 2s. 2d. per quarter, a hundred at 5s. per quarter. Here we see foreshadowed the more elaborately graded scale of fees in operation at Manchester Grammar School, North London Collegiate School and other such direct-grant schools with which we shall be concerned in a later chapter. Help was also provided with the cost of university education for poor scholars, among them the poet Edmund Spenser. The following is one of three such entries in the accounts bearing his name: '1596 28 Aprill. To Edmond spensore scholler of the m.chante tayler school at his gowinge to penbrocke hall in chambridge – x s.' [10].

It is tempting and all too easy to dismiss the pretensions of these early grammar schools to be 'free' and for 'poor scholars' as so much hypocrisy or self-deception. But we must remember that their founders had no state help for financing their schools; they could not laugh off heavy costs and rising prices with a penny or twopence on the rates. Also they were religious men whose principles of revenue-raising were drawn from a source that contained the story of the Widow's Mite but not the Tales of Robin Hood. For all their imperfections and shortcomings, in the circumstances of the times they were doing their best.

Two other features of these early grammar schools should be noted. First, there was usually some prescribed academic qualification for entrance and at times, too, a condition of good behaviour. Winchester's 'poor scholars' had to be 'of good character and well-conditioned, of gentlemanly habits, able for school, completely learned in reading, plain song and old Donatus (the Latin grammarian) [3]. At St Paul's a boy had to be able to read, write and repeat the Catechism. Likewise at Merchant Taylors': 'But first see that they can the catechism in English or Latyn, & that every of the said two hundreth & ffyfty schollers can read perfectly & write competently, or els lett them not be admytted in no wise' – from Statute XXV [10]. Richard Mulcaster, the School's first headmaster, was quite positive about this. 'Everyone desireth to have his children learned.' But *only boys of real power* should be received, whether poor *or* rich; the latter by private help if the parents are wealthy, or by public aid if poverty pray for it' [7]. The other point to be noted is that although the grammar schools had their categories of 'poor scholars', local residents or whatever, to be educated free, this did not in many cases preclude their headmaster from taking other paying pupils, often boarded with him – indeed often enough he had every cause to do so to eke out a none too princely stipend. Winchester allowed ten such 'outsiders' (*extranei*) or 'commoners' – so called because, as at the universities, they paid for their food, or commons – to be 'instructed and informed in grammar within the said college, without charge to the college'. When Mulcaster tried to do this at Merchant Taylors' he was forbidden by the Company, but the Master added £10 to his salary (thereby doubling it) from his own pocket by way of compensation. Such inhibitions were rare, and it was this practice, coupled with the impetus given later to boarding education by Arnold's ideas at Rugby, that eventually led, more than anything, to the high fees and expensive terms of many of the independent boarding schools today.

The gradual entry of the state into the field of secondary education inevitably brought a change in the attitude towards fee-paying, especially after all state primary education was made free in 1918. The case for the abolition of fees in grant-aided secondary schools gained momentum in the period between the wars, and was forcibly and eloquently put by the Education Advisory Committee of the Labour Party and its spokesman R. H. Tawney [30]. Some of his arguments were emotive and specious; for instance that making elementary education free and charging fees for secondary education 'suggests that one is a necessity and the other a luxury'; and 'to charge a fee before a child is permitted to enter the second stage in its educational development is about as reasonable as it would be to impose a tax upon it because it had reached the age of eleven'. But the main burden of Tawney's case was unanswerable, particularly in the thirties. Despite the steady increase in local authority free places at grant-aided secondary schools, reaching 100 per cent in Bradford and Glamorgan even during the First World War and in Durham from 1923, it was clear that many children able enough to profit from a grammar school education were not receiving it because their parents could not afford the fees. Places were awarded by competitive scholarship examinations, and there were not enough of these scholarships to go round in many areas. Moreover any suggestion of a 'means test' to channel help where it was genuinely needed was anathema in those days of depression and slump. There may be a case, which we shall examine later, for such an arrangement in the affluent society of the sixties, but there certainly was not in the thirties. Tawney was able to argue overwhelmingly for an education system that would enable us 'to forget the tedious vulgarities of income and social position in a common affection for the qualities which belong, not to any class or profession of man, but to man himself' [31].

The abolition of fees for state secondary schools in the Education Act of 1944 was thus assured and was merely 'a completion of a process already far advanced' [22]. But if, as far as state secondary education was concerned, the first of our historical principles was thus guaranteed – for now no child could be deprived of secondary education through lack of parental means – the second began to be threatened. Would parents who no longer had to pay directly for education care enough about it? For rates and taxes were a less obvious and meaningful link with the pocket than the old terminal bill. In the event they reacted in two different ways. Some were suspicious and sceptical when what they had hitherto paid for was now offered free. Matthew Arnold, nearly a century before, had expressed their feelings precisely in *A French Eton:*

It is said that in education given wholly or in part by the State there is something eleemosynary, pauperizing, degrading; that the self-respect and manly energy of those receiving it are likely to become impaired.... How vain, how meaningless to tell a man who receives aid from the State for the instruction of his offspring that he is humiliated! Humiliated by receiving help as an individual from himself in his corporate capacity! He is no more humiliated than when he crosses London Bridge or visits the British Museum. But it is one of the extraordinary inconsistencies of some English people in this matter, that they keep all their cry of humiliation and degradation for help which the State offers. A man is not pauperized, is not degraded, is not oppressively obliged, by taking aid for his son's schooling from one of Mr Woodard's subscribers, or from the next squire, or from the next ironmonger, or from the next druggist, he is only pauperized when he takes it from the State, when he helps to give it himself! [32].

Many of these parents turned to the independent fee-paying schools as long as they could afford the fees. Others were wary at first of a kind of education of which they had had little or no experience, and hesitated to let their children waste their time, as it seemed, on subjects which appeared irrelevant to the business of earning a living, especially when they were actually expected to continue their studies after an age when they could otherwise be helping to swell the family budget. But in time, as a grammar school education was seen to be a gateway to the more attractive and responsible jobs in a technological and professional age, they began to accept and later demand it. At the same time some parents of the former type, convinced by the very success of the grammar schools that they were none the worse for charging no fees and unable, in any case, to pay the steadily rising fees in independent schools, began to return to the maintained-grammar-school fold. There arose a concentrated demand for a grammar school education for all.

But this demand could not be met. For one thing there were just not enough grammar school places available, and in any case not all children were considered suited to it. Selection there had to be, and it was given official blessing by the Ministry of Education booklet *The Nation's Schools* and defended by Ellen Wilkinson, the Socialist Minister of Education, at the Labour Party Conference of 1946. The instrument of selection was the notorious 11-plus examination, and the psychologists who operated it claimed confidently that they could predict at the end of the primary stage of a child's education which kind of secondary school, grammar, technical or modern, fitted him. In theory there was to be 'parity of esteem' between the three types of school, and children were merely being channelled to the appropriate school, however much misguided parents might talk – and how they talked! – of 'winning a scholarship to grammar school' and 'failing the 11-plus'.

But there were two serious difficulties. First the technical schools to all intents and purposes scarcely existed. As has been pointed out [22], for a genuine tripartite system we should need as many technical schools as grammar schools, whereas in fact there were in 1959 four grammar schools to every technical school and six grammar school pupils to every technical school pupil. Over 40 per cent of local authorities did not provide them at all, and in 1963 there were only 204 in the country, 16 fewer than the year before [8]. It is a paradox, but none the less true, that in an age that cried out for technologists and technicians, technical schools actually seemed to be withering away. Meanwhile the secondary modern schools were at a disadvantage to begin with through being in many cases housed in the buildings of the former senior elementary schools. This was to some extent offset by a concerted effort to give them new and imaginative buildings beside which many grammar schools looked shabby. But at first progressive ideas, contemptuous of examinations while the outside world was increasingly looking for the paper qualifications which they provided, robbed them of any prospect they might have had of competing on anything like fair terms with the grammar schools, and by the time second thoughts had begun to produce modern schools with General Certificate of Education and later Certificate of Secondary Education streams their image had been tarnished beyond repair. Yet these are the schools to which all from the age of eleven onwards go 'unless they can show cause to the contrary and there is a place for them in a school giving a different kind of education' [22]. So it comes to this: of the three types of school that make up the 'tripartite system', the secondary technical, the secondary modern and the grammar, the first is virtually non-existent, the second is that to which most go and nobody wants, the third all want and few can have. This 'tripartite system', sacred cow of a Socialist Government in 1945 and scapegoat of a Socialist Government in 1965, could thus with some justification be defended by Lord Attlee in the familiar words used in defence of the Christian religion: it has never been tried.

It could have been tried, given time, by various measures. Technical schools could have been expanded, not allowed to fall away. Secondary modern schools, after their teething troubles, could have been allowed to develop on the promising lines many of them are now following. Grammar school places could have been increased and more evenly distributed over the country to redress the present ludicrous maldistribution we have noted in the Introduction.* *Educating the Intelligent*, in setting its sights at the top 40 per cent of the intelligence range of our children [21] implies reasonably enough that this is the percentage that could profit by a grammar school education. Yet only about the top 25 per cent in fact qualifies for it. Above all the 11-plus examination, which produces this result and the much publicized anomalies which accompany it, could itself be examined.

The problem has been aggravated by the phenomenal growth, in post-war years, in the demand for higher education. A product of the 'bulge' (of the 1946–8 birth-rate) and the 'trend' (towards staying on at school), it shows statistically in the fact that between 1954 and 1966 the number of school leavers with the minimum qualification for university entrance rose from twenty-four thousand to sixty-six thousand. Much of the credit for this expansion, particularly in the field of mathematics and science, belongs to the grammar schools, and it is a recurrent theme in both the Crowther [22] and Robbins [45] Reports. To meet this demand Conservative governments have instituted a vast programme of university expansion. But the mere provision of university places, even if their number were adequate, still leaves the problem unsolved lower down, and there are two conflicting claims which seem hard to reconcile. On the one hand, the better the prospects school leavers have of securing a university place, the less willing the majority of parents become to see their children 'out of the race' at the age of eleven; on the other hand, those parents whose children do secure a grammar school place are anxious. Some of them, it may be, merely fear the loss of hard-won status in a world of grey uniformity:

> When everyone is somebodee,
> Then no one's anybody.

But with others the motive is more respectable. Any dilution of

*Since these words were written the anomalous situation has been even more strikingly illustrated thus: 'In Pembrokeshire a boy or girl whose I.Q. is round about 115 was probably perfectly safe for a grammar school place; in Putney he would have had a reasonably good chance; but just four miles away at the other end of the boat race at Mortlake he would have been a poor bet.' David Ayerst, *Understanding Schools*, Penguin Books, 1967, p. 216.

sixth-form standards could lead to a decline in the numbers qualifying for university education, and to high hopes at 11-plus being disappointed at 18-plus. With higher education increasingly regarded as a birthright, the resentment of the apparently disinherited presents a growing challenge to the fears of the heirs apparent. Meanwhile the problem of discovering and training the maximum quantity of national talent without sacrifice of quality becomes more urgent if we are to enter the European Common Market and pit our brains against the formidable continental products of *Lycée* and *Gymnasium*. All the more reason, therefore, to explore fully the possibilities of reforming the 'tripartite system' mentioned in the previous paragraph, and others besides.

None of these possibilities, however, is now being considered, much less implemented. Instead there is a more attractive proposition. Grammar school education in the past had to be paid for, an arrangement which, for all the objections to it, did at least ensure that those who used it cared enough to find out what they were buying and, so long as fees were reasonably low and adequate provision was made for those who could not afford them, was perhaps not as iniquitous a system as the facile phrase 'selection by the purse' implies. It has now become free to ticket holders, and inevitably the demand for tickets has far exceeded the supply. To increase the supply, or improve the method of distribution, is costly, slow and tedious. How much easier to smash the ticket-machine! This is the attraction of the comprehensive school. It removes the hated 11-plus and the three kinds of school of the 'tripartite system', with their unhappy associations, at a single blow; as such it is a politicians' dream. We must now examine it as an educational reality.

CHAPTER TWO

THE COMPREHENSIVE CHALLENGE

THIS chapter may at first seem an impertinence: for readers of
Penguin Books will be aware that there is a companion volume on
The Comprehensive School by Mr Robin Pedley [33] giving a full
and well-documented account of comprehensive experiments in
this country and elsewhere in much more detail than is possible
here, and there are other such books, many of them attractively
illustrated. But these writers, in their anxiety to win converts,
overstate their case in two ways. First they over-idealize it.
Memories of our own school days die hard and have been further
deglamourized by the literature of disenchantment that has grown
up around school life, and as we move from happy comprehensive school to school, with its eager children and enlightened
teachers, scepticism mounts. The 'best years of our life', we feel,
could not be that good. Secondly many of them wear their
political hearts on their sleeves. If the Church of England is the
Tory Party at prayer, the Comprehensive School is apt, these
days, to be the Labour Party in the pulpit. The comprehensive
debate is essentially an educational one. There are some who
believe that going comprehensive is 'one of the most worthwhile
changes that ever have or ever can be brought about in this
country' [34]. Others fear that we may be selling our grammar
school birthright for a mess of comprehensive pottage. The
politically uncommitted reader who wants to assess the argument
on its educational merits is merely distracted or irritated by ill-
concealed Party rosettes.*

Our aim in this chapter is to state the comprehensive case as
fairly and objectively as can be before we examine it critically.
Therefore, while much of the material in it is derived from Mr

---

* Mr Pedley's bias even insinuates itself into his Glossary of Educational
Terms, where the 'tripartite system' is described as 'an ugly phrase for an
ugly arrangement' [33].

Pedley and other committed writers, we shall temper it by other less prejudiced sources, in particular the excellent series of articles published in *The Times* in April 1965 [35]. Moreover many of the books written by advocates of the comprehensive case ante-date the election of a Labour Government in 1964. After that, understandably, they have felt that their mission has been accomplished and that Circular 10/65 [47] is worth a thousand books. But a good deal has happened since then, and of this we must take account to get a proper perspective.

DEFINITION

What is a comprehensive school? No one could better answer this question that Sir Graham Savage, formerly Education Officer to the London County Council and master-planner of London's post-war comprehensive schools, for it was he who coined the name. 'Everyone,' he tells us, 'was calling these schools multi-lateral then, and I thought that was an awful name.' When asked what they should be called, 'I said "comprehensive". For two reasons: one because they will cater for every activity; two, because all children from a given area, regardless of ability, will go to them' [35].

In this sense all state primary schools are comprehensive, and the comprehensive secondary school, as Mr Pedley points out, is 'simply an extension of the comprehensive primary school, and has the same aims' [33]. But it is not quite as simple as that, for though the age ranges of primary (5–11) and secondary (12–18) education embrace roughly the same length of time in a pupil's school life special interests begin to develop at the secondary stage, and a wide range of courses must be offered to meet them, particularly at sixth form level. That is why, if any sort of economic staffing ratio is to be maintained, secondary comprehensive schools are almost inevitably large. A school which must cater at once for a specialist interest in, say, landscape gardening and the inscape imagery of Gerard Manley Hopkins in viable teaching groups is almost bound to be a four-figure affair.* But

---

*For a well-argued case that this is not inevitable see David Ayerst, *Understanding Schools*, Penguin Books, 1967, pp. 227–32.

as most existing grammar and secondary modern schools are
built for an average of 450 pupils and many are far smaller this
immediately raises a difficulty. Expensive new buildings are
required and multifarious and no less expensive equipment to
furnish them. To meet this problem some subdivision of the
secondary stage has been suggested and tried, and this solution
will be considered later. But such 'two-tier' comprehensives, as
they are often called, are not truly comprehensive schools in the
sense intended by Sir Graham Savage, for though they may be
comprehensive 'horizontally' they are not so 'vertically', and
though they may do much to solve the problems of cost and size
they raise others just as formidable, as we shall see.

Before considering in more detail the implications of Sir
Graham's definition we must dispose of a popular heresy. It is
sometimes claimed, particularly by politicians and 'personalities'
in B.B.C. programmes such as *Any Questions?*, that the 'public
schools' are really comprehensives 'for those who can afford the
fees'.* This is firmly denied both by the former Headmaster of
Eton and the educational correspondent of the *New Statesman*
[36], and in the face of such improbable accord little more,
perhaps, is needed than a clinching Euclidean Q.E.D. But it
is worth pointing out that all 'public schools' demand the
Common Entrance Examination as a qualification for entry
(though there are variations in pass mark from 35 per cent to
above 60 per cent) and that even to make a showing in this
examination with its academic syllabus including subjects like
French, Latin and Mathematics (not merely Arithmetic as in the
11-plus exam) it is essential to begin an academic training,
usually in an independent preparatory school, at a considerably
earlier age, even allowing for the fact that it is taken at 13-plus,
than is necessary to gain entry to the maintained schools. Moreover the curriculum in 'public schools' differs little from that in
state grammar schools, and all follow courses leading to O-level
and (for increasing numbers) A-level in the General Certificate of
Education. What people who claim that 'public schools are

*That the usually penetrating Insight feature of the *Sunday Times* (16
October 1966) should have fallen into this heresy is a measure of the widespread misconception about educational matters these days.

comprehensive' are trying to prove is difficult to see. Is it the naïve syllogism: Eton is a good school; Eton is a comprehensive school; therefore comprehensive schools are good schools? Or is it the familiar complaint that the rich can get in anywhere? Whatever the motive, the statement is just not true, and need not further detain us.*

In Sir Graham Savage's definition of the comprehensive school two qualities stand out. First, *they cater for every activity*. Of this there can be little doubt, and the breadth and range of the courses they offer is a strong attraction. To take two examples: at Binley Park School, Coventry, by the age of fourteen:

In the more academic forms, all pupils take English and mathematics, nearly all take French and some branch of science. Children choose three or more subjects from Scripture, German; commerce, accounts, shorthand/typing; art, music, needlework, woodwork; domestic science, metalwork, geometrical and engineering drawing. The pupils enter for the General Certificate of Education, or for the new Certificate of Secondary Education. The less able children can still do academic subjects – and may plod on and reach G.C.E. level a year late. Others join a variety of courses – technical, domestic. commercial, arts and craft, or rural science. [35]

One of the newest London comprehensive schools, at Woolwich,

offers its fourth year a choice from English, mathematics, physics, chemistry, biology, German, French, history, geography, commerce, typing, book-keeping, shorthand, retail trading, woodwork, metalwork, technical drawing, engineering, cookery, needlework, art, pottery, music, physical education, religious education, surveying and drama. There is also a specialist for remedial work with backward children [37]

*A more serious question is whether pupils who fail the 11-plus could, given the academic training of an independent preparatory school, pass the Common Entrance Examination and thereby gain access to an academic course. In fact there are some boys in 'public schools' who, for one reason or another, have passed Common Entrance and failed the 11-plus, and many of them go on to get respectable results in G.C.E. This problem is solved by the good comprehensive school and also in secondary modern schools like those in Surrey which have G.C.E. courses. Elsewhere there might be a case for some sort of 'integration' of private preparatory schools to give such pupils whose parents cannot afford the fees a chance of an academic education, though the problem of selecting them would be difficult. But the question of 'integration' at other than secondary school level is outside the scope of this book.

Mr Pedley gives an even more impressive list, including Russian, but I suspect this is intended to be exhaustive rather than typical. At least a random check of a well-known comprehensive school on the matter of Russian produced the reply that they used to offer it but now have no one to teach it. Perhaps this was untypical. Certainly the very size of a comprehensive school, often enough held against it on human grounds, makes possible the pursuit of a wide range of subjects supported by expensive ancillaries such as up-to-date science and language laboratories and closed-circuit television. Any measure thus to enrich the curriculum offered at the secondary stage is to be welcomed, and it is perhaps here more than anywhere else in the *educational* sphere that these schools are making their greatest contribution at the present time.

Secondly, according to Sir Graham's definition, *all children from a given area, regardless of ability, go to them*. This is a much more controversial matter, for it presupposes the abolition of selection of any kind, and the only place where this is absolutely true at the time of writing is in the County of Anglesey and in the Isle of Man. Elsewhere it is the common complaint of the advocates of comprehensive schools that the abler pupils are 'creamed off' by maintained grammar schools or direct-grant and independent schools and this applies particularly in the London area. That this is so must be frankly admitted in this chapter which is concerned with facts. Whether it should be so will be considered later. At this stage, however, it is also worth pointing out that comprehensive schools are also 'creamed' – or perhaps the word is 'dredged', though nothing derogatory is intended against the unfortunate people concerned – in another sense. For throughout the country there are special schools – not enough of them indeed – for the mentally retarded and physically handicapped, and these children, wherever possible, are therefore excluded from comprehensive schools. It is worth noting that the comprehensivists raise no objection to this practice, no doubt because it does not touch their obsession about keeping up, in terms of academic prowess and examination successes, with the grammar school Joneses whom they hope, eventually, to liquidate. Still, the fact remains that the comprehensive school, except in

Anglesey, is at present lopped at either end and in this sense Sir Graham's definition is not completely valid. Implicit also in the definition is the social comprehensiveness that complements the educational. If all children from a given area, regardless of ability, go to them so do all children regardless of class. Many supporters of the comprehensive principle lay great stress on this, arguing that it is not only a desirable piece of social engineering but also has an *educational* role since social mingling is itself educative. How far the comprehensive neighbourhood school achieves this is examined critically in Chapter 4.

THE 'ALL-THROUGH' COMPREHENSIVE – ANGLESEY AND THE PROVINCES

Though other countries, especially the United States and Canada, the Soviet Union and Scandinavia, have had comprehensive schools, usually under other names like 'high-school', for many years, in Britain they are essentially a post-war development. It should be pointed out, too, that they originated here not, as some of them would perhaps like us to believe, with the politicians, but with a problem and a pioneer.

First the problem – that which faced the County of Anglesey. Just after the war the island possessed four grammar schools, two of them with a high reputation but all too small to offer a sufficiently wide range of courses, especially in the sixth form. 'One, at Amlwch in the barren north of the island, carried on day by day in an austere church hall. Classes were held on the stage and in kitchens and cloakrooms; yet good teaching still got good results' [35]. For the 11-plus 'failures' there was only the prospect of an extended primary education in 'all-age' schools. How then could the demand of the 1944 Education Act for 'secondary education for all' be met in a rural, rate-starved county? The problem was solved by establishing four comprehensive schools. This was educational experiment at its best. There was no political campaign, with words like 'under-privileged' and 'deprived' being bandied around – no appeal to class distinction and envy. The people of Anglesey simply faced up to the problem of providing the best education possible for their sons and daughters on a limited budget in the spirit of the 1944 Act. They have been amply justified in the result. In ten years the number of O-level candidates has doubled and A-level trebled; and their determination to invest in success is shown by the willingness of a population of 50,000 to spend £1,600,000 on education in 1965 [35].

Within a general pattern of success there are, of course, as with all worthwhile experiments, criticisms and qualifications. Practices vary and reports are somewhat chequered. The David Hughes School at Menai Bridge accommodates 900 children divided into six houses of 150 each with a housemaster and housemistress who receive extra pay for the general and pastoral care they give their charges. Pupils are streamed for academic but not for non-academic subjects. Ability groupings are assessed twice a year and children move up or down accordingly. In the planning and arrangement of buildings much was 'learned from the mistakes' of earlier schools. Holyhead, on the other hand, scattered over the town in old buildings, is ruefully described by its headmaster as a 'prize example of how not to go comprehensive' [35]. It delays streaming until after two years, when it is introduced under the pretentious pseudonym 'progressive-differentiation' but seems to operate none the worse for that. The special feature of Llangefni is the organization of its four houses on a territorial basis according to the complex of villages from which the children are drawn. A roving teacher has the special task of arranging extra-mural activities in the various villages in turn – for instance a house will put on a play one night at each village, and the school receives a grant of £200 a year from the Welsh Church Arts Council for the purpose. Amlwch, with about 800 pupils, rather resembles an overgrown grammar school, conducting its own tests on entry at 11-plus and streaming immediately on the evidence of these and primary school records. Its headmaster, though he now has some doubts about the value of streaming, is convinced of the value of comprehensives: 'We have about 300 pupils of grammar school level, but we provide a much greater variety of advanced level courses than could a grammar school of this size. There is no evidence of bright children being pulled down by the dull. Fortunately the school is not too large; I would not fancy being head of a school of 2,500' [35].

Naturally enough, too, individuals are critical. At Holyhead, the largest, there was an example of what has now become a sort of 'comprehensive chestnut' – a master, when about to rebuke two boys for smoking, was asked by them who he was. It is interesting that the reason given for favouring the 'old split' was rather a sympathy for the effect on the 'not-so-bright', and this recalls the advocacy of a smaller school community for such children in the Newsom Report, *Half our Future*. But the value of the Anglesey experiment, carried out before the comprehensive issue was clouded by the class-war or perverted by politicians, cannot be overestimated. Indeed other education authorities were quick to profit by its experience.

Thus Lawrence Weston School, situated on a new housing estate just outside Bristol, has followed up the idea of the school as a community centre developed at Llangefni. Here a compact housing estate has immense advantages over a scattered group of villages. The school, in fact, operates a sort of voluntary shift system: daytime for the children, evenings for the parents as well: 'In the large craft room mother, father and teenage daughter bend over a bench. Mother is doing pottery; father and daughter are painting. The daughter's work is easily the best, but father is coming on' [35].

It was an imaginative stroke, too, that housed Lawrence Weston's public library inside the school. Lack of parental interest is perhaps one of the biggest educational diseases of our time, and while so many writers and speakers in this debate are concerned to make parents envious or resentful we should welcome this practical measure to encourage them to become involved. With so many families 'the greater part of the educational journey the children undertake must be unaccompanied' [22]; indeed the real clue to the undoubted advantage which the much-maligned middle-class parent enjoys in the scramble for good schooling lies not so much in his money, or even his education, but in the fact that he cares.

Though not wishing, in this brief survey, to rewrite Mr Pedley's book for him I shall mention, before turning to the London schools, one other provincial comprehensive school, Binley Park

School, Coventry. This school is of special interest because of its outstanding success, and that despite its lack of one qualification on which Mr Pedley strongly insists and its possession of another which he regards as of dubious value. Some consideration of it is essential, therefore, if we are to get our perspective right.

The academic success of Binley Park, a mixed school of 1,040 pupils, is quite striking. Of the 40 pupils taking A-level in 1965 two thirds were 11-plus rejects, and a third of the O-level candidates had failed that exam. We have already noted the range of its curriculum. Yet its site is unattractive – a village that once served as a coal pit. The base from which it grew, Binley Park Secondary Modern School, had an unsavoury reputation. And in Coventry the 11-plus still remains to attract the brighter children to four maintained or direct-grant grammar schools in the city centre. Now this 'creaming' by grammar schools is, as we have seen, something of which the comprehensivists complain bitterly. Mr Pedley's words are typical: 'All urban comprehensives suffer to a greater or less extent in this way from creaming by the grammar schools' [33]; and again, in more militant mood, 'comprehensives in the towns cannot be content with indefinite deprivation' [38]. For a more general consideration of the principles involved in these views, and the technique of 'hidden persuasion' by which they are propagated, the reader is referred to Chapter 4. But Professor John Vaizey, though generally a supporter of comprehensive schools, expresses a somewhat different point of view [9]. 'Such schools,' he says, 'resemble the more progressive, newly-built and excitingly-run secondary modern schools.' And later:

We know that many of the children in the modern schools are able to undertake sixth-form work with reasonable prospects of success. In such a situation the 11-plus will lose many of its terrors, and (one may ask) what would be the point of carrying on a battle about comprehensive schools – especially as it is extremely difficult to tell the difference between adjacent areas where one has a grammar school and a comprehensive school and the other a grammar school and a big modern school? So long as the schools are big enough to carry a varied and qualified staff (and 600 is surely the minimum for an effective secondary school) then any school can take its pupils to A-level.

On the evidence of Binley Park School Professor Vaizey, it seems, comes a good deal nearer the truth than Mr Pedley.

There are many other features of the school that deserve praise – its lavish equipment, its value as a community centre, its magnificent music and other out-of-school activities. But space limits us to only one – its house system. We have seen the value of this already at Llangefni, but Binley Park was purpose-built for its house system. Each house of 150 pupils is a 'key social unit in the school' [35]. It organizes indoor games and other activities and has a house assembly, instead of the school assembly, twice a week. The heads of houses deal with pupils' personal problems, supervise their general progress, keep records and work closely with parents, each house having its own parent-teacher association. In the words of the headmaster: 'The object of these is to establish a rapport between parents and school so that parents have confidence in the school and come to regard it as a help and not a hindrance' [35]. The houses are subdivided into tutor groups of 25–30 children of about the same age but embracing the whole range of abilities. Each tutor gets to know his pupils intimately. An article by one of the housemasters of Binley Park in *The Times Educational Supplement* [39] gives an informative account of the valuable work the house system can do in a comprehensive day school. It was of special interest to me, as a housemaster in an independent day school, to compare notes on how youth, 'privileged' and 'under-privileged' alike (to use the fashionable jargon) can be helped by a sympathetic housemaster or tutor, and how frequently their problems are similar. But Mr Pedley has doubts. 'I am not yet convinced that [the house] in a day school is necessary,' he says, and quotes a headmaster who 'is uncertain whether this panders to fashion or is of real value' [33]. He cites difficulties such as lack of continuity of staff, as careerist teachers shop around in search of greater responsibility, pay and an eventual headship, and loss of contact between a non-graduate housemaster and many of his senior boys whom he no longer teaches (a special problem in comprehensives). Of course there are difficulties, as there are for a parish priest. But he must soldier on all the same, and, as my opposite number at Binley Park would doubtless confirm, so often the help one can give is of a confidential nature that escapes the notice even of headmasters, let alone itinerant educationists. Indeed it was a criticism of a student who did his teaching practice at a comprehensive school with a house system that the house spirit is almost too fierce and personal (recalling Mr Chowdler's régime in *The Lanchester Tradition*), and loyalty to house overshadows loyalty to school. Yet it is so often objected that children in comprehensive schools suffer because the community is too big and impersonal. Between the doubts of Mr Pedley and the certainty of the Binley Park housemaster and myself the reader must make up his own mind. It is worth noting that when I put to the headmaster of Tulse Hill Comprehensive School, which has a strong and well-developed house system, that this, by its administrative and pastoral decentralization, left him with the vision to do his own job more effectively, he warmly agreed.

THE LONDON COMPREHENSIVES

From the problem (see page 72) we now turn to the pioneer, whom we have already met in the person of Sir Graham Savage, author of the name 'comprehensive' and of our definition. In 1925, when he was still a young inspector at the Board of Education, an exchange visit to Canada took him also to the United States, where he studied the American high schools of New York and Indiana and recorded his impressions in a 200-page report published by the Board of Education in 1928 [40]. Much of what he said there was critical, particularly his strictures on the retarding influence of the senior high schools on abler pupils. These views can hardly please comprehensivists of the Pedley persuasion, but more detailed consideration of them is reserved till later. Broadly, however, Sir Graham was impressed by the American non-selective system and eager to see it tried in this country. In due course the moment came to match the man. When Labour gained control of the London County Council in 1934 one of its first measures was to brief its Education Committee to inquire into and report on the arrangements for post-primary education in the schools under its jurisdiction. This report came out in favour of a system that would function as an integral whole, and of 'multilateral' schools which would cater for all pupils from 11-plus without any special competitive or scholarship examination. Like Sir Graham the compilers had reservations about American schools because they were concerned with national integration whereas the L.C.C. aimed at the individual development of each pupil according to his capacity. 'So we turned to Scotland, where, because of their different system of administration, they were able, in some of their secondary schools, to combine academic and technical education with the education of the less gifted pupil. And we thought that if it could be done successfully in Scotland, it could, once the regulations permitted, be done in London' [41]. The 1944 Education Act provided the machinery and Sir Graham, who by now had moved from the Board of Education to become Education Officer of the L.C.C., provided the expertise and personal energy to translate plan into action. In 1947 he produced the London School Plan which was the blueprint for London's comprehensive schools. In 1948 five experimental comprehensive schools were established, two mixed and three single-sex, but they were housed in existing buildings, sometimes scattered, as the post-war priority in building was repair of the ravages of war damage and the more urgent restoration of wrecked primary schools. These schools were an amalgamation of former senior elementary and selective central schools but nowhere absorbed a grammar school. The reason is significant. London possesses, in the words of a former L.C.C. chairman, an 'undue number' of voluntary secondary schools [41] – 'London's main headache', in Mr Pedley's engaging phrase. The reader will recall, from Chapter 1, the unselfish initiative and generosity that produced such schools and note, for future reference, the sour impatience that any suggestion of independence calls forth in some educational planners. This impatience Sir Graham, to his credit, did not share. He visualized that his Plan must be a long-term one, requiring perhaps thirty years to implement, and his attitude, at least towards direct-grant grammar schools, is, as we shall see later, much more tolerant and appreciative [35]. In any case the voluntary element on the governing bodies of the London grammar schools, in the majority in the 'voluntary aided' schools and to be reckoned with even in the 'voluntary controlled' (see page 37), objected to being taken over, as they saw it, and, to quote the former L.C.C. chairman again, such schools 'by the provisions of the Act cannot as yet [menacing words] be incorporated' [41]. The new comprehensives had to manage without a grammar school element, and though a system of 'county complements' was devised to work in conjunction with the voluntary schools it was not a success and these 'county complements' have since become fully comprehensive with their own sixth forms.

Meanwhile building restrictions were relaxed and the brand new London comprehensive schools began to appear, the first of them Kidbrooke school for 2,200 girls at Blackheath, opened in 1953. Today London has seventy-seven fully comprehensive schools and plans to create as soon as possible others for the remaining secondary modern schools. In quality and character these schools show infinite variety. At one end of the scale is Kidbrooke, purpose-built and something of a showpiece, of which the following description gives a striking impression:

Its architecture expresses both the idealism and the size of the concept, and the atmosphere of a brave new world of schooling. It is a huge triangle of buildings of brick and glass and cedar-wood, with a low copper-covered hall in the middle of it, big enough to hold all two thousand girls at prayers every morning. Inside there are rows of glassy, brightly painted classrooms, including a room of typing girls, a room of dressmakers, a row of model kitchens, a pottery, a model flat, laboratories, libraries and three gymnasia. It certainly has some of the appearance of mass-production: there are long rows of pegs, numbered from 1 to 2,200, two thousand steel chairs in the hall, two thousand girls dressed in identical light grey skirts. The school timetable, showing the criss-crossing of fifty different classes, looks like a Continental railway timetable. But it shows the freedom, as well as the intimidation, of bigness: it is clear at Kidbrooke, as it is far from clear at most British schools, that you can do almost anything and find any kind of girl. And the school is split up into smaller units: there are eight houses (Dolphin, Salamander, Unicorn etc.), which cut across classes and ages, and a huge range of unacademic activities, like an orchestra, an Old Vic Club, rounders or fashion shows. Behind a yellow door in the entrance hall is a light office more like a sitting-room – with a loud-speaker, a microphone, and a mass of charts and timetables – inhabited by the headmistress [1].

Then there is Holland Park, a mixed school of 2,040 pupils. Housed in what seems to be becoming a Ministerial catchment-area, with three Ministers' sons there already and now no less a prize than the two step-daughters of the Secretary of State for Education, it bids fair to become the Eton of the New Establishment and has amenities to match. At the other end of the scale is North Paddington, recently visited by the Queen, accommodated in dingy, scattered, makeshift Victorian buildings with a depressed and multi-racial catchment area and every sort of problem to contend with; and then, before the Inner London Education Authority closed it, there was Risinghill. Not surprisingly some of these metropolitan comprehensives have from time to time become the centres of publicity and controversy – the observations of Miss Lang of Kidbrooke, the closing of Risinghill, perhaps above all their relationship with that thorn in their flesh, the neighbouring grammar schools. To these we shall return later when the issues they raise come to be discussed. But whatever the differences of opinion raised by such matters of principle few will dispute that the London of the sixties without its comprehensives would be a poorer place, or grudge recognition to Sir Graham Savage, the educational pioneer who, more than anyone else, made them possible.

ADVANTAGES OF THE ALL-THROUGH COMPREHENSIVE

At this stage it may be useful, before considering some variants of the comprehensive principle, to take stock of the advantages commonly claimed for these schools. Of these six seem to me to stand out:

(1) Schools that take all children of secondary age in a given area must be large, and this means new buildings, for most existing ones were designed for a three- and not a four-figure population. Mere size means a wider variety of courses and larger staffs, including graduates, which pupils in secondary modern schools see comparatively rarely. The staff, 'comprehensive' from choice as long as choice remains, are often enthusiasts, and

the new buildings and amenities further fire their enthusiasm.

(2) In the field of 'social engineering' they look attractive. The 11-plus 'failures' share many of the amenities of the 'successes' such as games, social activities and non-academic subjects. The wearing of the same cap helps to mask the differences immediately beneath it, and while the segregation of the 1944 Act appeared to accentuate class barriers, a single school for all seems to break them down.

(3) In the academic field late developers can be better cared for. Though most British comprehensive schools are streamed, with none of the 'all-ability' classes of the American high schools, transfer between streams in the same school is easier than between separate schools. There is some evidence, too, of academic success, though we shall consider later whether these have been perhaps tendentiously exaggerated.

(4) There are some successful comprehensive schools which existed before the Kidbrooke vintage – in rural Anglesey for instance – where the 'grammar school population' was too small to produce a viable selective institution.

(5) Sheer size makes necessary the decentralization of head-masters' contact with individual pupils through housemasters, and this is proving beneficial as it has long done in most inde-pendent boarding and day schools.

(6) They have value as community centres, particularly by encouraging parents who might otherwise be apathetic about their children's education to become involved.

But the educational advantages that stem from the very size of the new comprehensives are also an economic liability. No government, even one committed, as at present, to mass com-prehensivization, can escape some compromise between the desirable and the financially feasible, and in the educational field alone the competing claims of primary and higher education rule out any prospect of expenditure on a scale adequate to honey-comb the country with Kidbrookes overnight.* Some interim schemes, making full use of existing buildings while still moving

* Merely to bring existing primary and secondary schools in England and Wales up to modern standards would cost £1,368,000,000 (*The School Building Survey, 1962,* H.M.S.O., January 1965).

some way towards 'the reorganization of education on comprehensive lines', have therefore been devised, and to these we must now devote some attention.

THE LEICESTERSHIRE PLAN

We have seen that for a comprehensive school to produce a sixth form of reasonable size it needs over 1,000 pupils, while existing secondary school buildings, grammar and modern, accommodate on average only about 450. If therefore vertical division according to ability is to be avoided the alternative is some form of horizontal split, thus making the secondary stage a 'two-tier' affair. The former secondary modern schools assume responsibility for the lower division as junior comprehensive schools, catering for *all* children from leaving primary school to the age of fourteen. Then all who wish go to the grammar schools, which with their established sixth forms are particularly suited to the later secondary stage, provided that their parents undertake to keep them there for at least two years. The rest remain at the junior comprehensive school to complete their education. Quite simply the scheme puts 'existing small and medium-sized schools end-on to provide secondary education in two stages', in Mr Pedley's words. It was, in fact, he who first suggested the idea in 1956 and to his description of it, cautiously realistic and free here from political bias, the reader is referred for further details [33].

A year later Leicestershire decided to adopt this plan in two areas, Wigston and Hinckley, officially describing it in these terms: 'Three links in a continuous chain of education – Primary School, High School, Grammar School, and boys and girls move naturally from one to the next. At no point is the next step forward dependent on an examination' [43]. Broadly the County followed the lines adumbrated by Mr Pedley, but with one difference:

A small proportion, corresponding to the fast streams in the grammar schools which will probably take the General Certificate at ordinary level at 15, will be able to transfer a year earlier, just as they are now able to enter under age for the '11-plus'. . . . The admission to the high school of high fliers at the age of 10 would be an internal matter for discussion between the heads of the primary schools, the high schools, and the grammar schools [43].

At first this intake of high-flyers was a fixed small percentage (somewhere between 8 and 10 per cent) but now it is entirely on the recommendation of heads of high schools. It has been said that 'all children but a few "flyers" go to the same high schools until fourteen' [1], but this gives the false impression that the 'flyers' by-pass the high school altogether and, as a corollary, that there is some form of selection. Perhaps this error arose because during the first transitional two or three years problems of accommodation made it necessary to select the top $12\frac{1}{2}$ per cent direct for grammar school by the old 11-plus examination, but this now no longer applies. Again some people, when speaking of the Leicestershire plan, talk loosely of junior and senior high schools, but the County are precise in their terminology, insisting that the lower schools are *high schools* and the upper schools *grammar schools*. This may seem mere semantic hair-splitting, but I believe it is more important than that. The retention of the name 'grammar school' is deliberate and valuable, and helps to make the Leicestershire plan the excellent compromise or half-way house (according to one's point of view) it is between the selective and fully comprehensive systems.

This shows itself in three ways. First, the name 'grammar school' for the upper tier stresses the basically academic orientation parents who opt for it are giving their children's education, and does much to allay the anxieties ('prejudice' [35] is perhaps not quite fair) of grammar school teachers. Secondly, the recognition of the existence of 'high-flyers' is a welcome admission, in these egalitarian days, that in academic ability some children are 'more equal than others'. Thirdly, the introduction of parents' choice, with at least minimal 'strings' in the form of the guarantee to keep the child at grammar school for at least two years to ensure that it is a responsible choice and not merely 'for the sake of status' [33], is something which scarcely exists under a comprehensive system or, despite the protests of its champions, in the selective system either.

The Leicestershire plan is still relatively in its infancy, for the first A-level results of pupils who have been right through the new system were not due until Summer 1966, and the first O-level results suffered from extraneous difficulties associated with the building of a new school, though the later ones are more encouraging [44]. There are obstinate problems to settle – for instance, what to do with those who elect to stay at high school for one year, when the school leaving age is raised to 16 in 1970 making it statutory to stay for two years. The time for final judgement on the Plan is clearly not yet, but perhaps it is not too early to see in it something of the best of both systems. For instance streaming is firmly established at the outset in the high schools. An entry of nine forms is divided initially into three waves, A, B and C, on the evidence of junior school reports. Streaming within each wave takes place after one term, and thereafter there is ease of transfer between streams, though not between waves as the syllabus in each subject varies according to the wave. Broadly the A wave is reckoned to be equivalent to a normal grammar school entry at 11-plus. There is little belief in mixed ability groups : to quote one high school headmaster, 'I just can't see a child who is retarded and has an I.Q. of 70 learning maths alongside a child with an I.Q. of 140' [35]. This, and much else, would gladden the heart of the most diehard 'segregationist'. On the other hand Mr Pedley modestly sees in the Plan much to praise: it makes possible a smooth and rapid transition from selection at eleven to a fully comprehensive system; it can be introduced by a local education authority without reference to the Minister unless, as is unlikely, it involves the opening, closing or substantial enlargement of a school; and it prepares the public for fully comprehensive education. Furthermore the balance-sheet of advantage and disadvantage as between this plan and the 'all-through' comprehensives is so evenly poised as to be almost self-cancelling, as can be seen if we summarize Mr Pedley's pros and cons in tabular form [33]:

FOR THE PLAN	AGAINST THE PLAN
(1) The high school helps the gradual transition from the all-purpose class teacher of primary schools to the specialist teacher of secondary schools.	(1) A break after only three years is harmful. Some pupils take nearly a year to adjust to new teachers and environment. Continuity and undisturbed growth are essential in the education of adolescents.

(2) In a high school boys and girls can remain boys and girls and avoid the sophisticated influence of older pupils. They have a bigger say in running their own affairs and the intimacy of a small community. Equally the grammar school provides a more mature grown-up community for older pupils.

(2) It is the high school boys and girls who at fourteen and fifteen are the most flighty and least responsible. They need the steadying influence and example of the seventeen- and eighteen-year-olds.

(3) A bigger range of optional courses can be provided in the grammar school than in a 'through' school of the same size.

(3) The standard of teaching and the personal quality of teachers in the high schools tend to be average and rather mediocre. The influence of the real scholar is needed, both among his colleagues and on the most gifted pupils.

Again, while some argue that the high schools lose their potential leaders, whom they need as prefects, to the grammar schools, others claim that prefects drawn from the fourth-year high school pupils make better prefects than sixth-formers because they show less sophistication. When even Mr Pedley suspends judgement at present on what is predominantly *his* Plan perhaps the last word on it may be left to him: 'Both forms of organization [i.e. "Leicestershire" and "all-through" comprehensive] are needed, according to different local conditions' [33].

OTHER FORMS OF TWO-TIER ORGANIZATION – THE WEST RIDING

Not all have shown this tolerance towards Leicestershire. Sir Alec Clegg, for instance, Education Officer of the West Riding of Yorkshire, objects to the Plan because it is not truly comprehensive and retains selection. Moreover he is something of a paternalist in education, believing that parents cannot be trusted to choose what is educationally best for their children and that to replace selection at eleven by parental choice at fourteen is to replace one evil by another [35]. He has therefore devised for the Hemsworth division of the West Riding a scheme among schemes – for he is by way of being an alchemist of educational experiments, which include the successful 'Thorne' scheme for selection to which we shall refer later – which, starting from September 1968, contains three comprehensive schools, from 5 to 9, 9 to 13, and 13 till 16 and beyond. Revolutionary as this seems, with its departure from the traditional age-division between primary and secondary schooling, it has one strong argument in its favour. The Plowden Report [56] has now recommended that the age of transfer from primary to secondary school school should be 12-plus instead of 11-plus, and as a consequence the Leicestershire high schools, if they cater for the two years between 12-plus and 14-plus, will be little more than educational transit-camps. Sir Alec, foreseeing this, conducted a private referendum among fourteen of his headmasters asking them when the break should be made. Ten chose 13, two 14, one 11 and none 12. The majority who favoured 13 considered that two years in the Leicestershire grammar school before G.C.E. is 'not enough, and that "playing up" by children in secondary modern schools usually starts at 13' [35]. So the West Riding scheme is a piece of inspired anticipation, and it is worth noting that it corresponds to the common practice in many independent schools, with their nursery schools from 5 to 9, preparatory schools from 9 to 13 and 'public school' from 13 onwards after Common Entrance, and the general satisfaction of their clients suggests that the arrangement has much to commend it.

Hemsworth, where the experiment is to be tried, is an ill-favoured mining area which is one of some thirty divisions in the West Riding. The top tier, from 13 to 18, will be catered for in three high schools, one an extension of an existing grammar school, another an existing secondary modern school, also to be expanded, and the third an entirely new school. Each of these three high schools will be served by four or five intermediate schools for the ages 9 to 13, mainly in existing secondary modern schools; and each of these three groups of intermediate schools will be fed by six or seven primary schools covering the ages 5 to 9. The scheme is due to begin in September 1968, but any worthwhile assessment of it will be impossible before 1970. Three things, however, can be said now. First, Hemsworth is a neglected area with much arrears of building to be made up, and this scheme, like the scheme it supersedes which is mentioned in the next paragraph, suggests that it is an area that is receiving much administrative cogitation and paper when the real need is for bricks and mortar. Secondly, the intermediate schools present a special problem in that they are both an appendage to the primary stage and a preparation for the secondary. At this level there is a straddle not only of the existing primary/secondary division but also of the transition from 'form' to 'subject' teacher. To be successful this will require a new kind of head and probably assistant teachers as well who can be both 'form-minded' at the earlier stage and 'subject-minded' at the later and can move easily over the frontiers that more or less neatly coincide, under present arrangements, with the frontiers between primary and secondary schooling. Much thought and research is needed on what emphasis is to be given to each approach at each stage from 9 to 13; a mere willingness to teach any child of any ability anything, though showing the spirit of the willing horse, will not be good enough if the scheme is to have a fair trial. Thirdly, in the context of neglect at Hemsworth, a Cinderella where any change can only be a change for the better, hasty generalizations when applied to other better-favoured areas would be quite misleading.

Another arrangement in the West Riding, that at Doncaster and Bradford, follows more closely the Leicestershire pattern, but their junior high schools from 11-plus to 13-plus are followed by a move for *all* pupils, to senior high schools for those who propose to follow an advanced course, high schools for those who will leave at fifteen. At Hemsworth, in an earlier scheme, now suspended but appearing as an acceptable plan in Circular 10/65, two districts were to have a senior high school fed by a number of junior high schools all of whose children were to transfer to it at fourteen and thus get 'a taste of the superior opportunities and more adult atmosphere of the senior school' [33]. More interesting still is the experiment at Mexborough, but this brings us to a fundamentally different outcome of comprehensive experiment.

THE SIXTH-FORM COLLEGE

We have seen that one practical difficulty of comprehensive reorganization lies in the size of 'all-through' school necessary to produce a worthwhile sixth form. Yet another solution is to separate the sixth-form stage altogether. This idea had its origin before, and independently of, the comprehensive debate. The Crowther Report, for instance, gave it a cautious welcome: 'There may be room for a special junior college parallel with, but not in place of, Sixth Forms, enrolling only full-time students, offering a wide variety of courses both academic and practical.' The Report visualized 'an institution with the adult atmosphere of a technical college but with a much wider range of curriculum and with terms of reference nearer to those of a school, in that equal weight would be attached by the staff to the subjects taught and to the personal development of the students' [22]. The proviso that it should not *replace* sixth forms in schools is important, and was underlined again in the Robbins Report [45]. Sir Geoffrey Crowther himself pointed out [46] that his own children would welcome the more adult atmosphere of such a college, and there is no doubt that it could be valuable to many young people of about sixteen who, though not tired of education, are bored with school. All the same it is the comprehensive issue, and the proposal of a sixth-form or junior college to replace an assortment of inadequate sixth forms in the group of schools it serves, that has brought the idea of the sixth-form college more into public notice and translated it into bricks and mortar for the first time at Mexborough. (Atlantic College, at St Donat's Castle in Glamorgan, though its foundation antedates Mexborough, is an independent international establishment and therefore not in the same category, nor is the War Office's Welbeck College.)

Strictly speaking Mexborough is an excrescence on an existing grammar school (the implications of this are examined in detail in Chapter 5) but the college and lower school are in more or less separate buildings. They share laboratories, workshops, gymnasia and playing-fields, but the college proper is out of bounds to school pupils. Its remaining buildings enclose a courtyard and consist of common room and cloakrooms on one side, the main teaching block with centres for specialist studies in various subjects on another, on a third a great hall for dining, drama and the larger social functions. A splendid library adjoins that of the school and includes individual study cells for the students. The college, though largely fed at present by the lower school, is to be comprehensive for all who wish to continue full-time education to eighteen. School and college share the headmaster, senior mistress and senior master and have teaching staff in common, but day-to-day affairs in each have their own special master in charge. There is a house system running through both, and some pooling of resources in the matter of school societies and prefects. The facilities in the college are impressive. The common room is equipped with Scandinavian furniture, there is a self-service restaurant with a choice of dishes and the privilege of inviting guests. Morning coffee and afternoon tea are served in the common room. There is no supervision and the only rules are a ban on smoking and stiletto heels in the school and eating in the street, and compulsory attendance at morning prayers [35]. It cost the West Riding authority £750,000, but though it has its critics, including some teachers who fear it may create a new élite within the profession, the general view is that it was well worth the money.

There was an earlier but abortive plan for sixth-form colleges at Croydon, and Essex are working out a comparable idea in their South-East Division. Stoke-on-Trent also has a plan which has received Ministerial approval and is included in their building programme for 1966–7. Mr Pedley describes the plan as 'exciting', but on this word, which Ministerial Circular 10/65 [47] also applies to general progress in the comprehensive direction, a note of caution should be sounded. Someone has observed that when *avant garde* architects are about to launch a new experiment on the general public they frequently describe it as 'exciting' or 'challenging'. Likewise schemes which educational planners and administrators find 'exciting' on paper can often prove sheer purgatory to the unfortunate teachers whose lot it is to operate them. Broadly, Stoke's scheme is for a college of some 750 students, perhaps larger if demand justifies it. As an interim measure the new Longton High School is to be used as a co-educational school with an enlarged sixth form to specialize in A-level studies for those with suitable O-level qualifications.

While paper plans for sixth-form colleges accumulate, mention should here be made of a report by a voluntary study group formed from the staff of Luton County Technical School [48], of special value because it has the down-to-earth practicality of teachers actually engaged on the job. The report deserves reading in its entirety by all interested in sixth-form colleges, but one or two of its realistic recommendations may be briefly referred to. It favours some specialization between colleges, with perhaps a 'grammar school based' college to concentrate on classics and the rarer languages and a 'technical school based' college to supply the crafts and technology, though both should offer the more popular A-level subjects. It does not approve the 9 a.m. to 9 p.m. routine practised at Mexborough, but rather 9 a.m. to 5 p.m., thus avoiding the risk of becoming a 'knowledge-factory with a late shift'. It stresses the limitations of language-laboratory and teaching-machine, reminding us that in America, after extensive experiments, these are already 'on the way out'. Discipline should be the personal responsibility of the principal and not organized on a university system of self-government, and it cites the problems encountered by Atlantic College, Glamorgan, through 'having too democratic a form of student government and control'. Finally, a most practical point in our affluent society, a large car park with easy access is insisted on.

THE ORGANIZATION OF SECONDARY EDUCATION – MINISTERIAL CIRCULAR 10/65

The comprehensive debate has now come to a head in the demand of the Minister to local education authorities to submit to him their plans – fifteen copies by 12 July 1966 – for the reorganization of secondary education on comprehensive lines. For their guidance the Circular lists six patterns which 'have emerged so far from experience and discussion' and gives comment and advice on each [47]. These six headings serve as a convenient summary to this chapter. For the reader's guidance names of areas where the various schemes are being operated or planned as described above are added in italics and the diagram (Table 1) aims at further clarification. It is emphasized that neither parentheses nor diagram are the Minister's.

(i) The orthodox comprehensive school with an age range of 11–18. [*Anglesey* and, with qualifications, *London, Bristol, Coventry* and elsewhere.]

Table 1: Comprehensive Show-Case

SYSTEM	AGE 5–8	9	10	11+	12	13	14	15	16	17	18
Selective Education Grammar & secondary moderns most common	Primary			Grammar Schools (*or free places at direct-grant or independent schools*)							
				Secondary modern (*some to G.C.E. O level*)					STOP		
(i) *True Comprehensive* (a) Anglesey only (b) London, Bristol, Coventry etc., with reservations.	Primary			Secondary Comprehensive *New buildings usually needed*							
(ii) *Two-Tier Comprehensive* Hemsworth (earlier scheme)	Primary			Junior Comprehensive School			Senior Comprehensive School				
(iii) *Two-Tier Comprehensive* Leicestershire and some variants	Primary			High School		? ?	Grammar School				
(iv) *Two-Tier Comprehensive* Bradford, Doncaster.	Primary			Junior Comprehensive School			Senior High School / High School				
(v) *Sixth-Form College* Mexborough. Stoke-on-Trent modified and building.	Primary			Grammar School / Secondary Modern School					Sixth-Form College		
(vi) *Two-Tier Comprehensive* Straddles primary/ secondary age range. West Riding – Hemsworth (later scheme)	Primary			Junior High School			Senior High School				

SYMBOLS: ⎏⎏⎏ examination 'hurdle'.
       ???? parents' choice.
       – – – generally free access.

SOURCE: Based on a diagram in *The Times* of 6 April 1965, but brought up to date and title supplied.

(ii) A two-tier system under which *all* pupils transfer at 11 to a junior comprehensive school and *all* go on at 13 or 14 to a senior comprehensive school [a footnote explains that 'junior' and 'senior' refer to the lower and upper secondary schools in two-tier systems of secondary education]. [*Hemsworth* – earlier scheme.]

(iii) A two-tier system under which *all* pupils on leaving primary school transfer to a junior comprehensive school, but at the age of 13 or 14 *some* pupils move on to a senior school while *the remainder* stay on in the same school. There are two main variations: in one, the comprehensive school which all pupils enter after leaving primary school provides no course terminating in a public examination, and normally keeps pupils only until 15; in the other, this school provides G.C.E. and C.S.E. courses, keeps pupils at least until 16, and encourages transfer at the appropriate stage to the sixth form of the senior school. [*Leicestershire* and variants.]

(iv) A two-tier system in which *all* pupils on leaving primary school transfer to a junior comprehensive school. At the age of 13 or 14 *all* pupils have a choice between a senior school catering for those who expect to stay at school well beyond the compulsory age, and a senior school catering for those who do not. [*Bradford, Doncaster.*]

(v) Comprehensive schools with an age range of 11 to 16 combined with sixth form colleges for pupils over 16. [*Mexborough* and, modified and still building, *Stoke-on-Trent.*]

(vi) A system of middle schools which straddle the primary/secondary age ranges. Under this system pupils transfer from a primary school at the age of 8 or 9 to a comprehensive school with an age range of 8 to 12 or 9 to 13. From this middle school they move on to a comprehensive school with an age range of 12 or 13 to 18. [*West Riding, Hemsworth* – later scheme.]

This Circular will be further considered in Chapter 4. For the moment the reader is merely reminded of what was said at the end of Chapter 1: that the comprehensive school was attractive to politicians because it abolished selection. Yet in a sense this Circular has merely replaced one form of selection by another. The examiner is now no longer a teacher or psychologist but the Minister himself; the candidates are not now the pupils but the schools; and 'comprehensiveness' has ousted intelligence or ability as the criterion for selection. How the wholesale invasion of education by politics has brought this situation about will be the theme of our next chapter.

CHAPTER THREE

POLITICAL BATTLEGROUND

EDUCATION AND POLITICS

THE striking thing about the oft-repeated appeal to 'keep education out of politics' is not so much what it says as who says it. From a grammar school headmaster threatened with comprehensive reorganization, from a headmaster of an indepedent school anxious about integration, from a direct-grant school headmaster reeling under a Ministerial 'shot across the bows' it comes as no surprise. But coming from a champion of the comprehensives it gives us pause; for to reject the blessings of politicians who support his cause seems like looking a gift-horse in the mouth. Yet Sir Graham Savage, to whom London, as we have seen, in large measure owes its comprehensive schools, is quite emphatic: 'Damn it. I wish education could be left out of politics. The Conservatives were all against it. They opposed it simply because the other side proposed it. . . . Mind you, I can see the position where the Labour group would have opposed it, if it had come from the Conservative side' [35].

Miss Green, headmistress of Kidbrooke, likewise pleads: 'I wish we could keep politics out of it' [1]; and a master at Binley Park School, Coventry, 'believes that one of the troubles of the comprehensive system is that it is the chosen vehicle of one of the major political parties' [35]. The politician's blessing, it seems, is as embarrassing as his curse. In a sense this is understandable; for to the schoolmaster, seeking to go unobtrusively about his business, the noisy arena of politics where, in the current jargon, one's opponents' activities are 'manoeuvring' or 'tom-foolery' while one's own are a 'crusade' seems utterly alien. But a natural antipathy between pedagogue and politician does not of itself explain certain recent developments in the interplay of education and politics, and this matter must now be examined further

We have seen in the first chapter that government involvement in education since the middle of the last century had been cautious and reluctant. Conflict on narrow party lines had been rare, and complaints rather of lack of action than of the wrong action. The 1944 Education Act was a bi-partisan affair, and even in 1950 Sir John Newsom could claim with truth: 'No one political party has a better educational policy than any other – apart from a number of pious platitudes they exhibit a woeful lack of interest in the whole subject' [49].

But since 1960 there has been a dramatic change for which both leading political Parties must share the responsibility. The Conservative Party, steadily growing more complacent in contemplation of vistas of apparently endless office, by instinct prodigal over Defence and parsimonious over Education,* and in any case dedicated by conviction and electoral calculation to progressive tax-reduction, inevitably left undone in the educational field many things it ought to have done. The temptation to any Opposition in these circumstances to do at least one thing it ought not to have done was irresistible. We have seen that a sense of the unfairness of selection at 11-plus was growing in the fifties, and with it the increasingly strident claim that comprehensive schools provided the panacea. Here was a word tailor-made for a Signpost for the Sixties. There might, to the perceptive, be countervailing dangers. The Frogs, in Aesop's fable, complained to the Gods of their King Log because he did nothing. They were given King Stork instead, a king more dynamic and purposeful, a king indeed who

*That this is not quite fair to the modern Conservative Party is apparent from the following figures, for which I am indebted to Sir Edward Boyle:

Educational Expenditure as a Percentage of Gross National Product (*excluding* school meals and milk)

1954–5	1956–7	1957–8	1958–9	1959–60	1960–61	1961–2	1962–3	1963–4	1964–5	1965–6
3.2	3.6	3.9	3.9	4.0	4.1	4.4	4.8	4.9	5.1	5.3

Even the final figure for 1965–6, though under a Labour administration, no doubt stems mainly from Conservative planning. Moreover the Conservatives could cite, among other things, their achievement in university expansion and technical education to refute the charge of 'thirteen wasted years' in the educational sphere. Nevertheless the then Labour Opposition managed to make this image of the Conservatives credible, and it still carries some conviction in defiance of facts and figures.

abolished selection; he devoured them all. Whatever the moral of this tale the impact of politics on education had certainly taken a new form. Not that the Conservatives were opposed to comprehensive schools: by the time they left office 175 had been opened, most of them under their stewardship, and several Ministers spoke in favour of them. But the Opposition was now committed to the universal imposition of a comprehensive system, and for the first time a political party was prescribing a particular and exclusive form of secondary school organization. It was now no longer a question of how much of the gross national product should be devoted to education, but also how precisely it should be used.

Can we, and should we keep education out of politics? In this simple form the question is academic for two reasons. Politics, derived from the Greek word *polis* or 'city-state', is the business of man living in a community. A man's education, as Plato saw, affects his place in and contribution to society and to it, therefore, the politician cannot remain indifferent. But it is also of concern to himself as an individual and to his parents, and it was this aspect of it which, until the nineteenth century, accounts for the reluctance of British politicians to become involved. Once they did it was not easy to pull back. But, more important, involvement meant spending public money, and the amount has steadily increased until now it threatens to rise astronomically. In 1946 it was £189 million, now it is £1,500 million and the National Plan estimates that it will be £2,000 million by 1970, an average annual increase of £100 million over the next five years. Sir John Newsom puts it bluntly: 'One of the silly things that is often said is that education ought to be taken out of politics. That is barmy, because you cannot spend £1,500 million of public money and not be involved in politics' [50].

Nevertheless it is possible to rephrase the question as one of degree. For if the extreme position of non-intervention is untenable the opposite extreme of total take-over leads to totalitarian systems of education like those advocated by Plato and Karl Marx or practised with unenviable results in some countries today. How far, then, should government be involved in education? Here we meet two difficulties. First it is a vast and shifting question to which no definitive answer, valid for all time, can be given. State participation in education is a matter of evolution, and what may be accepted in 1966 as a matter of course would have been regarded as an intolerable interference with liberty in 1866, or even in 1900. Indeed even to describe it as evolution is in some sense to beg the question, for there are some who feel that the evolutionary process should be reversed – for instance Dr E. G. West in his recent book *Education and the State* [58], to which we shall return later. Secondly many schoolmasters are reputed to show in this matter an attitude of rugged independence and their views are therefore suspect. All the same two principles can, I think, be fairly applied in forming a judgement on this controversial issue.

First, such government participation should be unequivocal and honest. It is possible, for instance, for a government to believe, with Dr West, that it can best serve the community by progressively withdrawing from the sphere of education. If so, it should openly admit it, perhaps even to the extent of calling its department a Ministry of Educational Disengagement. Equally it is possible to regard a government's part in education as not primarily to further the cause of education at all but rather to redress the balance of social injustice. Thus a modern novelist, after a recital of the all-too-familiar evils – violence, crime, racialism and so on – that mar contemporary British society, continues: 'It is these deeper social evils as well as an inborn dislike of injustice that makes me support the comprehensive system with its coeducation, its heterogeneous communities, its interwoven streams of ability, its wide range of subjects offered' [51]. If a government accepts this, it should establish a Ministry of Social Engineering. But to have a so-called Ministry of Education and Science which is not concerned primarily with education and science at all but with other purposes, however laudable, is to mislead the public and set off on the slippery downward path to a dishonest administration.

Our second principle is that the proper concern of any government in the sphere of education is with ends, not means. Thus the 1944 Education Act, justly acclaimed on many counts as a model piece of educational legislation, charges local education authorities to do a number of things; it does not tell them precisely how to do them. If this seems an over-simplification of a complex problem, the present controversy over comprehensive re-organization provides a good illustration of its application. We have heard much lately about the 'groundswell of opinion' in favour of such a policy. This expression will be later examined more closely (see Chapter 4) as an example, among others, of high-pressure political salesmanship in the education market, but let us suppose, for the moment, that such a groundswell really exists.

First of all it could still be wrong. It is a function of demo-cratic government to distinguish between majority and informed opinion, and this is as important in the field of education as, for instance, in the matter of capital punishment, where legislation has run clean counter to mass feeling as revealed in opinion polls. Nor is Establishment opinion, whether of the Right or the Left, any more infallible. The warning of Mr Kingsley Martin is pertin-ent here: 'When a great many very important people say something over and over again very solemnly you can be pretty sure they are wrong' [52]. There was a groundswell of opinion among the Bourbons, the lemmings and the Gadarene swine.

Again, even if such a policy is correct the Opposition may not think so, and may be tempted to commit itself to the reversal of it. We have seen the results of this in industrial relations, with political battles over nationalization, de-nationalization and re-nationalization inflicting damage and uncertainty on the economy. Nothing could be worse than a similar conflict over education, with the two major Parties adopting diametrically opposed views, words like de-comprehensivization and re-comprehensi-vization being bandied about and politicians gambling not now with the national prosperity, which is bad enough, but with the futures of powerless children. It is to the credit of Sir Edward Boyle, the 'shadow' Minister of Education, that he has fore-stalled the danger to some extent by announcing in advance that he would not withdraw Ministry Circular 10/65. His bizarre picture of directors of education otherwise having 'two drafts in their locker', one for Conservative-controlled and another for Labour-controlled local or central government, is not entirely fanciful. Even so there is no guarantee that a subsequent

Conservative Minister would be as accommodating or that if Sir Edward, in reply to the Circular's demand for local plans for comprehensive reorganization, received from certain authorities a laconic 'none' (fifteen copies) his reaction would be quite the same as Mr Crosland's.

Finally it could well be that the best solution lies not within the strictly comprehensive terms of reference of the Circular but in a variegated pattern of regional or local differences. We have seen that Anglesey went comprehensive for cogent reasons in a climate of tripartite orthodoxy. Yet what may well be right for rural Anglesey could equally be wrong now for urban Bournemouth or suburban Croydon even though a Government of the same political colour has shifted its ground from tripartite to comprehensive. The varied advance reactions of local authorities to the Circular rather confirm this, and if the Government complain that these variations closely match political patterns it does not follow that they are wrong, and in any case only serves to underline the point I am making. A Government that treats a problem of educational organization as a political question has only itself to blame if it receives a political answer.

These are, it seems to me, compelling reasons why a government's concern in education should be with ends rather than means. The only means that should exercise it, indeed, should be not organizational but financial, and these it should will as far as it can. It is doubly unfortunate, therefore, that the present Government has dictated the means in the former sense and denied them in the latter, and excuses about the inheritance left by its predecessor are beside the point.

THE PARTY LEADERS

We turn now from political principles to politicians. It is fair, in this matter, to consider their pronouncements in the pre-election period of 1964, and to give pride of place to the Prime Minister himself. In a television performance at that time Mr Wilson promised the electorate that the grammar schools would be abolished over his dead body. This observation from the leader of a Party committed to a policy of wholesale comprehensive reorganization has not yet received sufficient attention in the education debate. To me it seems there are two possible explanations of it. The first is that Mr Wilson had failed, for once, to do his homework. For the *New Statesman* leaves the matter in no doubt:

> In this period of change, much confusion surrounds the future of the grammar schools, created largely by the reassuring speeches of some Labour politicians to the effect that these schools are to be 'preserved and strengthened' and that their 'traditions are to be valued'. If this means that it is desirable to make use of the staff and the buildings, this is generally true (though not always, when you think of some of the buildings – and indeed some of the staff). But it needs to be said more frankly that, while a grammar school in a comprehensive system may be the kind of school it was in Tudor times, it cannot be the kind of school it has been since 1944. And if the comprehensive idea means what I take it to mean, *the dominant tradition of the present grammar school ought not to be valued but discarded* – for it is a tradition of élite education.
>
> There are various things you can do with a grammar school. . . . What you cannot do, if you believe in a genuinely comprehensive system, is to maintain it alongside an adequate comprehensive and let it continue the 'creaming' process, whether by formal or informal selection. At that point, *the grammar school will have to go.* Perhaps some authorities should be preparing themselves and preparing public opinion for this event more consciously than is yet the case. Perhaps a Labour Secretary of State should too [53 – italics supplied].

He was hardly helped by his Leader. It is true that these words were written nearly a year after Mr Wilson made his pronouncement. But all the facts that lie behind them were available in 1964 and long before, and given the comprehensivist premise the logic of the *New Statesman* writer seems irrefutable.

The other explanation is that Mr Wilson had indeed done his homework, but his chosen course of study had not been the *New Statesman* or indeed his Party's manifesto but Michael Young's *The Rise of the Meritocracy* [54]. To this book, much praised for its satire but under-praised for its prophetic insight, we shall return later. But broadly its theme is that a socialist government, though first toying with the comprehensive school as a vote-winner, would later reject it in the face of concerted opposition from parents, children and teachers and then devote all its efforts to developing the grammar school, even awarding the present Minister of Education a knighthood in advance, presumably for his part in a delicate volte-face. If Mr Wilson accepted the thesis of this book or reached the same conclusions independently, his Delphic words may well have been telling the electorate more than they knew and his Party more than they bargained for. It might seem that to abandon the dogma of comprehensive education after so much propaganda in its favour would scarcely be politically feasible. We shall see. A brief resurrection on television of the grammar schools issue during the 1966 Election campaign brought an unequivocal answer no nearer. Mr Wilson parried the question by a deft rapier-thrust at his opponents – scarcely any of them had ever *been* to a grammar school – but the rest of his reply merely illustrated and underlined the *New Statesman's* criticism.

The impression given in 1964 by the then Conservative Leader left no such doubts. In a similar pre-election television interview Sir Alec Douglas-Home made the surprising and surprisingly little noticed observation, when defending parental choice in education, that if parents wished to *pay for* a grammar school education they should be allowed to (italics supplied). The charitable explanation is that this was a slip of the tongue, but one wonders. Conservatives may well object that their leader is now an ex-grammar school boy who knows what he is talking about. But the fact remains that there are still too many Conservatives who look upon the state schools as other people's schools while the 'public schools', where most of them were educated, are in some peculiar way their own, and even these are more valuable for their cachet than for their curriculum. The albatross of Eton still haunts them – a wasting asset to which their opponents can point the finger of scorn whenever they please, as Mr Wilson did in 1966, to sidetrack the central issue of the future of the grammar schools.

It is, then, a sad fact that in the pre-election exchanges of 1964 on the subject of education neither Party Leader emerged with much credit, and in 1966 education scarcely became an issue at all. Described not unfairly as a referendum in which Mr Wilson got his resounding *Oui*, it offered little to tempt the Opposition, who realized that grammar school parents form a minority of the electorate, while for the Government there were richer electoral dividends to be reaped elsewhere. In any case the Minister of Education was recovering from an attack of hepatitis.

THE MINISTER OF EDUCATION

Perhaps, however, it is unfair to tax the Party leaders with their shortcomings on matters of education. They have, after all, many other preoccupations and the proper person to turn to is the Minister of Education himself. Here we are at once faced with an occupational hazard to which politicians and political theorists are particularly prone when they make pronouncements on education – that of both expecting too much of it and blaming it for too much. Mr Crosland is in good company, for it has been said of Plato:

> One may perhaps ask whether education really has quite the power to transform society that Plato and others have thought. There are so many other influences that determine both society and the individual; and anyone engaged in the business of teaching who keeps his sense of proportion will perhaps view his work with a little greater scepticism and a little more saving humility [55].

Amen to that, from one schoolmaster to another. But the Labour Minister of Education has even less excuse than the Greek philosopher, for he has enjoyed the benefits of training not only in philosophy but also in politics and economics. Yet the following is his indictment of a small, if influential, part of British education:

> It is again no coincidence that Britain, the only country with a national élite system of private boarding schools from which its leadership is still disproportionately drawn, should be falling so badly behind other democratic countries in the achievement of widely accepted national goals – behind Western Europe in economic performance, Scandinavia in social welfare and urban planning, the United States in technology and innovation [4].

The independent boarding schools, as we all know, have their faults. But are they really, rather than the Common Market, the cause of our falling behind Europe's economic performance? Are they really, rather than the Scandinavians' avoidance of direct military involvement in major wars together with long periods of socialist government, responsible for our falling behind these countries in social welfare and urban planning? (It is surely ungracious for a socialist Minister thus to begrudge credit to fellow-socialists where credit is due!) Have not the vast American material and financial resources more to do with their success in technology and innovation than their comparative lack of private boarding schools?

Nor is this all. These same boarding schools, after the short-comings of Oxford and Cambridge have been superimposed on their products, are responsible for the deficiencies of the Civil Service. In particular, 'The Ministry of Education takes decisions for or against different types of school without conducting any research into their different consequences, and has little idea of how many teachers we need to carry out its own policies' [4].

Plus ça change, plus c'est la même chose. Mr Crosland is now at the Ministry himself with the following results. The Ministry has gone comprehensive on a hunch, to be justified by *post facto* research which will be concerned with comprehensive schools only, and not with a comparative investigation into the merits of alternative forms of secondary organization. Even such research as there is has received scant attention. The Ministry's own Plowden Committee which was to advise on the age of change-over from primary to secondary education and now recommends 12-plus [56] has not been awaited; and the Ford Report on com-prehensive reorganization in Bristol [62] has been dismissed as incomplete on the dubious grounds that partial research is worse than no research at all. It still seems that the Ministry does not know or dare not say how many teachers it will need to carry out its ambitious policies fully and such proposals as have been made to attract new recruits are unimaginative and seem unlikely to achieve their full purpose. Finally Mr Crosland has committed himself to comprehensive reorganization on a standstill budget, a policy which, whatever the merits of the case, seems guaranteed to secure the worst of all worlds.

One other sample of Mr Crosland's educational thinking

deserves attention. We are told that 'education is not a private good, like a washing-machine, to be left to the push and pull of market forces' [4]. In this kind of argument it is better to let one expert economist answer another:

The confusion here is in the judgement of the vehicle by the things it carries. One might just as well object to the provision of schools by municipal organization on the grounds that it is unthinkable to treat education as something that can be put on the rates – like refuse disposal. The market in fact is used for all kinds of professional services including medicine, insurance and law. While these services share, with soap (or washing machines) the same type of exchange mechanism, all similarities end at that point [58].

The question of the method of provision of education is, of course, a controversial one and we shall return to it in the chapter on independent schools. But confusion of the product and its method of distribution only clouds the issue. If Mr Crosland insists on his analogy the correct statement of it would be this: he is offering one standard comprehensive washing machine, to the exclusion of all competitors, at tax-payers' and rate-payers' expense, and this a machine that many consumers would (in the language of *Which?*) regard as a very dubious 'best buy'.

So much for Mr Crosland's ideas in areas where, as an economist, he can claim some expertise. It will come as no surprise, therefore, that when he is acting as a layman and politician in the hands of advisers he will be found to be on even shakier ground. Three examples will be mentioned now and considered in more detail in their proper places. First, he has gone comprehensive on the advice of educationists who tell him what he wants to believe against that of practising schoolmasters and, I suspect, Ministry Inspectors, whose ideas are less palatable. Secondly, at a time when psychologists are becoming less positive about the degree to which intelligence is inherited rather than acquired, he has chosen the advice of those who favour the emphasis on acquired intelligence because they better suit his political thinking on the evils of selection and the advantages of a universal comprehensive system. Finally he exhibits confused thinking on the integration of independent schools. For while admitting that the complete abolition of fee-paying in these schools would be impracticable and 'such interference with private liberty would be intolerable' [59], he still clings to the hope that the erosion of their independence resulting from integration on his terms would be acceptable to these schools. And his attitude to what measure of independence the direct-grant schools have left is hardly reassuring. Indeed it is surprising that one who has, through *The Future of Socialism*, done so much to rid his Party of their inflexibility on the subject of nationalization should, in his views on education, be so doctrinaire. 'Mr Crosland,' we are told, 'in his heart of hearts is not convinced beyond a doubt of the wisdom of the policy he is pursuing' [60]. On the evidence above this sounds more like a pious hope than a true appraisal of the facts.

PARTY POLICIES

From politicians we turn to policies. It is no part of my purpose to set forth in detail the plans for secondary education of the various Parties, but rather to highlight those aspects of them which have transformed the 'pious platitudes' and 'woeful lack of interest' (see page 94) of 1950 into the atmosphere of clash and conflict of today. This metamorphosis was brought about, in the main, by the Labour Party through their manifesto *Signposts for the Sixties*. After reproaching their opponents with the theory that 'The mass of children ... are second-rate material, which should be given what is left over when the very best has been provided for the educational élite', the argument continues: 'Our socialist attitude to education is based on the conviction that there are great potentialities of hidden talent in the British people, which can only be revealed by ensuring that every child is given more than one opportunity in the course of its life to show an aptitude for higher education.' The means of achieving 'genuine equality of opportunity' in so far as they affect secondary education are 'to reorganize the State secondary schools on comprehensive lines, in order to end the segregation by the 11-plus examination which is now almost universally condemned on educational as well as social grounds' and 'to deal with the problem of the private, fee-paying sector of education' [61]. But even comprehensive schools have their dangers if – as most of them do – they continue the practice of streaming. So, at the Blackpool Conference of the Labour Party in 1965, a composite resolution on education was passed, though not debated, which included the significant statement that 'the education system could become genuinely comprehensive only if the practice of selection (i.e. streaming) was actively discouraged' [62]. The *New Statesman*, which can often be relied upon to anticipate the next Labour Party manifesto but one, warns similarly that streaming 'on both educational and social grounds is something to watch' and goes further: 'Parity of esteem, which became a sour joke when applied to grammar and secondary modern schools, ought to be a serious consideration as between comprehensives . . . there is need to watch the balance – and especially to see that inequalities do not coincide too neatly with "nice" and "undesirable" neighbourhoods' [53]. While not going all the way with the conclusion of a B.B.C. commentator that in effect parents would be allowed to send their children to any school they choose provided it is comprehensive and no comprehensive is different from any other [63] it is difficult to avoid an impression left by these quotations that in secondary education socialists are concerned not, as they profess, with 'genuine equality of opportunity' but quite simply with equality. At first they believed that comprehensive schools would achieve the latter under the guise of the former. Now they are not quite so sure, and modification and rethinking of their policy has already begun. Moreover the tone of many socialist pronouncements on education does suggest that they are more concerned with the eradication of privilege than with the extension of opportunity. In this objective they may, of course, be right; but the cautious reader will be wise to look behind the manifestos for manifestations of ultimate intent.

The Conservative counterblast *Putting Britain Right Ahead* is too subtle merely to defend selection and attack the comprehensives. Indeed they can claim with justice that many new and well equipped comprehensive schools have been opened during their period of office. After some unexceptionable generalities about giving an opportunity to all young people to travel along the education road as far as their ability and perseverance can carry them and a pledge to preserve the voluntary aided and direct-grant schools and extend the latter the manifesto continues:

> We have long recognised that 11 is too early an age at which finally to decide the kind of course of which a boy or girl may be capable. But while acknowledging this, and accepting that a comprehensive pattern is best suited to certain areas, we do not believe that the academic standards set by our grammar schools, which are widely admired outside this country, can be maintained if all these schools are to lose their separate identity. The Labour Government's attempts to spread comprehensive education throughout the country are a regrettable and, in places, a damaging irrelevance [64].

Mr Iain Macleod puts it more briefly. 'Let both comprehensive and grammar schools flourish together. It is possible and there is no need for the artificial division which seems to have been set up' [65]. Much of this sounds good pragmatic sense – indeed one of the themes of this book is that the 'tripartite' and comprehensive systems need not be mutually exclusive. And yet the objective observer of thirteen years of Conservative government will be wary. He will know that Conservative policy on education must be viewed against the background of their other policies; for whenever, as inevitably with all British governments since the war, there comes a time of retrenchment, education is apt to be an early Conservative casualty. And here the outlook is far from encouraging. Despite the radical thinking of Mr Enoch Powell on Defence we still too often hear the old cries about honouring our commitments and these, in Conservative terms, could all too easily mean expensive defence projects whose cost, if applied to the educational budget, could have transformed British education beyond recognition. Promises of tax cuts are another danger signal. And the recent talk about the £1,500 a year man who wants to own his own car, buy his own house and pay for his children's education by people who find these things difficult enough on incomes far above this leads all too easily to the conclusion that so long as independent schools flourish the state system can be left to manage as best it may. It was Sir Edward Boyle who once put the matter bluntly: 'We all know parents who can afford to educate their children privately and yet let them go to a state grammar school – how many parents do we know who could afford to send their children to public school, and yet chose that they go to a state secondary modern?' [37]. The answer to that question is clear enough, but it is Sir Edward Boyle's Party who, if they search their consciences, can furnish the reason why.

When we turn from Sir Edward's Party to Sir Edward himself, the prospect is more encouraging; he is refreshingly free from a dogmatic approach to the comprehensive school. Following the Crowther Report [22], he sees its value in densely populated areas where a variety of schools can be accessible, in new housing-estates, and in thinly populated country districts or small self-contained industrial townships where one good all-purpose school may be better than two separate institutions with inadequate equipment and staffs. Education, he argues, is a local government service and local education authorities must have reasonable freedom to decide what is best for their own areas. He has no time for what has been called 'the deplorable business of agglomerating a group of widely separated buildings and calling them a school'. But an argument has been put to me against such thinking which deserves consideration. It runs like this. Political and social change tends to happen through the direct involvement of the vociferous and intelligent middle-class minority. This minority is, in the Britain of today, overwhelmingly urban. If the choice between comprehensive and non-comprehensive education is to be left entirely to local initiative, it is not impossible that the result will show a very clear pattern. In the urban areas of dense population, where the great majority of the middle-class is to be found, the middle-class preference for grammar schools will give non-comprehensive education. In the more rural areas, where few middle-class people live and most send their children to private schools, the middle-class will raise no objection to comprehensive education. There could result from this a state of affairs in which educationally Britain was divided, in practical reality, into first-class and second-class education nations with the urban centres being the first-class citizens and the rural remainder of the country second-class. Britain could become a nation of city selectives and country comprehensives. Two things may be said in reply to this. First the premise – that comprehensive schools produce second-class citizens – would certainly not be accepted by the comprehensivists, and to the uncommitted it is still too early to say. Secondly, it can be met by the scheme of parental choice, with boarding provision in rural areas, adumbrated in Chapter 7. The result of this could still conceivably be city selectives and country comprehensives, but if it were the result of choice it would at least be a voluntary social revolution, and as we are now begging two questions – would comprehensives produce second-class citizens and would country parents necessarily choose them – the matter is better left open, perhaps as a piece of homework for the Conservative Research Unit.

There remain the Liberals who, we are told, 'have an important role as the conscience of our political system – reminding us of what really matters as distinct from stressing only what wins votes' [66]. A promising testimonial this for educational policy. The reader will recall, too, the Party's great tradition of educational reform and more recently attractive ideas like 'going into Europe' long before others seriously thought of it, co-ownership, and taxing site values as a step towards an answer to exorbitant rates. Anticipation will be increased by the fact that the Liberal spokesman on education is Mr A. D. C. Peterson, to whose stimulating ideas on the sixth-form curriculum we have already referred (see page 55) and who offers some refreshingly radical thoughts in the final chapter of *A Hundred Years of Education* [15]. For instance he argues persuasively that it would have been better had it been decided in 1946 that one single and simple reform, the rebuilding and re-staffing of primary schools, should have precedence over everything else for the next five years. Or again, he speculates about the unlikely possibility of a local education authority, in revolt against Parkinson's Law, reducing its staff to a bare skeleton and packing off all the other officials to teach in the schools in its area. 'A lot of records would go uncompiled, a lot of letters would go unanswered – many of them such as need never have been written – a lot of silly questions would get no reply, but I find it hard to believe that for that term the children would not be better educated' [15]. Here, it would seem, is promise of a 'ginger group' to get something done in political terms to improve the primary schools, while the other

Parties merely make the right polite noises, or streamline the top-heavy administrative superstructure of education that all too often tempts or drives good teachers away from teaching. But the Liberals, on educational issues, have been a sad disappointment. Their advocacy of comprehensive reorganization closely follows the Labour Party pattern, while perhaps laying rather more emphasis on the Leicestershire experiment, and though the author of *A Hundred Years of Education* ventilates ideas which are stimulating and liberal, as a Liberal educationist he is scarcely distinguishable from a socialist.*

A CONSENSUS?

The central issue to emerge from this brief glance at Party policies is whether, as Labour and Liberals urge, comprehensive reorganization should be imposed as an exclusive dogma from the centre or whether, as in the Conservative view, it should be allowed to develop from local initiative while not excluding co-existence with some form of selection. Whichever policy is right the prospect for the maintained secondary schools is not a healthy one: selection alternately abolished and resurrected, a 'general post' between schools at each change of government – the possibilities multiply and horrify. The reader who cares more for education than for politics may well feel nostalgia for the benevolent apathy that obtained before the sixties and sigh hopefully for some sort of *modus vivendi* between the Parties. There is slight encouragement to be drawn from the existence of common ground between them. Sir Edward Boyle and Mr Crosland, for instance, are probably closer together in their attitude towards reorganization than either of them are to the extreme wings of their respective Parties. Moreover we have heard a good deal lately about the 'politics of consensus' [67]. There are sentences in all three manifestos for 1966 which, if torn from their context, would not be easy to assign to their correct Party. Mr Wilson even claimed on television that his was a national Government and was actually seen to usurp a Conservative prerogative by making

*In the 1966 Liberal Party Conference the subject of education was not even on the agenda.

the occasional speech from a platform draped with the Union Jack. Sir Winston Churchill observed long ago that four fifths of each major British Party agree about four fifths of the things that need to be done. The trouble is that after *Signposts for the Sixties* and *Putting Britain Right Ahead* the organization of secondary education seems to fall obstinately within the non-overlapping fifth. The true test will come when Mr Crosland shows his hand towards those local authorities who submit recalcitrant replies to Circular 10/65, and his more recent circular refusing financial support for new secondary school building other than in a comprehensive context is not auspicious. Nobody would be more delighted to be proved wrong about this than the present writer, and the plan outlined in Chapter 7 to break this deadlock through genuine parental choice is offered tentatively to this end.

EDUCATION AND POLITICS
AT LOCAL GOVERNMENT LEVEL

It is part of the brief of Circular 10/65 that in formulating plans for comprehensive reorganization teachers should be consulted and parents informed. Attendance at a parents' meeting with the latter purpose (details of time and place are spared) proved illuminating. The following were its highlights:

(1) A party-political tone was set by Young Conservatives distributing leaflets in the foyer.

(2) The meeting opened with a *suggestio falsi*. There was no choice, we were told, about comprehensive reorganization because the 1944 Education Act demanded a 'varied and comprehensive service in every area' (Section 1, Subsection 1). It was not made clear that in the Act 'comprehensive' meant 'all-embracing' and had not its present connotation.

(3) The meeting was held in the beautiful and attractively furnished hall of a secondary modern school. But we were told that grammar schools, since 1944, had been favoured by the best buildings.

(4) A questioner who expressed anxiety about rising rates was chided not to 'talk of filthy lucre when considering our children's future'.

(5) Another, asking why there was a 'brain drain' from not yet comprehensive Britain to already comprehensive America, received the evasive answer 'because there is more money there'. (The information sought was not, of course, why our scientists go there but why the Americans want them.)

(6) The Chief Education Officer, when asked what would be the future of a particular grammar school, replied that this would depend on what proved a 'viable comprehensive unit'. Someone murmured 'I want my child to go to a school.'

(7) In a similar 'follow-up' meeting a questioner who asked how far grammar school teachers were represented on teachers' working parties to advise on reorganization was told that these working parties had been 'well sorted out'. Someone interjected 'I bet they have.'

The brief of Circular 10/65 is that teachers should be consulted and parents informed. But the impression left by such meetings is that teachers are being insulted and parents conformed – or misinformed.

Nor have the Conservative side anything more to be proud of. Many of their meetings have shown as rigid a determination to sabotage comprehensive reorganization as the above meeting did to impose it. A councillor, in reply to a request that the general public be admitted to meetings of his executive, protested that he was 'fed up with people poking their noses into things which do not concern them' [68]. At a meeting of a divisional executive not far from the meeting described above a local plan for comprehensive reorganization was put to the vote. Not one Conservative voted against it and the only dissentient voice was a Liberal's. The general view was that it was a thoroughly bad plan, but this is no reason for abstention. One would have thought a bad plan to carry out what Conservatives profess to believe is a wrong policy is doubly deserving of a protest vote. But local elections were imminent. The more likely explanation is that the Conservatives, sure of their own supporters, did not want to alienate possible converts from the other side by going on record against the comprehensives. Neither side, therefore, emerges from these local battles over comprehensive reorganization with much credit; but perhaps it is better to appear partisan than pusillanimous.

Further light is shed on the attitude to teacher consultation by what has happened at Liverpool. There is no need here to recount in detail the unhappy and still unfinished story of a great city's attempt to go comprehensive or explore the strange Ministry decision that gave help and approval in the area where it was least needed – in the middle and outer bands of the city – while denying it in the inner downtown areas. More significant and ominous is the fundamental difference of outlook between the teachers and the Labour-controlled Council. The latter interpreted their un-questioned responsibility for determining policy as carrying with it the right to lay down the type of schooling desirable and the date at which it should be introduced. The teachers, on the con-trary, maintained that policy should be restricted to a general commitment and that after that it was 'for the experts, the teachers and the education office to decide just what was feasible' [69]. Though this situation occurred with a Labour-controlled Council, Conservatives have little cause for complacency about the course of events at Croydon. Here comprehensive education had been approved in principle as early as 1956, but recently the Conservative-controlled Council first proposed an unsatisfactory two-tier scheme involving also the taking up of 1,700 places in local direct-grant and independent schools. It then withdrew it under pressure from parents not only of grammar school children but also of children in secondary modern schools in the southern districts of the borough whose new buildings and O-level courses made them a more attractive proposition than the pro-posed two-tier comprehensives. Temporary political victory it may have been but was it also an educational one, and where, in all this, did the teachers stand or for that matter the children? Neither Labour Liverpool nor Conservative Croydon emerge here with much credit; yet the underlying cause is the violation by central government of our second principle of state participation in education – that it should concern itself with ends and not means. When the comprehensive principle is dictated from the centre, however varied the choices offered in Circular 10/65, a sympathetic local government, robbed of its power of decision in its proper sphere – that of organizational means – is tempted in its turn to invade the sphere of operational detail that belongs properly to the experts on the ground, as occurred at Liverpool; while a hostile local government, as at Croydon, is conversely tempted to drag its feet within the centrally dictated framework and welcome eruptions of local opposition as a pretext for rejecting it out of hand.

BRISTOL

But if there are dangers apparent at local government level in the preliminary stages of going comprehensive, the experience of Bristol, where comprehensive reorganization has already reached an advanced stage, is even more instructive. The record of Bristol's progress towards comprehensive education is given fully and impartially in a special report commissioned by one of its local newspapers [57]. Briefly the Development Plan of its Council, framed in 1951, aimed to make full provision for secondary education in the city by 26 comprehensive schools, and of these 17 were in operation by 1965. These were in the residential suburbs where they were easier to build in the process of new development, particularly as an enterprising Chief Education Officer had secured large sites for them. Nearer the centre, however, there were difficulties, among them the problem of finding sites in a closely built-up area and the existence of a large number of schools, among them no less than seven direct-grant schools, one voluntary controlled and six maintained grammar schools, and eighteen secondary modern schools. Matters came to a head when plans were submitted in 1964 to complete the remaining nine comprehensives and it became clear that the Government's school building grant for the next three years would scarcely cover one new comprehensive school, let alone nine. This was hardly the Minister's fault. Sir Edward Boyle, then the Minister is no enemy of the comprehensives, but he had to fit the demands of Bristol into the national context and funds were limited. The Chairman of the Bristol Education Committee, however, visualized that it would take ten to fifteen years to complete the City's comprehensive provision, and to quote his words that have since become notorious, 'we are not prepared to wait'. As a temporary measure, therefore, the non-comprehensive areas are to be organized in three self-contained schemes while the comprehensive schools are assigned their closed catchment areas and become neighbourhood schools.

In East Bristol, containing about 15 per cent of the City's secondary school population, a version of the two-tier Leicester-shire scheme is to be operated with secondary modern schools as lower tiers from age 11 and grammar schools as upper tiers starting at 13. Transfer to grammar schools would be by 'joint agreement of heads and parents' and children not transferred will 'complete their education with courses of a somewhat less academic character'. The objections to this scheme, as Professor Ford points out, are threefold. First it involves for some transfer from mixed primary schools to single-sex secondary schools and then back to mixed-sexed upper secondary schools, for others a mixed-sexed intermediate secondary school and then a single-sex upper school – either fate bewildering and unsatisfactory for the children. Secondly the two-year intermediate schools can be little better than transit camps or, in the words of a chief education officer, 'corridors' [70], if even the three year term of the Leices-tershire high-schools is felt by some to be too short. But perhaps worst of all it is visualized that some 60 to 75 per cent will move on to the upper schools. Yet if, in the national 'tripartite' system, some 80 per cent feel a sense of failure when 20 per cent are selected, what will be the feelings of the 25 to 40 per cent who thus become, in Professor Ford's phrase, 'the odd-failures-out in the midst of a successful crowd'?

In Central Bristol, comprising two areas called North-Central and South-Central with some 20 per cent of Bristol's secondary school population, similar proposals for a two-tier system met with such opposition from the teachers that they were abandoned, and selection will continue with the existing bi-partite system. Allocation will be based on primary heads' assessments together with a verbal reasoning test which all children in Bristol will take, not only those in the two central areas, partly in the interest of fairness and partly to provide comprehensive heads with a basis for streaming. The difficulties and frustrations of such an area of selection surrounded by yet insulated from a comprehensive cocoon can well be left to the reader's imagination, or he can see them spelt out in Professor Ford's report. We need only add here that a bad situation is made worse by the fact that North-Central Bristol contains three grammar schools and two secondary modern schools, so that the grammar school headmaster who objected to a two-tier system because he had neither facilities nor staff to cope with the really less able looks like having to live with some of them after all.

Finally, so that the outer ring of comprehensives shall no longer be 'creamed' of abler pupils, the Council proposes no longer to take up its quota of places at Bristol's direct-grant schools – including the famous Bristol Grammar School – and would so limit the catchment area and thereby widen the ability range of Colston's voluntary aided girls' grammar school that the school has now opted to become independent. The Council, of course, are perfectly justified in making such a decision, but it need not have been so hasty and abrupt. The situation has been further aggravated by the fact that all three of Labour's leading comprehensive campaigners sent or send their children to fee-paying schools [71] and has been reflected in the signing of a protest against the comprehensives by 28,000 residents out of a city of 450,000 and in the retention by the Conservatives in 1964 (though not in 1966) of the two marginal constituencies of Bristol North-East and Bristol North-West.

The reader may wonder why this review of Bristol's comprehensive reorganization, already so well-advanced, was not included in the previous chapter, though reference was made to one of Bristol's comprehensives, Laurence Weston School, as a model and a success *within its local context*. But that chapter was entitled 'The Comprehensive Challenge', and the story of Bristol is no challenge – rather a nightmare, and an object lesson on the perils of going comprehensive on a shoestring. For it was the inadequacy of financial support from the Government at a critical stage that caused most of the trouble. Yet it is just this problem that will be multiplied all over the country as a result of the present Government's policy of comprehensive reorganization with no extra money now nor, in the present economic climate, much prospect of it. As a reminder, therefore, of what may be in store for other local authorities when comprehensive reorganization gets under way we may thus summarize the Bristol situation:

(1) A ring of seventeen comprehensive schools, purpose-built and on the whole successful, have at the very moment when they were gaining popularity and prestige become strictly neighbourhood schools from which those living outside their catchment areas are excluded.

(2) A two-tier system in East Bristol modelled on Leicestershire, but with none of the virtues of new buildings and an atmosphere of experiment; rather a makeshift, temporary expedient openly admitted to be such, with two-year transit-camps or 'corridors' masquerading as schools at the intermediate level.

(3) The preservation of selection in Central Bristol, forced on the Council by the opposition of teachers but accepted with reluctance and little faith in it, and further complicated by the existing provision of schools.

(4) The termination of local authority free places for academic high-fliers at Bristol Grammar School and other direct-grant schools and, as a result, the prospect of these schools becoming independent. Thus, while the Government sets up a Commission to integrate independent schools into the state system, in Bristol semi-independent schools are moving in the opposite direction of enforced disengagement.

(5) Colston's voluntary aided girls' grammar school is becoming independent, and thus open only to those who can afford the fees.

(6) The attitude of the Chairman of Bristol Education Committee, epitomized in his words 'we are not prepared to wait', is a microcosm of the Minister's. Doctrinaire, given to thinking with the heart rather than the head, and convinced that comprehensive reorganization will of itself achieve social justice, both have forgotten that you cannot have social justice on the cheap. As a consequence the next five years may well see events in Bristol East and Bristol Central repeated on a national scale.

Furthermore Bristol enjoys a local advantage which will not obtain everywhere. The opposition Citizen Party, though in conflict with the present Council over the complete abolition of selection and its termination of free places at direct-grant schools, is not opposed to comprehensive schools in principle and seems prepared, on the evidence of the Ford Report, to work within a largely comprehensive context in something near to a bi-partisan approach. The special problem of Bristol is further considered in Chapter 7, with a suggestion for a possible solution. There is no guarantee that other cities will be so fortunately placed in local swings of the political pendulum.

FABIAN TACTICS

As local authorities ponder their plans for reorganization a contribution from Sir Alec Clegg, Chief Education Officer of the West Riding, will not have passed unnoticed. In an article in *Education* [72] he listed means whereby education committees could delay, impede, put a spoke in the wheel of or foul comprehensive reorganization. For example insistence on an 'all-in' 11–18 school rather than a two-tier system or the introduction of sixth-form colleges would 'thwart Mr Crosland's Circular almost indefinitely' owing to the shortage of capital for buildings implicit in the National Plan. Also if direct-grant schools resisted the Circular the Minister would have to explain why he wanted 20 per cent selection removed from maintained grammar schools while schools he supported directly could get away with 1 per cent selection. 'Waiting for Plowden' could also be a useful delaying tactic,* and bad schemes would be the most effective way of fouling the introduction of good schemes. Thus could the Government be frustrated by 'an orgy of double-talk and treble-think that could go on for years'. Though Sir Alec insists that he was being ironical [73] he was taken seriously by the education correspondent of a quality Sunday newspaper who described the article as 'the first sign of a major revolt of local authorities against the Minister's plans' [74]. Ironic or no Sir Alec should know that attempts to disarm potential criminals by telling them that you know their plans in advance can have a boomerang effect. And there is nothing ironical about these words:

A diplomatic resistance, the skilful use of delaying tactics, a certain haziness in plans presented for the future are weapons which local authorities can use to effect when satisfied that their present provision of

*No longer so, since its publication in January 1967 [56].

secondary education is efficient and just. If the power of central authority is increasing it does not follow that authority in the locality has ceased to exist [75].

Intentionally or unintentionally Croydon has shown the way, and I know at least one headmaster who believes that administrative chaos will delay comprehensive reorganization for a generation. A sinister unanimity between journalists of two quality newspapers of opposite political colour lends credence to this view. The first, in an article on what he calls 'The Local Jungle of Education' thus warns: 'To clear the jungle is the first task of any reorganization of education in this country: to call for comprehensive plans is simply to sow fertilisers in the jungle' [76]. The other is no less depressing:

At present a child of, say, twelve can move schools twice in a year and find himself in the same type of school. In five years, perhaps, he will find himself successively in the last year of a junior school, the middle year of an intermediate school, then the first year of an all-through comprehensive. In some schemes an element of choice will linger on. In some there will be no leeway. Some areas will have their direct-grant schools partially integrated, in others the bastions of élitism will soldier on untouched. For one, probably two decades, we shall have a patchwork-quilt system of schools based only tenuously on the same principle [77].

SUMMARY

Whatever side is taken, then, in the comprehensive debate its emergence as a political issue has had effects that nobody genuinely concerned with education can welcome. The intrusion into the sphere of education of the emotive language of politics and Party postures does nothing but harm. The prospect of political battles over comprehensivization resembling those over nationalization may flatter politicians' egos, but can do children little good. The concomitant fashion of regarding education as a universal scapegoat and, in the hands of the enlightened, a panacea, is unrealistic and dangerous. Doctrinaire insistence on a monolithic comprehensive system carries with it some of the implications of the 'closed shop' in industrial relations, and has already made current the dubious maxim 'act now, research afterwards'. Government dictation of an exclusive pattern of educational reorganization increases the growth of power at the centre and threatens to spread what has been called 'the gospel according to Curzon Street' [78] in a situation when we cannot be sure how far the Minister and his permanent advisors are synoptic. And finally the effects on local government arrangements for secondary education have been shown to be frightening enough even in this chapter where we have only touched the fringe. Keeping education out of politics may well be, as we have seen, an impractical dream; but extricating it from the stifling political net that now enmeshes it seems likely to become a formidable and pressing problem of the next decade.

CHAPTER FOUR

THE CASE AGAINST THE COMPREHENSIVES

It is fashionable these days to call for a Great National Debate, and one has already begun on the Organization of Secondary Education. But the last chapter serves as a warning that such a debate, if it follows narrow party lines, will prove misleading and sterile. It is unedifying to hear socialists, with obvious embarrassment, defending the comprehensive system when their private life and conduct shows that in their heart of hearts they are meritocrats who send their children to private schools; or conservatives suddenly revealing a crusading eagerness to defend maintained grammar schools to which they would never send their children as long as there was a 'public school' whose fees they could meet however dubious its academic standards. Maudie Littlehampton's complaint, in Osbert Lancaster's cartoon in the *Daily Express*, that Brighton at the time of the 1965 Conservative Conference was full of old-Etonian delegates who were claiming to have been educated at a little-known grammar school near Slough was fair comment on this sort of thing. If the comprehensive debate is to achieve anything it is essential to forget party allegiance in the cool search for truth. That is why it is so refreshing, and all too rare, to hear a Sir Edward Boyle championing the comprehensives from the Conservative side, or the generally left-wing Baroness Stocks, from the eminence to which the Prime Minister raised her in admiration of her 'sensible views', [79] delivering her intermittent diatribes against those who would destroy the grammar schools. This debate can only become real and constructive when we hear more Conservative champions of 'comprehension' and more socialist supporters of selection, and this demands a more honest appraisal of the facts by both sides.

Towards such an objective, non-party debate this book is intended to be a contribution. Our review of the development of the grammar schools makes no attempt to conceal that, valuable though their part has been in the spread of secondary education in Britain, they have weaknesses and shortcomings which the comprehensive experiment attempts to remedy. In an imperfect world it would be strange if the comprehensive school had not, in its turn, limitations and failings which, in honest debate, must be squarely faced. This we shall now attempt to do, but first it is necessary to dispose of two forms of misrepresentation into which comprehensivists, understandably in their partisan opposition to what they regard as an Establishment institution, have fallen. First, they have adopted, consciously or unconsciously, the techniques of propaganda and 'hidden persuasion' to further their cause; and secondly, in their natural delight at such academic success as their pupils have achieved, they have made more extravagant claims than the facts seem to warrant.

'HIDDEN PERSUADERS' IN EDUCATION

One of the more striking developments of the second half of the twentieth century is the application of the discoveries of psychology and sociology first to the field of advertising and salesmanship and then, more recently, to politics. This 'technique of mass-persuasion through the unconscious' has been brilliantly and frighteningly analysed by the American writer Vance Packard in *The Hidden Persuaders* [8]. Though America is far ahead of ourselves (if that is the right expression) in this field, the super-market and the 1966 General Election have provided examples in plenty of public-relations experts and politicians 'engineering our consent to their propositions' and of 'the intensive use of symbol manipulation and reiteration on the voter, who more and more is treated like Pavlov's conditioned dog' [85]. What J. B. Priestley called 'admass' is paving the way for Orwell's 'proles' or Aldous Huxley's 'gammas'. It would not be surprising if something of this technique were subconsciously used by some supporters of the comprehensive idea in their eagerness to persuade. Though not as refined or sophisticated as in the world of business or politics this practice is none the less misleading and dangerous. Education, we are often told, is the business of learning to think and we should not allow ourselves to be influenced, in the matter of its organization, by the weapons of non-think. The reader must be on his guard, therefore, when comprehensivists employ emotive words to anaesthetize thought, often enough their own included, and pander to irrational feelings.

Fortunately if one writer has diagnosed the disease another suggests the cure. In my undergraduate days I remember being impressed by a book by R. H. S. (now the Right Honourable) Crossman which he called *Plato Today* [81]. In it he reconstructed, at places in imaginary dialogue form, what might be the Greek philosopher's attitude to contemporary problems. Now behind Plato, as master to disciple, lay the personality of Socrates, whose great service to his times and to all time was to insist that words be defined before being exchanged. His spirit is acutely needed today in politics – 'If politicians were compelled by law to define any term they wished to use, they would lose most of their popular appeal, their speeches would be shorter, and many of their dis-agreements would be found to be purely verbal' [81] – and even more in the comprehensive debate. One of the commonest com-plaints of the comprehensivists is, as we have seen (page 75), that their schools are 'creamed' by the grammar schools. Now this word 'creamed' is just such a 'hidden persuader' and we shall give it the full treatment of the Socratic dialectic. Other such words we shall analyse more briefly, but again in the spirit of Socrates, in a sort of glossary of 'hidden persuaders'. If this book achieves no other purpose than to cause the ghost of Socrates to walk even briefly across the educational scene of the sixties, it will not have been written in vain.

A DIALOGUE ON CREAMING

COMPREHENSIVIST: It is a scandal that comprehensive schools should be creamed by the grammar schools.

SOCRATES: What do you mean by 'creamed'?

C: Being deprived of their ablest children, like cream off the top of the milk.

S: Why do you object, then, to cream being removed from the milk?

C: Because it is the best part of it.

S: So you would say that you are being left with skimmed milk?

c: Yes.

s: You compare yourself, then, to a customer in a dairy who demands that the commodity he is buying shall be of a certain standard? But your analogy breaks down, unless you are purchasing children whom you propose to devour like a bottle of milk, cream and all. I take it your aim is to educate them.

c: Of course.

s: So parents are sending their children to you for a service, and you are claiming to perform it for *all* children better than anybody else regardless of what the parents think. But are not the grammar schools more experienced than you in educating the abler children whom you call 'the cream', since they have been doing it for four hundred years or more, and have more teachers who specialize in this kind of work?

c: Yes, but then these children are privileged. They would be taken from other children, like cream from milk, and this is against social justice.

s: So you are saying that you want these children not so much for what you can give them as for what you can deny them.

c: Some people must be denied special treatment so that all can have fair shares.

s: Now let us look at it another way. You have in Britain, I believe, a National Health Service.

c: Our National Health Service is the envy of the world.

s: As I understand it, when somebody is ill he goes to his doctor. If this doctor cannot cure him he sends him to the local hospital, and if the specialist there cannot deal with him he sends him to a super-specialist in a London hospital, or some other big centre. Is that correct?

c: Yes, in our Health Service the poorest man can have the best possible treatment if he needs it.

s: Would you say, then, that the general practitioner is 'creamed' of his best patients by having them sent to hospital? Or the local hospital 'creamed' by the London hospital?

c: That is different. If a man has a special illness he needs a specialist to cure him.

s: How is it different? You are saying that if a man's body is peculiarly sick he must be singled out for special – in education

123

you would call it 'privileged' – treatment. But if a man's soul, or brain as you would call it, is peculiarly healthy it should not have the special treatment it requires.

c: No, that would be unfair. He must stay in a comprehensive school where he will improve the quality of others and have no more than his fair share of education.

s: So if a man is very ill he can receive the privileged treatment his body needs, but if his soul or mind requires specialist treatment this must be denied him.

c: You are twisting the argument. No wonder the Athenians condemned you to death.

A GLOSSARY OF 'HIDDEN PERSUADERS'

Words are fluid things and can have three levels of use. First, their precise meaning by derivation; second, their 'usage' sense, sometimes less precise but none the less valid and meaningful; and thirdly, their emotive or associative value. Broadly speaking each level is a step away from thought and towards emotion. The purpose of the 'hidden persuader' is to push them from the first level to the third and where possible over the brink into propaganda. This is easier to do when the word has a usage sense because it is apt to be less precise, and emotional overtones can therefore be more readily exploited. The purpose of this glossary is to put the reader on his guard against the 'hidden persuaders' of modern educational polemic and help him distinguish between usage and abusage, argument and propaganda.

Democratic. An all-purpose word with a usage sense of vague approbation. Statements like 'grammar schools are undemocratic' are effective 'hidden persuaders'.

Deprived. Useful in expressions like 'deprived children' to excite a vague sympathy without the awkward necessity of specifying what they are being deprived of, or what good it would *do them* if they received it.

Élite. It is an odd feature of the English language that it sometimes uses French words to convey a pejorative nuance. Thus we call a person who is obsessed with equality an egalitarian, from the French word *égal*. Sometimes the French return the compliment, as when they call what we call 'French leave' *congé anglais*. This practice is being masterfully operated in the comprehensive debate with the word 'élite' and its even uglier derivatives 'élitist' and 'élitism'. 'Élite' stems from the same Latin root as 'elected' and basically has the same meaning: thus the England cricket team are an 'élite' and so are Members of Parliament, though they seldom remind us of the fact. So too grammar school pupils are elected or selected for a particular form of education by the 11-plus exam or some other test. But 'élite' has a usage sense of unfair or priviliged selection; so the opponents introduce a subtle smear when they call them an 'élite', suggesting to the unwary that in some unspecified way the choice is unfair. There is a good example of it in the quotation on page 118: 'the bastions of élitism soldier on' – with a mixed metaphor thrown in for good measure.

Equality. Effectively exploits a vague sense of grievance. It is useless, for instance, to speak of equality to a winner of the football-pools. Its value as a 'hidden persuader' is inversely proportional to the amount of thought it is allowed to provoke. For thought reveals the manifest inequalities in the distribution of human talent and, to quote a socialist, 'we do not want complete equality of incomes, since extra responsibility and exceptional talent require and deserve a differential reward' [59]. Statements like 'selection at 11-plus offends against the principles of equality' are persuasive provided no opportunity is given to probe into precisely what these principles are.

Fair Shares. Used much like 'equality', but with an added patriotic appeal to the British sense of sportsmanship and fair play.

Groundswell of Opinion. Used by the Minister himself and calculated to appeal to every man's instinct to go with the crowd and climb on a bandwagon. Has a fine democratic ring about it but obscures the fact that, in the search for truth, counting heads is less important than the quality of their contents. There is little to be said for a groundswell from Eatanswill.

Integration. By derivation means 'forming a whole from its parts'; but has the usage sense of making the resources of independent schools available to the general pool of educational requirements of the whole country. Commonly used, by comprehensivists and others, as a euphemism for nationalizing them. This whole question will be fully considered in a later chapter, but the word is mentioned here as a 'hidden persuader' because of its skilful avoidance of the full implications of nationalization and its half-promise, transparently false to the perceptive, of a 'public school' education for all.

The Nation and *National*. Prestige symbols for the Party in power. Thus the Labour Government's plan for the next five years was called The National Plan, and comprehensive reorganization sounds more respectable when described as 'national policy'.

Educational Need. Commonly cited as the criterion for entry to the 'public schools'. Confuses thought by usage associations of expressions like 'those in need' and 'the needy', which identify need with poverty. Adroitly begs the awkward question of who is to decide the need. If it is the State, then the independence of these schools has gone. Also an important factor in assessing educational need, if the phrase means anything, is ability, yet this, along with parents' income, would be 'entirely excluded' from their criteria by the self-styled 'Public Schools Committee' [82].

Privilege and *Under-privileged*. Derived from the Latin *priva lex* meaning a special law or exception to the rule, privilege is basically a neutral word. But it lends itself to emotional overtones. Disraeli made it a virtue when he said: 'Learned in human nature the English constitution holds out privilege to every subject as an inducement to do his duty' [83]. It has a usage sense of any unduly favourable situation owed generally to wealth. But more commonly the word is used to disparage any kind of special treatment and incite the envy of those who do not receive it. Thus grammar school education is described as 'privileged' education without pointing out that the pupils thus 'privileged' are expected to work long and difficult hours, in school and at home, on a dull and to them sometimes meaningless grind if they are to achieve any success at all. It is even used at times to denigrate any kind of intellectual distinction, as when winners of open scholarships at Oxford or Cambridge are dismissed as a 'privileged élite', though those who receive, after passing a some-what less exacting test, a treasure chest of £50 or whatever on commercial television are applauded for obtaining their democratic deserts. Finally a subtle *non sequitur* is slipped in by the use of the word 'under-privileged' to excite pity. For if privilege is such a bad thing then those who lack it, or enough of it, deserve congratulation and not sympathy. We are reminded of what Vance Packard called the 'sub-threshold effect' of flashing 'ice cream ads' on the screen for split seconds during the showing of a regular film [80]. The inconsistency of the use of 'under-privileged' is not consciously recognized, but its effect is absorbed by the subconscious.

Progressive. Effective in statements like 'progressive educationists favour the comprehensive idea'. 'Progressive' means advancing step by step, and in this sense all education should be progressive – we learn to walk before we learn to run. It also has the usage sense of serious experiment along lines formulated by an educational philosophy. But 'hidden persuaders' use it to imply that any innovation is forward-looking and give the specious impression that it is admirable without specifying the experiment or the philosophy on which it must be judged.

Public. A woolly multi-purpose word for inciting emotions to taste. In 'the public schools' it is anathema, but in 'the public interest' and 'public ownership' it acquires a misty halo. 'The public will not tolerate . . .' is a useful formula for discouraging one's personal dislikes.

The Rich. Extended from its absolute sense to any who are prepared, by economy, intelligent housekeeping or self-denial to spend money on their children's education rather than passively accept what the State dispenses.

Rat Race. A pejorative term for competition. Particularly used in expressions like 'the examination rat race' to comfort the unsuccessful with the illusion that examinations are in some cruel way unfair. Has a valid usage sense of unhealthy competition, but 'hidden persuaders' distort it to suggest that *all* competition is unhealthy.

Selection and *Segregation.* Used partly to stir the envy of the unselected, but more subtly to feed a guilt-feeling in the selected.

Applies in reverse the advice on selling technique cited by Vance Packard:

> If you tell the housewife that by using your washing machine, drier or dish-washer she can be free to play bridge, you're dead! The housewife today ... is already feeling guilty about the fact that she is not working as hard as her mother. You are just rubbing her the wrong way when you offer her more freedom. Instead you should emphasize that the appliances free her to have more time with her children, and to be a better mother [80].

Constant repetition of terms like 'selection', with their usage nuance of social exclusiveness (as in the expression 'select hotel'), 'segregation' and 'élite', plays upon the guilt feelings of their beneficiaries and so seeks to undermine the prospects of survival of separate grammar schools.

Social Justice. 'Justice' of itself conveys a relationship between society and the individual and between individuals in a society. 'Social justice' is therefore etymologically tautologous; but it has a usage sense which is strong, though somewhat vague and imprecise. Some, who confine 'justice' to a narrowly legalistic sense, reserve 'social justice' for something like the wider concept of 'equity'; for others it connotes a condition of society which only socialism can achieve. It is thus the perfect tool of the 'hidden persuader', who through it can push his brinkmanship to the point of propaganda. For example I found myself in the Introduction using the expression 'manifest social injustice' in my desire to put the case of the anti-grammar-school-lobby as persuasively as I could. Statements like 'It is unjust that M.P.s should have had a rise in salary while workers' wages are frozen' and 'It violates social justice that M.P.s, etc. . . .' differ only in that the latter is more persuasive because 'social justice' sounds more sacrosanct than 'justice' alone. So with statements like '11-plus selection violates social justice'.

Society (or *The Community*). These are often used, like The Nation, as prestige symbols for the Party in power. Thus the 'Public Schools Committee' objected to any scheme of state bursaries to independent schools on the lines of the Fleming proposals on the following grounds: 'The measure would represent a state subsidy to schools over which *society* could exercise no measure of control and, in fact, the *community* would receive the worst possible bargain' [84 – italics supplied]. All that this really said is that the Government would not be securing absolute control over these schools, but words like 'society' and 'community' make the concealed expropriation sound more palatable.

Educational Trust. This was the original name of the body suggested (e.g. in *Signposts for the Sixties*) to take over the independent schools, no doubt to give the impression that it could be trusted. It has now been changed to a 'Commission', perhaps because its acquisitive purpose might involve the brushing aside of so many established Trusts inherent in the foundation statutes of those schools that the whole thing would have become a palpable mockery.

To innoculate himself against the insidious effects of this kind of 'hidden persuasion' the reader is invited to try the following simple test. Written by an imaginary journalist who advocates comprehensive football, the passage gives his reaction to a Cup Final in which the best team won:

So Whitehall Wanderers have won the Cup! Once again this privileged élite, thanks to its faceless managers who flout the principles of equality to cream off more than their fair share of able footballers, have exploited the under-privileged to gain a victory in the football rat race against the demands of social justice. The public will not much longer tolerate this undemocratic survival of privilege. There is a groundswell of progressive opinion that this rich élitist club should no longer be allowed to deprive the Nation of its fair share of football talent. The crime of selection and segregation must end forthwith. A Football Trust should be established without delay to assign players to teams according to athletic need, and integrate Whitehall Wanderers into the Nation's football system. Only thus can society benefit from their victories and the community be helped to breach the bastions of élitism.

All twenty of these 'hidden persuader' expressions are there, some more than once. Any reader who fails to discover ten or more is urged to treat any literature advocating mass comprehensivization or the 'integration' of the 'public schools' with extreme caution. It should perhaps be mentioned that if the presence of a good football team is felt to be a genuine social necessity, then the ability of one locality to buy footballers at astronomical prices while others have to make do with local talent would be a genuine example of 'social injustice'. It is in this fairyland that the 'hidden persuader' strives to make us believe.

It is only fair, at this point, to utter a warning. The reader may have noticed that I have, from time to time, used the words 'comprehensivist' and 'comprehensivization' in this book, and shall do so again. My purpose in this has been to avoid excessive repetition of clumsy periphrases like 'supporters of comprehensive schools' and 'the imposition of comprehensive reorganization'. Now 'comprehensive' is a 'good' word – prefixed to the name of your subject it will even help to sell a textbook. But 'comprehensivist' and 'comprehensivization' are ugly words that smack of doctrinaire posture and monolithic policy. They may have a side-effect of 'hidden dissuasion' against what they stand for. I happen to believe that these words do reveal, in some of the people and much of the practice to which they apply, things which are doctrinaire and monolithic. But the reader, if he comes to be persuaded of this too, should search his conscience that it is the evidence and arguments in the book, and not any 'hidden persuasive' quality in this or other parts of its vocabulary, that have influenced him. Nothing would be worse than for the author, after all that has been so far said in this chapter, to deserve the reproach 'physician, heal thyself'.

THE COMPREHENSIVES AND THE GENERAL CERTIFICATE OF EDUCATION

Another way in which supporters of comprehensive schools have been led, through resentment at being 'creamed' or 'deprived' of able children by the grammar schools, to overstate their case, is by dramatizing their results in the General Certificate of Education. The following, in its defiant pride and imputation of unworthy motives to the opposition, is typical:

The bright children at Kidbrooke, at Forest Hill, Sydenham, Wandsworth and Woodberry Down ... have done as well as their equals at any other school of any type. Their examination results have delighted the protagonists of the comprehensive school; its opponents have expressed surprise and reluctant congratulation ... or ... they have chosen to ignore these successes; it is easier not to admit that one might have been wrong [85].

Now these claims of examination successes take two forms. The first, which might be called the 'Conversion Claim', purports to show that when a grammar school becomes absorbed with a couple of secondary modern schools into a non-selective comprehensive school the results, at O- and A-level, improve strikingly on their previous record as separate entities. The second, which I shall call the 'National Average Claim', compares favourably the number of O-level passes or 'good passes' (five or more subjects) gained by comprehensive schools with the nationally averaged performance of grammar and secondary modern schools taken together. We shall examine these claims in turn.

First the 'Conversion Claim'. This, with its 'before and after' appeal, looks quite impressive to those who know little of the post-war history of the General Certificate of Education. Here are two examples taken from an impartial survey [35]. O-level rather than A-level performance is considered here to be fairer to the comprehensives, which have a larger proportion of early leavers than the grammar schools:

Table 2

Converted School		1952 Grammar School	1964 Non-selective Comprehensive
Holyhead	Number in School	850	1317
	Passing 5 or more O-levels	30	45
Wandsworth	Number in School	531	1,908
	Passing 5 or more O-levels	15	49

From these figures it would appear that results improve roughly proportionately to the increase in numbers and this, bearing in mind that the new intake to the nucleus school would be mainly of secondary modern calibre, seems to reflect great credit on the new comprehensive schools. But this conclusion assumes to be constant a factor which, over this period, has been far otherwise – the G.C.E. O-level pass. In fact it, like the £, has been subject to creeping inflation. Indeed: 'To compare grammar school results obtained in 1951 and 1952 with comprehensive results in 1964 is roughly comparable with comparing the dividends of a firm in a year of profound depression with those obtained during a runaway boom, and then claiming that the difference is entirely due to superior management' [86]. Briefly what happened is that in 1947 the old 'School Certificate', with its low pass-mark and group subject requirement, was scheduled to be replaced by the General Certificate of Education, a *subject* examination designed to be a qualification for university entrance and explicitly not a leaving certificate. To ensure this it was originally intended that the minimum age of entry be 17, but under pressure from schools it was reduced to 16, and the pass-mark raised by nearly 15 per cent. 1951, the first year of the new examination, produced a vast crop of failures and 1952 was even worse. But a concession was soon wrung from the Ministry that candidates could be entered before reaching the age of 16 provided their headmaster signed a declaration that this was in their best interests. Meanwhile the number of candidates taking O-levels was rising spectacularly, and in an examination in which the percentage of passes remains more or less constant this was enough to ensure, from about 1955 onwards, a steady inflation in the O-level pass. Indeed if anything there is a tendency to *raise* the pass percentage and thus further accentuate the inflation. For instance I can vouch, as a member of the Classics Sub-Committee of a G.C.E. Board, that there is some pressure to increase the pass percentage in Latin. Representatives from schools argue cogently that since candidates taking Latin are 'doubly selected' – for they are mostly from grammar schools and by no means all grammar school pupils are deemed capable of taking Latin – a high proportion of them ought to pass. Whatever one may feel about debasing academic standards the logic of this is difficult to resist. So, in G.C.E. terms, after 'the bleak age of the fifties, the sixties are the affluent society'. Indeed one schoolmaster claimed that 'the day is not far distant when we can successfully enter a trained seal for this examination' [86]. The implication of this for the 'Conversion Claim' of the comprehensivists, based as it is on the 'slump' of 1951–2 and the 'boom' of post–1960, is obvious; yet these are the people to whom the Minister lends a receptive ear.

What of the 'National Average Claim'? Here the performance of comprehensive schools in gaining 'good O-levels' (five or more passes) is compared with the national average of maintained grammar schools and secondary modern schools taken together. This method is favoured particularly by Mr Robin Pedley ([33] and [38]), and has been given an aura of authority by at least one popular handbook for parents which suggests that on his figures 'the academic argument is all but settled' [8]. Now while the 'Conversion Claim' ignores the post-war history of the G.C.E., this 'National Average Claim' overlooks another important factor in post-war British secondary education. Mr Pedley claims that whereas the system of separate secondary schools produces about 10 per cent (or 11 per cent if direct-grant schools are included) of each age group getting 'good O-levels' after five years, comprehensive schools are on average achieving about 14 per cent and some a good deal better. But he gives his case away by an admission that in the orthodox secondary schools of East Sussex the average over 1959–61 was over 18 per cent and goes on: 'It may be significant that there are G.C.E. courses in all the "modern" schools of this county. This naturally enlarges the opportunity for all children to show that they can do well in external examinations' [33]. It may indeed be significant. For it was deliberate policy in the first secondary modern schools that their curricula should be 'child-centred' and free from the cramping demands of external examinations. Only comparatively recently has it been realized, as we noted in the Introduction, both that proof of educational achievement by examination qualifications is increasingly demanded by prospective employers and that few children will work without this stimulus. Gradually secondary modern schools are developing G.C.E. courses and learning the professional technique of gaining success in them. Results are beginning to show. In 1964 in East Sussex there were actually more O-level candidates from secondary modern schools than from grammar schools. In September 1965 nearly one sixth of the pupils (104 out of 672) in that county entering grammar school sixth forms were from secondary modern schools, and to qualify for this good O-level results would be essential [87]. In the same year the number of successful O-level candidates in all maintained schools in Surrey was as high as 42 per cent, and about a third of the secondary schools in the county, in addition to the grammar schools, run A-level courses. Doncaster has · G.C.E. courses in its secondary modern schools and, as a consequence, a high proportion even from working-class homes stay on at school after 15 for advanced courses [88].

Table 3.

Type of School and Date	Number of Schools (a)	Number of O-level Candidates (b)	Average number of Candidates per School ($\frac{b}{a}$)
Comprehensive			
1959	19	1,845	97
1962	33	3,487	105
1965	51	4,563	89
Secondary Modern			
1959	202	3,886	19
1962	337	8,039	23
1965	467	15,039	32

This trend is confirmed by Table 3. A random sample – random by the accident of taking the London University G.C.E., whose thoroughgoing statistics make this breakdown of the figures possible – shows the following growth-rate of O-level candidates from comprehensive and secondary modern schools at three-year intervals from 1959 [89]. It will be noticed that while the number of schools and candidates show a marked increase over the period, the number of secondary modern candidates between 1962 and 1965 is almost doubled. Furthermore while the average number of candidates per school for the comprehensives fluctuates somewhat, first increasing then decreasing, that of the secondary moderns shows a steady rise – and the rate more than doubles between 1962 and 1965. This is precisely what other developments tend to show: the secondary moderns have 'discovered' O-level, and similar figures for A-level show they are beginning to discover that too.

Now Mr Pedley's 'National Average Claim' was based on figures up to 1962, before the momentum of the secondary moderns towards taking O-levels had properly got under way. Up till then the grammar schools were maintaining their traditional successes in the G.C.E. while the comprehensives, anxious to win their spurs in the academic joust and so justify their protest against being 'creamed', were also inclined to put everything and everybody they could into the competition for O-levels. But the secondary moderns at this stage were, from policy and choice, virtually non-starters. Small wonder that the performance of the O-level conscious comprehensives looked good beside a 'national average' based on 20–25 per cent grammar school candidates, admittedly with the advantages of 11-plus selection, and 75–80 per cent secondary modern pupils, who, being almost all non-candidates, ranked statistically as 'failures'. What is surprising, and a tribute to the grammar schools, is that thus saddled with a load of statistical failures three times their own number they still managed to achieve 10 per cent* 'good O-levels' (or 11 per cent with the direct-grant schools included) beside the comprehensives' 14 per cent.

*The latest Volume of Statistics published by the Department of Education and Science (H.M.S.O., 1966) gives, for the year 1963–4, the national average gaining five or more O-level passes as 18·5 per cent with regional variations between 25 per cent in the South East and 14·1 per cent in the North East. In the Report of the Inner London Education Authority, *London Comprehensive Schools, 1966*, the average of pupils in the 77 comprehensives gaining five or more O-level passes (subjects unspecified) in 1964–5 was 5·8 per cent of G.C.E. entry, and in seven specially selected schools (Appendix XXI) such 'good O-level passes' varied between 4·7 per cent and 21 per cent of entry, with an average of 14 per cent, well below both the national average of 18 per cent and the 25 per cent in the South East, where London belongs. The matter is somewhat complicated by the fact that the nationa average and I.L.E.A. figures are not exactly comparable: for the former are percentages of all leavers, the latter of all candidates entered for the G.C.E. by the I.L.E.A. comprehensive schools. But I have shown in a letter to *The Times Educational Supplement* of 17 March 1967, so far without contradiction, that this incomparability rather flatters the I.L.E.A. results.

Table 4: *Hillingdon Borough Schools: G.C.E. Examination Results –*
July 1965

Numbers of Pupils with Two or More Passes

Schools	Ordinary Level G.C.E.			Advanced Level G.C.E.		
	Number of Passes	Pupils 15–17	% Pass	Number of Passes	Pupils 17–19	% Pass
Grammar	677	938	72.1	269	347	77.5
% Total Pupils		28.1			10.4	
Secondary Modern	532	1,282	41.5	27	53	51.0
% Total Pupils		14.6			0.61	
Comprehensive	102	224	45.5	12	30	40.0
% Total Pupils		23.5			3.15	
Combined Grammar and Secondary Modern	1,209	2,220	54.3	296	400	74.0
% Total Pupils		18.6			3.35	

Now that the secondary moderns have started to take O-levels
in earnest the picture is somewhat different. Table 4, showing the
O- and A-level performance of all secondary schools in the London Borough of Hillingdon, speaks for itself [90]. This borough
contains 5 grammar schools, 17 secondary modern schools and 1
comprehensive. In this latter it is particularly favoured for, as Mr
Pedley tells us, the school (Mellow Lane, Hayes) enjoys many
advantages – a reasonable staffing ratio (1,120 mixed pupils with
56 staff), a staff of high calibre – 'in nine years no fewer than
eleven members of staff have gone to be heads elsewhere' [33] –
and a big range of social activities (the carol singing of their
choir was particularly impressive). It is said to be 'handicapped
by poor buildings' but my own observations leave me in no
doubt that many a grammar school would settle for such a
handicap. Yet the figures above show that this comprehensive

school does little better than the neighbouring secondary moderns at O-level, rather worse at A-level, and in both trails badly behind the secondary modern and grammar school figures combined, which is the basis of the 'National Average Claim'. Mr Pedley complains that Mellow Lane Comprehensive School 'loses the cream of the local 11-plus entry to the grammar schools'. These figures suggest that both the cream and the milk have their compensations.

But even if the 'Conversion Claim' and the 'National Average Claim' are thus exploded by the facts of 1965, comprehensivists may still argue that though the secondary modern schools are beginning to show their paces in the G.C.E. there is still a great deal of leeway to make up. In a comprehensive school, therefore, more pupils might be encouraged to take O- and A-levels and with a better chance of success. Let us once more look at facts, and here again London University G.C.E. can help us in that at O-level it provides separate statistics for the three types of school with which we are concerned – comprehensive, secondary modern and grammar. First, with regard to the prospects of taking the examination, if we assume the average size of a secondary modern school to be between 450 and 500 pupils, and the average comprehensive around 1500,* a rough computation from Table 3 (page 134) shows that in 1965 the chances of a pupil in a secondary modern school being a candidate at O-level were about the same or fractionally better than in a comprehensive school (1 in 14 or 15 against 1 in 16).

Once entered, what are the chances of success? Table 5 gives the comparative performances in the London University G.C.E. at O-level of the three types of school, subdivided into boys and girls. It would be a breach of confidence to give a list of the schools, but I can assure the reader that the fifty-one comprehensives whose collective O-level performance is here set out include

*The national average size of a comprehensive school is just over 1,000 (199,245 pupils in 195 comprehensive schools, *Statistics of Education 1964*, 1, H.M.S.O., 1965), but the figure 1,500 given above is weighted because many comprehensives taking London G.C.E. are the large London schools, some of which exceed 2,000. Similarly, though the national average size of secondary moderns is 420 (1,640,549 pupils in 3,906 schools) this has been increased to 450–500 because metropolitan schools tend to be larger.

Table 5: London University G.C.E. Results - Ordinary Level - Summer 1965
Comprehensive, Secondary Modern and Grammar Schools Compared

| | | COMPREHENSIVE SCHOOLS | | | | MODERN SCHOOLS | | | | GRAMMAR SCHOOLS | | | | Boys + Girls | |
| | | Boys | | Girls | | Boys | | Girls | | Boys | | Girls | | | |
No.	Subject	E*	P%†	E	P%	E	P%	E	P%	E	P%	E	P%	E	P%
1	Accounts, Principles of	38	44.7	61	54.1	55	58.2	154	44.2	53	56.6	80	63.8	133	60.9
2	Art	303	60.4	390	69.2	1,948	60.1	1,482	62.8	3,052	61.8	6,421	68.9	9,473	66.6
3	Biology	224	53.6	538	60.0	470	37.0	1,142	41.2	4,929	68.2	11,427	70.3	16,356	69.7
4	Biology, Rural	—	—	10	50.0	26	53.8	8	62.5	12	75.0	15	100.0	27	88.9
5	Botany	2	—	2	50.0	9	44.4	—	—	85	68.2	50	52.0	135	62.2
6	British Constitution	18	83.3	2	50.0	143	48.3	98	49.0	365	66.6	317	70.7	682	68.5
7	Chemistry	323	49.8	88	35.2	491	41.1	100	43.0	6,917	62.4	3,008	60.4	9,925	61.8
8	Commerce	69	44.9	85	36.5	98	48.0	227	53.7	25	68.0	84	61.9	109	63.3
9	Domestic Subjects (Cookery)	—	—	172	70.3	6	33.3	988	68.3	9	33.3	3,135	67.9	3,144	67.8
11	Domestic Subjects (Needlework)	—	—	128	71.9	—	—	816	63.4	—	—	1,905	60.9	1,905	60.9
12	Economics	127	67.7	98	56.1	162	34.6	53	26.4	1,740	57.3	644	61.5	2,384	58.4
13	Elementary Surveying	16	43.8	—	—	12	41.7	—	—	69	76.8	1	100.0	70	77.1
14	English Language	976	31.5	1,180	44.1	3,753	31.6	2,919	48.9	14,975	62.9	18,683	77.3	33,658	70.9
57	Spoken English Test	233	29.6	515	36.9	844	32.5	931	44.3	5,710	52.6	8,032	67.1	13,742	61.1
15	English Literature Test	307	51.8	650	58.9	1,192	47.3	1,651	69.7	7,067	62.3	12,639	78.7	19,706	72.8
16	English Literature (Syllabus B)	173	66.5	213	73.2	395	49.4	519	65.1	2,660	62.4	3,700	80.4	6,360	72.9
17	French	312	41.7	589	49.4	478	29.1	776	42.3	11,719	59.3	14,524	75.3	26,243	68.2
18	General Science	39	41.0	32	18.8	701	37.2	204	32.8	454	52.4	728	67.0	1,182	61.4
19	General Science, Additional	—	—	—	—	12	66.7	1	100.0	23	60.9	21	42.9	44	52.3
20	Geography	623	43.2	578	37.0	2,322	43.5	1,277	41.1	9,218	68.6	10,854	72.5	20,072	70.7
21	Geology	7	42.9	18	50.0	26	11.5	4	—	400	56.3	165	65.5	565	58.9
23	German	78	59.0	153	49.7	34	38.2	51	60.8	2,622	55.4	4,006	68.5	6,628	63.3
24	Greek	6	50.0	1	100.0	—	—	—	—	179	66.5	203	85.2	382	76.4

		COMPREHENSIVE SCHOOLS				MODERN SCHOOLS				GRAMMAR SCHOOLS					
		Boys		Girls		Boys		Girls		Boys		Girls		Boys + Girls	
No.	Subject	E*	P%†	E*	P%†	E*	P%†	E*	P%†	E*	P%†	E*	P%†	E*	P%†
25	Greek Literature in Translation	1	—	6	100·0	11	72·7	14	92·9	127	80·3	739	84·2	866	83·6
26	Handicraft (Embroidery)	—	—	—	—	—	—	36	69·4	1	—	123	74·8	124	74·2
27	Handicraft (Metalwork)	313	54·0	—	—	1,987	64·0	3	33·3	932	66·0	3	33·3	935	65·9
28	Handicraft (Woodwork)	263	59·7	—	—	1,494	64·7	—	—	1,469	58·7	4	25·0	1,473	58·7
29	History	426	57·5	457	58·4	1,471	48·2	1,220	47·0	7,595	54·6	10,651	64·3	18,246	60·2
30	History, Ancient	—	—	—	—	1	—	1	—	11	100·0	26	57·7	37	70·3
32	History, British Economic	36	58·3	28	46·4	259	40·5	190	48·9	613	42·1	646	51·9	1,259	47·1
35	Human Anatomy, Physiology	—	—	—	—	—	—	—	—	—	—	—	—	—	—
36	Hygiene	35	34·3	105	64·8	54	31·5	302	50·0	237	48·1	1,401	64·9	1,638	62·5
37	Italian	3	100·0	26	73·1	3	66·7	14	64·3	40	75·0	239	82·0	279	81·0
38	Latin (Syllabus A)	57	45·6	107	64·5	9	77·8	31	64·5	3,322	61·5	5,473	75·3	8,795	70·1
39	Latin (Syllabus B)	—	—	—	—	—	—	—	—	82	36·6	183	78·7	265	65·7
40	Logic	—	—	—	—	—	—	—	—	47	68·1	1	100·0	48	68·8
41	Mathematics, Pure	171	53·8	187	30·5	1,632	58·6	716	46·5	5,572	73·0	4,794	69·4	10,366	71·3
42	Mathematics, Pure (Syllabus B)	650	56·3	368	39·7	1,812	50·9	595	38·7	7,841	71·4	9,031	69·2	16,872	70·2
45	Mathematics, Additional	229	39·7	39	59·0	390	52·1	37	43·2	3,766	68·7	1,163	69·0	4,929	68·8
46	Music	35	62·9	80	58·8	66	53·0	121	46·3	531	58·0	1,276	68·4	1,807	65·4
47	Physics	410	55·4	46	56·5	1,802	39·1	111	32·4	8,426	70·8	2,586	69·6	11,012	70·5
48	Physics with Chemistry	161	43·5	71	53·5	538	41·3	57	54·4	1,769	48·8	2,441	70·8	4,210	61·5
49	Religious Knowledge	62	14·5	162	40·7	9	44·2	830	64·3	1,046	58·1	4,266	77·6	5,312	73·8
50	Russian	2	—	5	80·0	—	55·6	3	33·3	202	50·0	201	73·6	403	61·8
51	Spanish	21	42·9	61	57·4	29	27·6	51	35·3	491	57·0	1,326	73·0	1,817	68·7
52	Technical Drawing	488	69·3	15	33·3	3,567	63·2	16	68·8	2,408	69·6	32	50·0	2,440	69·3

*Numbers entered. †Percentage pass.

some famous and impressive names. Let us be as kind as we can to the comprehensives and compare their results, quite simply, with the secondary moderns'. It will be seen that in some subjects their performance is distinctly better: in Modern Languages, for instance (where the better provision of staff and language laboratory equipment in what, after all, are largely new schools, no doubt has its effect) and in Economics. In Religious Knowledge, on the other hand, there would appear to be more joy in heaven over the secondary moderns than the comprehensives. But in subjects where they compete more or less as equals there is little to choose. In English Language the boys of the secondary moderns do fractionally better, the girls considerably. In Pure Maths the secondary moderns do better in one syllabus, the comprehensives in the other, and in Additional Maths (a harder option) the boys of the secondary moderns but the girls of the comprehensives get the better result. In History a better performance by the comprehensives offsets a better performance by the secondary moderns in Geography. But as aspirants to become the exclusive, monopolistic pattern for secondary schools the comprehensives hardly stand out.

In this comparison I have made no mention of the grammar schools. Parents who fancy their children's chances to gain entry to one while they still survive can draw their own conclusions from the columns on the right without any guidance from me. Incidentally, now that we are told the possibility of sex determination of our children is on the horizon this table contains some interesting data about the relative performance of boys and girls.

Before we leave this topic one other thing needs to be said. Success in public examinations is by no means the only, or perhaps even the most important element in secondary education. It is the comprehensivists who have chosen to join issue on this point. But now they have forced the facts into the open the question of examination results must play its part in assessing their claim to 'preserve', in the language of Circular 10/65, 'all that is valuable in grammar school education'. And it must be frankly added that in this day and age all that is valuable in grammar school education does, for many parents, mean five O-levels and a couple of A-s as a passport to university and the prestige job that graduate status brings. Of course it should not, but it does, and the parents are the voters who have to decide. Yet in this matter the comprehensivists have fallen into a circular argument. They claim that their results are better than those under a separatist system and therefore their schools should not be 'creamed' of abler pupils. If in fact their results are better they can afford to carry the handicap of 'creaming' and do not need to monopolize the abler pupils to prove their point. But if, as the evidence above suggests, their claims have been exaggerated, can they be trusted with the abler pupils or even, given the emergence of the secondary moderns in the field of public examinations, with the less able? This is a factor to be borne in mind as we move to consider the wider academic claims of the comprehensivists.

ACADEMIC PERFORMANCE OF THE COMPREHENSIVES

The chief claim of the comprehensive school, almost in origin its *raison d'être*, is that it abolishes selection at 11-plus. From this a number of advantages are said to follow. It extends educational opportunity to all children, allowing the able to move ahead as they do now in a grammar school and the less able to profit by their example. Thereby everybody's capacity for 'acquired' intelligence is improved, and Britain's 'pool of ability' used to the full. The best buildings and equipment become available to the greatest number; and above all the best qualified teachers are shared by all instead of a limited number in the grammar schools. Now the latter claim is important and will be considered separately later. But the other pretensions in the academic field add up to a claim that what is now available only by selection at a grammar school will be offered to all children of secondary age – that in effect comprehensive schools mean grammar school education for all able to benefit from it.

Now if it were still true that selection at 11-plus could only be by a single examination on a single day, and irrevocable, this would indeed be a denial of educational opportunity to the many, as even Conservatives admit. How far this is true, in precisely these terms, will be considered in the next chapter. But let us assume for the moment that it is – that there is no alternative to the 11-plus except a universally comprehensive system. The comprehensives, by embracing all children in their area, do indeed dispense with selection, but at what cost to the child? Here are six typical schoolboys; their names are fictitious but they will be no strangers to any schoolmaster of experience, and they have their female counterparts. First there is Abel: as his name implies he is a high-flyer; he can and wants to work, and will achieve the satisfaction and self-display so important to all children through academic excellence crowned, with a little luck, by an Oxbridge scholarship. Then there is ebullient Bill: a capable fellow who could do well if, as the pundits say, 'motivated'. His parents are ambitious for him and much will depend on the lead he is given. Charles is a critical case: he would just manage selection to a grammar school, but academic work will always be a struggle for him. Derek is academically slow and a certain '11-plus failure', but good with his hands, a good games-player and capable of learning if given the right sort of encouragement. Eric is dull and diffident, easily led, and has little prospect at school in work or games. Fred is fractious: a rebel against school, a worry to his parents who are glad to get him off their hands, and a potential delinquent.

Under a separatist system Abel, Bill and Charles would all be in a grammar school. There Abel will set the pace; Bill, spurred by competition, will endeavour to keep up with him and Charles, though some way behind, will struggle along and strive, for the sake of his self-respect, to achieve something in the academic context. Meanwhile, at a secondary modern school, Derek will find success in his games and craftsmanship, become a leader and perhaps head of the school and even discover, given the right teaching and encouragement, that he can manage two or three O-levels. Eric, faced with the modest target of keeping up with Derek, has a chance to gain confidence and find something he can do, some satisfaction from his schooldays. Fred will always be a problem in any school. But perhaps there is more hope for him, as the Newsom Report suggests, in the smaller community of a secondary modern school and contact with a dedicated schoolmaster at the right time may be the makings of him.

But what if they are all lumped together in a large comprehensive school? Even if there is streaming, the ability range will be much wider and Abel will begin to mark time, feel frustrated because he is not intellectually stretched, and become restless. Bill finds he can take life more easily and even Charles can relax a little. Meanwhile Fred gets to work on Abel, whom he would never meet under a separatist system, tries to persuade him that school work and homework are 'square' and 'sissy', and begins to set the tone. Derek and Eric, who in a large comprehensive can easily become nonentities, meekly follow Fred's lead, and the stage is set for their early leaving.

This picture is of course over-simplified and presents the contrast in extreme form. It is also assumed, at this stage of the argument, that these children will not change radically over the next few years. What happens when they do is considered in the next chapter. Much can be done in a large comprehensive school through the house or tutorial system to lessen the dangers, and the employment of streaming and fast streams can help to counteract what might be called the intellectual attrition of Abel, Bill and Charles. But it should be noted that the trend in comprehensive schools is against streaming. A paper by the Institute of Community Studies at Cambridge argues forcibly that the advantages of abolishing the 11-plus will be cancelled out if comprehensive schools continue to stream their pupils [91]. The headmaster of David Lister School at Hull, which prides itself on being the only comprehensive school with a thorough-going non-streaming policy, argues thus: 'Labelling human beings, A, B, C, D and so on is anti-Christian and immoral. Streaming is a self-fulfilling prediction – if you tell someone he's a C person often enough, he'll come to believe it and act like one' [92]. Even where there is streaming a good deal of the timetable overlaps. Thus a colleague of mine was told by a comprehensive school mathematics master during a conference that though pupils in his subject were streamed they were able to test all streams by a common examination. Some adjustment in the marks was, however, necessary owing to the difficulty the lowest stream had with reading. When all is said the fact remains, and is a commonplace to any working schoolmaster, that the wider the ability range of a class the less efficient his teaching. So long as the group is fairly close-knit they can all learn together and the spirit of competition raises the standard. But inevitably, if the ability band is widened to a point where the work is beyond the grasp of the lower group, they give up the struggle and – incurable exhibitionists as so many school children are – begin to assert themselves through ill-disciplined behaviour which has to be curbed at the expense of teaching time. Discipline, by derivation, simply means learning; but it is more commonly regarded as an auxiliary or even an alternative to it, necessitated by poor teaching or inefficient class composition. A comprehensive intake increases the risk of both by massive widening of the ability gap that has to be bridged.

This was the gist of the now notorious observations made towards the end of 1964 by Miss Lang, Head of the Music Department at Kidbrooke Comprehensive School for Girls. She maintained in effect that it is the non-academic majority in a comprehensive school that sets the tone, and their influence militates against a high level of scholastic achievement. Moreover she pointed out that though in theory transfers between streams after eleven were possible – and apparent from tables showing movement between classes from year to year in London comprehensive schools [33] – in fact such transfers from stream to stream were seldom made [93].* What is most striking here is that the observations were made by a member of the music staff. Those who have substantial experience of the inner workings of a school will realize that the music staff are usually the least vociferous members of a teaching team – they mostly prefer to carry on unobtrusively with their job and not fish in the troubled waters of educational policy or public relations. They do, however, see the school at all levels and get the 'feel' of it, and the fact that Miss Lang was moved to speak out as she did and put her professional career at risk evinces a deeply sincere and heart-felt conviction.

What can we learn about academic standards from other countries where comprehensive education is already a *fait*

---

*The Plowden Report [56] also criticizes rigidity of streaming in comprehensive schools.

accompli? From America the evidence is consistent and long-established. As early as 1932 Professor E. L. Thorndike said: 'One of the serious criticisms of the American system is that in the zeal to provide identical opportunities for all the interests of the able students have been sacrificed' [94]. In the Harvard Report *General Education in a Free Society* the comprehensive school has been described as 'too fast for the slow and too slow for the fast' [95]. The Vice-Provost of one of the oldest American universities is quoted as saying: 'Our 17-year-old school leavers do not equal English 15-year-olds and this is a terrible waste of talents'[96]. A 'brain-drain' British scientist writes from America:

As the parent of a student who spent two very successful years in a British grammar school, followed by two years of complete stagnation in an American high school, I can confirm this is so. Not only does a comprehensive system *not* tap any latent talent, it wastes the obvious talent and intelligence. The only way a comprehensive non-selective education system for all can work is to provide education that everyone can achieve, so that everyone, brilliant and dull alike, have an equal opportunity to succeed. The only way this can be achieved is by lowering the standards to, at the very highest, the mediocre level. That is why there is such a demand for European trained scientists in this country [97].

Finally the reader is referred to the words of an American educationist in Appendix I (page 261). It is true, and has often been pointed out, that the Americans make up their academic arrears by their magnificent post-graduate courses. But can Britain in the sixties, with an increasing proportion of her population either pupils or pensioners, afford to shorten the productive life of some of her best brains by a further two or more years? Ph.D.s do indeed help us to pay our way in the world, but they cost precious time.

The Scandinavian countries, on the other hand, and Sweden in particular, seem to present a different picture. In Stockholm, some ten years ago, a controlled experiment in reorganization was carried out. The city was split, for educational purposes, into two. In the north a pattern of separate secondary schools similar to our own was retained, while in the south they introduced a comprehensive system. Tests in general ability, reading, writing, mathematics and English of a representative sample of 2,400 children taken equally from north and south revealed that though in the earlier stages those having a grammar school type education came out better the gap gradually diminished, and in the tests after the fifth year there was no difference at all. Moreover children of the secondary modern type were seen to do a good deal better in the comprehensive schools than in the separate schools of the south side ([33] and [35]). This was taken as a clear vindication of the comprehensive system, and plans for reorganization were given official blessing [98].

There can be no doubt that this is a powerful counterblast to the American experience in terms of *academic* achievement.* But before it is taken as *carte blanche* for comprehensive reorganization in Britain there are a number of special factors to be borne in mind:

(1) The Stockholm comprehensive schools in the south had new buildings and were well equipped. Our National Plan holds out little prospect of this on a country-wide scale.

(2) The Swedes insist on small classes – as soon as a class reaches 25 or 30, according to the age group, a new class is automatically formed [35]. Can we be sure we shall have the teachers or accommodation to make this possible?

(3) Teachers in the Swedish comprehensive schools at first employed examination papers to compare their pupils' standards with those in the old grammar schools. They were seldom found to reach the same level. In 1958 the use of examination papers was suddenly forbidden and the official reason given was that the papers did not suit the methods applied in comprehensive schools. Are we sure this could not happen here?

(4) There is a strong feeling among people engaged in secondary education in Sweden that comprehensive schools were introduced for social rather than educational reasons, and many

*The research on the results of the Stockholm experiment has since been subjected to damaging criticism, and it is fair to say that these results must now be considered inconclusive. See *Ability Grouping and Scholastic Achievement*, Almqvist and Wiksell, Uppsala, 1962, and Dr J. D. Koerner's article on Swedish educational reforms in the American *Saturday Review* of 16 July 1966.

regard them as a phase to pass through, not a final solution.

(5) These social considerations affect the course of study chosen. Originally about 70 per cent from primary schools in Sweden, much as in this country, wanted a grammar school education. It was believed that if comprehensive schools were introduced only 40–50 per cent would wish to enter the 'theoretical' (equivalent to our grammar school) stream as other streams would enjoy the same social status. But in fact 70 per cent still chose the 'theoretical' stream, with difficult courses in mathematics and English, and with German and French, for which many were quite unsuited. So re-thinking is in progress, with 1968 mentioned as a possible date for decision. Our own Minister of Education believes that the Scandinavian countries are the 'least class-ridden' in Europe [4]. But this subject class-consciousness recalls what Vance Packard in *The Status Seekers* (of which more later) said of America: 'The course of study a student chose in high-school was considered a good indication of status.... You couldn't "rate" if you took the commercial course and were somewhat handicapped if you took the general course.... The percentage of each class who took the Latin course declines with lower position in the class hierarchy' [99].

(6) Comprehensive reorganization 'is stimulating the establishment of private schools in a country which laughed at them ten years ago' [100], though the high rate of taxation imposed by the Swedish social-democratic Government precludes many middle-class families who would wish to from making use of them [101].

In what has been said here I do not claim to have dismissed out of hand the comprehensive case that it fully preserves academic standards. Clearly the matter is difficult and controversial, and comparisons drawn from other countries are not necessarily conclusive for what might happen here. Suffice it to say that even if, as is claimed in *Signposts for the Sixties*, 'segregation by the 11-plus is now almost universally condemned on educational ... grounds' [61], the assumed corollary, now Government policy, of reorganization on comprehensive lines is no panacea. Moreover there is another difficulty which we have not so far considered.

To students of Circular 10/65 it might seem that the problem of teacher supply under comprehensive reorganization presents no difficulty greater than the re-shuffling of a pack of cards. 'The changeover to a comprehensive system should not affect the numerical demand for teachers significantly.... Authorities should consider carefully how best to effect any redistribution of teaching staff which their plans may entail, and, in particular, how to ensure that specialist staff in scarce categories are deployed and used as efficiently as possible' [47]. But much more is at stake than the redistribution of existing teachers. One of the weaknesses of the secondary modern schools is their lack, compared with the grammar schools, of graduate staff. 'A sizeable proportion of the children at secondary modern schools will never encounter a university graduate throughout their education – even if they are the fairly bright children who in areas where there are plenty of grammar school places would certainly get one, but are excluded by the chances of geography' [102].

Now it is precisely this that the comprehensive school purports to remedy. Its advocates maintain that under the present system the grammar and independent schools are 'creaming off' more than their 'fair share' of graduate, and especially good-honours-graduate teachers. Moreover they seem, on the evidence of existing comprehensives, to have a case. Thus at Thomas Bennett School, Crawley, three quarters of the staff are graduates and six of them took Firsts – the headmaster admits that they did not just arrive; he went out to the universities to get them [103]. The London comprehensives boast of having a 60 or 70 per cent graduate staff, and at Binley Park School, Coventry, which expanded from a secondary modern school (see page 75), just over half the teachers are graduates and 'it is clear that the staff are of a high calibre, young, dedicated and mainly socialists' [35]. If, however, all secondary schools are to become comprehensive the hard facts of arithmetic will compel them to be content with teachers of a different political persuasion, or no political persuasion at all, and there will certainly not be as high a proportion of graduates. For the percentage of all graduates in the maintained schools in England and Wales is only 37·5 [104], and there are three reasons for believing that the ratio will become worse rather than better.

The first reason is a historical one. It was one of the great achievements of the 1944 Education Act to bring largely to an end the existence of what has been fairly called the 'two nation concept' in the teaching profession [105]. Broadly before that time there were two kinds of teacher: those who served a sort of apprenticeship, at one time as pupil-teachers, before teaching in elementary schools (which included the old senior secondary schools of unhappy memory), and those who read for a degree before teaching, often enough without any professional training, in grammar or independent schools. This move away from what was so often a status-conscious dichotomy towards a unified profession, though welcome, is nevertheless being achieved at some cost. Unity can be a façade that, at least at first, papers over real divisions, for which all too often both sides are to blame. The non-graduate teachers, elated at their new-found status, made provocative assertions, like the claim that 'any fool can teach clever children' (wide open to the riposte 'yes, if he is clever enough himself') or the challenge of the (graduate) headmaster of a comprehensive school: 'Of course being a teacher here is tough. ... That's probably why some grammar school masters object – they can't just preach in a comprehensive, they really have to teach' [35]. With its inevitable counterblast from the other side:

I find naïve, sentimental and unrealistic the notion – widely shared at the moment in 'progressive' educational circles – that only those who are prepared to teach a wide range of ability are worth their salt as teachers. ... As a well-qualified graduate I began my own career by teaching in a series of non-selective schools. After a few years I came to the conclusion that I was largely wasting my time; most of my pupils only understood the most elementary vocabulary and had little real intellect – and to teach them day after day was a kind of exercise in masochistic mental prostitution that I found increasingly burdensome [106].

Moreover this new-found professional unity has inevitably magnified its least common denominator. The largest teachers' organization, flooded by the big battalions of primary school teachers, reflects their anxiety, for instance, that the employment of class-room auxiliaries might threaten their hard-won professional status. Another result is the unified Burnham salary structure whereby the teacher in her first term at an infants' school and the head of a large grammar or comprehensive school are paid on the same basic scale, with graduate and responsibility allowances for the latter. Such allowances do not achieve as wide differentials as would the former system of separate graduate and non-graduate scales, and again the big battalions are there to ensure that they do not. Indeed the two most unpopular Ministers of Education among the teaching profession were the very two who tried substantially to increase these differentials – Lord Eccles and Sir Edward Boyle.

Now all teaching involves two elements – knowledge and presentation – but their relative importance varies with the level of teaching. With a sixth form preparing for university courses the former is dominant, with a class of recalcitrant juniors the latter. Both forms of teaching are equally valuable, both involve expertise. But the expertise required for sixth form teaching is scarcer and takes longer to acquire, and here the law of supply and demand begins to operate. Before 1960 five O-levels were enough to secure a place at a teachers' training college, normally at the age of eighteen, and two years' training equipped a teacher to start his profession. Since then the two-year course, where 'many students do not mature by living; they survive by hurrying' [107] has been extended to three years, and A-level qualifications are increasingly sought – 40 per cent already had them in 1963 [8]. But one wonders how long these standards will be maintained in the present shortage of teachers. Meanwhile the intending graduate teacher requires at least two years in a sixth form to secure two or three A-levels with good grades for university admission, and then four further years – three for a degree and a fourth for professional training – before he can commence teaching. Thus before 1960, and perhaps again in the future, the non-graduate teacher could be starting his first post while his graduate contemporary in academic terms was just leaving school with four further years' study ahead of him. The graduate's reward for each year of this much longer period of training is under ten shillings a week, or under £1 if he gains a first or second class honours degree; and while he has spent six years longer than the non-graduate earning this princely differential his non-graduate opposite number will have earned nearly £5,000, and reached a point on the scale where his increments outstrip the graduate's differential. It is true that the graduate has better eventual prospects of graded posts or headships, but these are in the future. Meanwhile whereas the non-graduate's training equips him only for teaching the graduate has many other openings in our graduate-hungry economy, and if he casts interested eyes outside the 'unified profession' he can hardly be blamed.

Under the present system graduate and non-graduate teachers have little contact as colleagues. In grammar schools graduates are a majority, in secondary moderns a minority, and this helps to compensate for the inadequacy of graduate differentials. But in comprehensive schools existing on a country-wide scale they would work with non-graduates, and the graduate, the good-honours-graduate in particular, would lack not only adequate differentials but also a special kind of school which matches his qualifications, protracted training and scarcity value. The point at issue here is not whether he is right or wrong – he can be dismissed easily enough as an arrogant status-seeker – but whether he will be attracted to teaching at all. Nor are graduates necessarily the best teachers. Indeed these latter are often to be found in the much-maligned 'prep' schools, with their only qualifications a little uncertificated learning and their human understanding. But graduates are the teachers parents increasingly demand for their children and comprehensivists assure them that, under their system, they are the ones they will get.

Even in the present situation there are ominous signs of difficulties ahead. I have heard of a comprehensive school where non-graduate staff have accused their graduate colleagues of wearing their gowns for display. Now I like to wear my gown when teaching – it is protective clothing (indeed this was its historic purpose) which helps to keep my modest tailor's bill down. I had not hitherto regarded this innocent practice as a form of ostentation. Yet if this kind of friction is already happening among colleagues who are in comprehensive schools from choice, what will happen when every secondary school becomes comprehensive by edict? Will there be complaints that a headmaster is assigning to his graduates more than their 'fair share' of 'privileged teaching'? Then there is the question of teaching auxiliaries. Some of the most successful schools in the country rely heavily for their first-class science departments and workshops on laboratory technicians and other assistants who play an invaluable part in freeing teachers from routine work so that they can concentrate on their teaching. Grammar school masters welcome such help and would like to see more of it. Are we to expect, in a comprehensive school, resentment and perhaps a threat of strike action from the non-graduate staff at the employment of such auxiliaries? In theory there is no Union objection to the employment of such auxiliaries *purely as technicians*. But the borderline between this and actual teaching is not always easy to define, and demarcation disputes in the teaching profession would not be a pretty spectacle.

This is a disagreeable argument. Brutally reduced it runs: We need graduate teachers. We must therefore pay them much more than non-graduates. Non-graduate teachers resent this. But if we make sure they do not come into contact with each other they will at best resent it less or at worst have less opportunity to fight. Non-graduates will naturally feel this lacks sympathy for or awareness of their case. The temptation to 'sweep it under the carpet' is strong, but this would not be honest. On the non-graduate side three things should be said. First, scarcity value has little to do with intrinsic value. If the criterion is teaching expertise, non-graduates as a whole probably make a better showing than graduates. The lesser academic demands of a teachers' training college leave more time to concentrate on professional skills and their importance receives greater emphasis. The travesty of teaching boasted of as a *modus operandi* by the young scientist on page 156 is practised unobtrusively by more graduates than should be, not all of them young and inexperienced, and the prestige value of a degree is no substitute for knowing one's job as a teacher. Secondly, the presence of non-graduate teachers in secondary schools is not a situation in which we should acquiesce. In Scotland secondary school teachers are all graduates whereas in this country 78 per cent of grammar school teachers are, but only 17 per cent in secondary modern schools and 45–46 per cent in comprehensive, bilateral and multilateral schools taken together [8]. In this situation the present move towards recognizing some of the courses in three-year training colleges by the grant of the Degree of Bachelor of Education is a welcome development. If the training college course is felt to be insufficient to rank for a degree, some plan of treating the first two years or so of teaching as an 'in-training' period with part-time study and a Part 2 examination to complete the degree (rather like the Articles in some professions) as suggested in *Educating the Intelligent* [21] would be a good solution. Mention of this book raises the third point in the non-graduate's case. Even for those whose training college course did not rank for a degree proper recognition by a truly professional salary scale is long overdue. The Burnham scale, though much improved in 1962 under Sir Edward Boyle when a small uniformly creeping rise was replaced by irregular increments, larger where a teacher's commitments and responsibilities increase, still does not meet this. Reform is needed on the lines of the 'H-Y scale' advocated in *Educating the Intelligent*, which is really two scales: Scale A for the teacher who earns steady increments merely by growing older in service, and Scale B for the really professional teacher who merits extra reward and responsibility. This latter can begin after seven years' teaching with a substantial rise (£250) and larger increments thereafter. It has the advantage over the present 'graded posts' that it belongs to the teacher, not the school, so that he takes it with him when he moves as long as his efficiency is unimpaired.

The non-graduate, therefore, has a triple case: he is by and large a better teacher, at secondary level anyway he ought not to be a non-graduate at all, and whether graduate or not deserves a truly professional scale that recognizes proved teaching merit. But all this would cost money; money for graduate allowances of the newly promoted graduates and for the 'H-Y' type scale. And the latter is merely one facet of the general lack of financial recognition of public servants which bedevils our welfare society – the National Health Service, for instance, and the Police have just as strong a case on these lines. But while their case is one of equity, the case for graduate differentials is a more urgent one of supply and demand. As has been said [15], it is not that calculus demands better *teachers* than simple addition, but better mathematicians. Good mathematicians are rare and much in demand elsewhere. All the same there was hope that teachers would stay on, resentful but resigned in a national crisis, non-graduates because they have nowhere else to go and graduates because they like it enough to stay. A realist government would gratefully leave it at that. But a policy of mass comprehensivization that would destroy the grammar schools seems likely to drive out anyway the good-honours-graduates (a warning that 25 per cent of teachers in Enfield intend to leave if comprehensivized should be taken seriously) and suggests that dogma has overridden pragmatic professions. Small wonder if the graduates, at least the younger of them, feel tempted to turn to pastures new – perhaps a sizeable part of the scarce and valuable 37·5 per cent of our teaching resources.

Nor are new pastures lacking for graduates in these days – and this brings us to the second threat to graduate presence in secondary education. In a gloomy article entitled *Departed Grammar School Glories* a headmaster has revealed the malaise of the grammar schools even before the full impact of comprehensive reorganization has been felt [108]. Before the war grammar school masters felt themselves to be 'the aristocracy of the profession'. Nowadays 'administratively and otherwise they are lumped in with all the rest'. While previously their salaries and status compared favourably with those in elementary schools and even at training and technical colleges and the universities, the extension of secondary education for all has narrowed the gap between themselves and other schools and expanding higher education has outstripped them. The result is 'a gradual run-down of grammar school staffs from their former high level of ability' and a threat that able children may be 'inadequately or badly taught' whatever kind of school they are in. The disclosure by the High Master of Manchester Grammar School that something like a fifth of his huge staff, apart from retirements, were leaving the teaching profession for posts in colleges of education, technical colleges and universities – an increase of 50 per cent in the number of masters leaving, a figure corroborated by a sample survey of a number of other grammar schools [109] – is a symptom of this widespread malaise.

There is much in the world outside teaching to attract the good-honours-graduate, in arts as well as science, and much inside it to repel him. Apart from the considerations above there is the ominous threat of re-distribution and re-deployment in the passage from Circular 10/65 quoted at the beginning of this section. No idle threat, it seems, for some authorities are already warning their specialist grammar school staffs that they are technically employed by the authority and not the school and may be moved around 'like members of a mobile labour force' [110] to suit administrative convenience. Most unsavoury of all, one local education authority has interchanged two of its headmasters, and for the one who was thought to be critical of comprehensive re-organization the interposting was hardly intended to be a promotion. In Manchester it is being said that after reorganization the Education Committee will only appoint supporters of the comprehensive principle as heads, deputy heads and departmental heads.* When we recall from Chapter 3 how comprehensive reorganization has become a political question, such a policy could even be the precursor of a kind of educational Macarthyism.

Thirdly, there is little prospect of this wastage of graduate teachers being replenished by new recruits. The following, from

*The early birthpangs of Manchester's secondary reorganization (as reported in *New Education*, February 1967, p. 9ff.) are hardly auspicious: the grotesque game of Box and Cox with the headships of secondary schools in the borough; the astonishing analogy of the Chairman of the Education Committee, '*When you are opening a butcher's shop*, you do not appoint a vegetarian as manager' (italics supplied) – to mention in the same breath comprehensive reorganization and the butchery business is the sort of *gaffe* any Opposition prays for – and finally, the unhappy story of the headmistress of Manchester Central Grammar School, denied the reappointment to her reorganized school for daring to criticize the pure milk of the comprehensive word and offered another she did not want. She has since become headmistress of an independent grammar school miles from Manchester, and who can blame her? When we are told that independent schools steal the cream of teaching talent (page 225), this episode is a reminder that a local authority can first turn the cream sour. But this, to quote Councillor Dr Kathleen Ollerenshaw, is 'only the tip of the iceberg, and nothing to what has yet to be faced' in Manchester.

Education and the Working Class [111], of which we shall have more to say in the next chapter, is the pedagogic philosophy of a young chemistry graduate and Ph.D. teaching at a grammar school:

I reckon I can do A level chem. in four terms. Four terms flat out, mind. We have to go really fast. We have tests twice a week, but we get the results. For instance, last year I got an open to Pembroke, Cambridge, and an exhibition at Trinity Hall, Cambridge, and then I got half-a-dozen places. I've got fourteen places in the last two years and then these opens. I do pretty well; my results are all right. The way we teach, we teach for results. I want the passes, the schols, and all those things. Tests all the time, and scrub the teaching methods, forget about the educational side. Yes, it *is* like that; not altogether of course, but there are two ways, aren't there? There's the one way I teach and there's another way. Well, let me give you an instance: if a boy asks a question it might raise some interesting matters. Now, the other way you'd waste the whole period and follow up those matters and that's all right. But that's not our way. We've got no time for any questions or anything that leads off the syllabus. You've got to get through it. I like teaching our A stream boys but you should see our C stream! They're shocking, absolutely shocking. I don't like teaching them at all, and I don't know what it can be like in the secondary modern schools. I'm not made out for missionary teaching. What I want now is a head of department in a really good school, and then I'd do what our head of department has done. I'd put on the pressure, really hard. Really work those children, tests, tests, tests, and get the results. Get them the results they should have, and that would establish me, wouldn't it? It would give me a reputation. People would know that I could do the job. I might slacken off when I got established – perhaps after ten years or so, I might start looking around and thinking more about the educational side. But you've got to establish yourself first, haven't you? Right?

Before we explode at such insufferable arrogance let us pause. This young man, for all his brash conceit, is the salt of the earth – we need hundreds more like him if we are ever to achieve the technological revolution. 'You should see our C stream. . . .' In a large comprehensive school he will be seeing our H stream. One fleeting glance will be enough to send him scurrying off to industry, there to use his chemistry for research, at double the salary, into a formula to make someone's detergent wash whiter than white, with perhaps at his heels a fugitive pack of arts graduates agog to persuade the washing public that it does.

It is computed that there are 31,647 good-honours-graduates at present in the teaching profession, 21,901 in grammar schools, the remaining 9,746 in comprehensive and other forms of secondary school [104]. Before the comprehensivists can get their redistributive hands on that coveted 21,901 they may well find that a sizeable proportion of them have melted away.*

COMPREHENSIVE SOCIAL ENGINEERING

For all their claims that the case for comprehensive schools is an educational one, I suspect that many comprehensivists, even if forced reluctantly to admit the validity of much of what has so far been said in this chapter, would still maintain that damaging though it may be to a few able children the comprehensive school is still worthwhile for its contribution to breaking down class divisions. The idea of the 'neighbourhood school' with its cosy classless ring is attractive, and without doubt a school like Laurence Weston, Bristol (see page 74) is doing valuable work in this field. In theory it sounds excellent that all the children of one neighbourhood should go to one secondary school and not be segregated according to ability. But there are two practical difficulties. First, a neighbourhood is itself often a reflection of class, so that neighbourhood schools merely emphasize class divisions rather than break them down. And secondly even in a heterogeneous neighbourhood the experience of American comprehensive schools and that most comprehensive institution, the British

*An article in the *Guardian* (23 August 1966) estimates that by 1980, if mass comprehensivization goes through, there will be between 3,000 and 5,000 comprehensive schools in the country, each with sixth forms of 70–120 doing A-levels. The Robbins Report [45] gives the 1961 total of good-honours-graduates in mathematics and science in maintained grammar schools as 4,500, and this figure is declining. Even if the decline does not become a walk-out this, in the unlikely event of perfect distribution, would give about *one* good-honours-graduate in mathematics or science per school by 1980 – not a rosy prospect for the technological revolution. As *The Times Educational Supplement* (26 August 1966) observes, 'It is figures like this which suggest that Mr Crosland and Sir Herbert Andrew are between them taking the country for a ride.'

primary school, suggests that in neighbourhood schools parents and children tend to underline and emphasize class differences from the very fear that they will become blurred. A neighbourhood school is in effect either itself a class institution or a catalyst to class-consciousness.

That neighbourhood reflects class is a fact so self-evident that it is surprising that it ever escaped the comprehensivists. The terms East End and West End applied to London and many another large city, the way many large towns which form two parliamentary constituencies return a Conservative from one end and a Labour member from the other with monotonous regularity, the experience of buying a house, all bring home this simple truth. Moreover attempts to counteract it have achieved scant success. The first New Towns of Hertfordshire were brave experiments in mixing people up in one cosy community, but they failed. Certain areas became 'better class' than others, and the latest development is that the New Town itself is becoming Non-U. In a recent survey of Crawley, Hemel Hempstead, Harlow and Stevenage it was found that few of the more highly-paid executives (at Stevenage only 11 per cent) live in the New Towns. Most prefer to live outside – those at Crawley, for instance, preferring Purley and Redhill [112]. In the New Towns, it seems, as much as in suburbia, promotion means locomotion. And workers paying a monthly rent regard themselves as a cut above those on weekly rentals. Indeed it is not uncommon to find snobbery between different and equally subsidized parts of the same council house estate [113].

Now segregation by ability does at least ensure that the abler children from a wide area will be mixed socially regardless of class. Lord James of Rusholme showed that 10 per cent of the pupils at Manchester Grammar School in 1960 were the sons of manual workers [1], and 'the grammar schools have been, with the trade unions, perhaps the most powerful agents of social mobility in the history of modern institutions' [114]. This, it is true, applies only to the abler children. But where the grammar school liberates, the neighbourhood school cabins and confines. What has been called the 'Berlin Wall of zoning' [58] limits a child's educational horizons to the class-determined accidents of residence. And these effects are cumulative. The smart, well-equipped comprehensive school of Euphoria Park will have the expensive buildings and amenities that high rateable values make possible, and the calibre of child and school will attract the best-qualified teachers; downtown at Gasworks Green where the rates are low there will be poorer buildings and facilities in consequence, and the less personable children will take their place at the end of the queue for teachers. The brilliant child from a tough area – the 'poor children with rich minds' – will inevitably suffer. Lord James emphasized this point in a debate in the House of Lords in February 1965:

If the school I worked in for sixteen years became a neighbourhood school, the social range of the pupils would be far less than it is today. Its greatest quality in my eyes was not its academic excellence but that it gave a boy from any home or background the opportunity to share that excellence. For every school there must be selection. What we have to decide quite simply is whether that selection shall be by birth, wealth, ability and aptitude or by neighbourhood, which is so often the same as wealth. It is because I believe that ability and aptitude are the right criteria that I view certain of these schemes of reorganization with so much misgiving. A society in which social class is unimportant is not achieved by educational means alone and certainly not by schools drawing on one neighbourhood [115].

The character of such a neighbourhood school from an undiversified social stratum is well illustrated in the account by Mr Michael Duane, headmaster of Risinghill Mixed Comprehensive School in London, of his experiences there before it was closed by the Minister [116]. As a chronicle of the good works of a sort of secular Father Borelli his story is moving, but one wonders how much time he and his staff could spare from their social problems for the education of the abler pupils capable of profiting from it.

Something more of the implications of neighbourhood comprehensives can be learned from the long experience of them in the United States. The American author of Appendix I emphasizes how these 'socially homogeneous schools that are called comprehensive . . . reinforce rather than combat class consciousness'. Some of their effects on American social life have been reported by Dr Kathleen Ollerenshaw after a recent visit to America [117]. Americans frequently change house and even change jobs to get the best education for their children. One in five, for one reason or another, moves each year. The turnover of pupils in some of the most disturbed schools is 70 per cent per year. Special schools for the ablest pupils are growing (for that matter accelerated courses are appearing even in the hitherto unstreamed comprehensive schools in Russia). Finally, in a country where 'public school' means what it says, 'private schools have never had it so good. They are mushrooming everywhere.' And here a Bristol-born wife of an American illustrates from personal experience the social effects of selection by residence in America:

A third possibility we all face – and one which has become the most popular – is to move to the outer grass-and-trees suburban areas where public schools are more up-to-date, better staffed, generally less crowded and not hampered with such severe racial or other problems as the city ones. Such 'nice' schools are a haven to so many parents fully aware of the possible horrors of a 'blackboard jungle'. But these moves bring hardship to the man of the family who has to meet a commuting schedule every day and night, and endure the long tiring trips into the city. Most men loathe the commuter trains and that cheery eager traveller is purely a myth – a product of the rolls of cellulose that make up a thousand screen comedies [118].

Circular 10/65 shows an awareness of this problem, and the Minister urges authorities 'to ensure, when determining catchment areas, that schools are as socially and intellectually comprehensive as is practicable. In a two-tier system it may be possible to link two differing districts so that all pupils from both areas go to the same junior and then the same senior comprehensive schools' [47]. To achieve this, ingenuity and inventiveness of a high order would be required, only to be frustrated by the more mobile – which in effect generally means the wealthier – citizens. But even if such socially and intellectually heterogeneous selection by catchment area is feasible, the American experience where true social mixing occurs is not reassuring. Here again it is the American writer Vance Packard who enlightens us with a well-documented account of American class distinctions in *The Status Seekers* [99], and his chapter on 'The Moulding of Tender Minds' contains some startling revelations. After illustrating how class distinctions enter into every facet of American educational life, culminating in the supreme illogicality of excluding students of Greek background from a sorority (or exclusive club) with a Greek-letter name just because they were Greek, and a Washington judge who confessed, 'I do not believe the Brotherhood of Man was intended to apply to social privileges', he thus sums up: 'Our educational system is a far-from-perfect incubator of democracy. If democracy is to be a reality in our nation, it should start in our schools. Further, I think the meanness of class-distinction is more painfully felt during school years than during any other period of people's lives.' If this is the picture in the United States – 'the most truly classless society in history' – what hope is there that comprehensive schools can achieve their purpose of social engineering in poor class-ridden Britain, however successful local authorities may be in carrying out the Ministerial behest to conjure with catchment areas? The experience of state primary schools, always comprehensive, is not encouraging. For the researches of Dr J. W. B. Douglas and others have shown a progressive decline in the performance of the children of manual compared with professional workers, and the assumption, without a shred of evidence or research, that this decline would be reversed at the secondary stage has little to commend it. It is all too easy, and fashionable, to blame the educational system for deep-rooted social problems of which it is merely a symptom, and cherish the optimistic belief that to reform it will solve them. Thus a 'teenage Rocker' is quoted as saying: 'Me, I failed the 11-plus and I felt bitter. From then on it was if you can't beat them with your brains beat them with your fists' [1]. The Minister expanded on this theme in a speech at Nottingham: 'A youngster from a slum went to the worst primary school in his city and at the age of eight would be put into a low stream. He would fail the 11-plus, leave school at the earliest possible age, go into a dead-end job and end up on the beaches of Clacton and Margate' [119]. The implication here is that streaming and the 11-plus are the cause of juvenile delinquency and that comprehensive reorganization will cure it.

But everyone knows that Sweden, by now nearing complete comprehensiveness, has a well-publicized social problem in her teen-age *raggare* and 'leather-jackets', and that even Russia is plagued with *stilyagi*, and that the United States, too, bears out to an astonishing degree the obvious truth that teen-age delinquency is a universal apparition and has about as much to do with the 11-plus as it has with jellied eels [119].

COMPREHENSIVIZATION ON A SHOESTRING

Though the foregoing are the chief objections to comprehensive schools there are others which are formidable if perhaps not insuperable. One commonly cited is their mere size. We hear, for instance, of a comprehensive school in Connecticut where teachers have three pads of coloured paper, pink, blue and green, which are handed out to pupils as authority to visit respectively the headmaster, the office or the lavatory [120]. Human ingenuity, aided by an efficient house system, can surely do better than this, and indeed does in this country at existing large comprehensives or at Manchester Grammar School and Eton (1,400 and 1,200 pupils respectively). More serious is the insistence on a monolithic comprehensive *system*, with its implicit exclusion of any other form of secondary organization. Competition is healthy and stimulating in education as much as in business, and the prospect of a massive comprehensive monopoly has its dangers. These are already evident, to some extent, in the attitude of some comprehensivists when they complain of their schools being 'creamed' or 'deprived' as if they were some divinely ordered institution resembling the Hegelian concept of the all-powerful, all-demanding State. We do well to remember, before swallowing the doctrine of the divine right of comprehensives, that they enshrine only one theory of educationists about how children should be organized for secondary education, to be judged on its merits alongside others. But, perhaps most serious of all, the comprehensive case rests chiefly on the evidence of the 'all-through' 11–18 school, generally housed in brand-new buildings with expensive, up-to-date equipment and, since there are still relatively few such schools, staffed by teachers who are there from choice, believe in what they are doing and include an artificially high proportion of graduates.

Now the one thing that is quite certain from the National Plan and Circular 10/65 is that such schools, on a national scale, cannot be provided in the foreseeable future. In terms of figures, however one looks at it, the money just is not there. More than £1,000 million is needed to bring existing schools up to date – to build new comprehensives would cost many millions more [35]. The Department of Education publication *Trends in Education* shows that while numbers in schools are expected to rise by 23 per cent (even not allowing for raising the school leaving age in 1970) the increase in the working population is unlikely to exceed 3 per cent. Thus to maintain existing standards in education will require both an increase in productivity from now until 1980 and an increase in education's share of the national budget. 'When fertility leaps ahead of productivity, education must either take a bigger share of a growing national income or allow its standards per head to fall' [121]. The implications of this for any grandiose or expensive scheme of mass comprehensivization are colourfully drawn by Sir John Newsom:

I think that in the next five years all our resources of manpower and womanpower and money will be required to keep the ship afloat. The chances of doing any structural alterations to the cabins, let alone hanging new chintz curtains in the captain's cabin, are not on. . . . For the most part our energies will be spent on preserving what we have got. . . . We will live in cloud-cuckooland if we think that there can be any dramatic improvement anywhere [50].

Since therefore we have so far been concerned with the 11–18 'all-through' comprehensive as we know it under ideal conditions, we must now mention briefly some special objections to the *ersatz* comprehensives with which, for many a long year it seems, we shall have to live:

(1) Two-year, and to some extent three-year schools (11–13 or 11–14 and 16–18) involved in the various two-tier systems suggested in Circular 10/65 present special problems. We have already seen them described as 'transit-camps' or 'corridors' (see page 114) in which children will be either settling in or preparing to move with scarcely any feeling of an established educational home in between. Nor would these two-tier schools, with the limited experience they offer, find it easy to attract good staff, and liaison between them and the staff of upper schools, while successful in the pioneering atmosphere of Leicestershire, could degenerate into

disgruntled wrangling when schools have been placed 'end-on' by administrative fiat.

(2) The sixth-form college, though successful when it is based on an established grammar school as at Mexborough, presents difficulties when it exists *in vacuo*. Quite apart from the problems of any two-year school mentioned above there are disadvantages in the concentration of specialist staff and senior pupils in such institutions. The former will lack variety in their range of teaching and their influence and inspiration will be missed in the lower schools; the latter will miss the experience of being an example to and responsible for younger pupils and run a greater risk of becoming a closed circle of selfish, self-conscious teenage introverts. Some of these difficulties are frankly faced in Circular 10/65 and the Minister cautiously visualizes only a limited number of experiments of this kind. They should prove instructive.

(3) Schemes which straddle the primary and secondary stages of education, like that at Hemsworth (see page 86) raise special difficulties connected with staffing and the whole philosophy of form *vis-à-vis* subject teaching to which we have already referred. To entertain such schemes, or indeed any two-tier scheme, without waiting for the Plowden Committee's recommendations on the age of transfer from the primary to secondary stages of education seems odd, and now likely to involve some local authorities in doing their homework twice over.

(4) Local traditions die hard. Two-tier schemes which involve, say, a younger brother attending a lower-tier school which he still regards as the secondary modern school which his older sister avoided, and then an upper-tier school which he still thinks of as the girls' grammar school she attended will make him feel bewildered and affronted on both counts. The march of progress may well demand it, but parents will need a good deal of assurance that the change is for the better. Reorganization that brings new schools is much easier to justify to local feeling than reorganization which merely renames, rehashes and, if need be, re-plumbs existing ones.

'Any judgement of English comprehensive schools at this stage must be made in faith rather than knowledge.' Such was the view of the Crowther Report [22] some seven years ago. Since then there have been many comprehensive experiments and it is right that there should be more, so that faith can be tested by knowledge. But is there yet enough evidence to justify the Government's mandatory 'Believe or else'? As the reader reviews the technique of hidden persuasion used to put the comprehensive case, its tendentious claims of examination successes, the serious doubts about academic standards, the problem of an adequate supply of graduate teachers, the ambivalent effects of social engineering by comprehensivization, and above all the shortcomings of make-shift schemes to circumvent financial stringency, he may feel entitled to wonder.

CHAPTER FIVE

THE CASE FOR THE GRAMMAR SCHOOLS

MOST people have two philosophies of education, one for their own children, another for other people's. The parents of the quarter or so of secondary school children who are selected for grammar school generally acquiesce in the non-selection of the remaining three quarters. The parents of the latter, not surprisingly, resent a system that appears to brand their children as rejects and are eager to see it changed, rationalizing or shrugging off any harmful effects of such a change on the selected minority. Hence the 'groundswell of opinion' that appears to leave the supporters of the present selective system in the posture of King Canute. Objections to it take two forms: that the process of selection is inaccurate or unfair, and that it should not exist at all. Both objections, by implication, threaten the continued existence of separate grammar schools. Two further lines of attack on the grammar school are often heard as well. First, that its whole ethos is middle-class and constitutes a divisive influence which, in a society that is or ought to be becoming increasingly classless, should have no place. Secondly, both in some of the subjects it teaches and in the way it teaches others it is an out-of-date survival from the first into the second Elizabethan Age and ripe for modernization – a process which, whatever other effects it had, would transform the grammar school as we know it beyond recognition. We shall consider each of these objections in turn.

IS SELECTION ACCURATE OR FAIR?

Selection, being a human activity, is prone to human error, and the 11-plus examination is no exception. According to the Crowther Report [22] research has shown that a fresh classification after four years (at about age 15) would have redistributed about 14 per cent of the pupils between selective and non-selective schools and concludes philosophically: 'This is what we should expect from the chances and changes of mortal life, and it seems increasingly clear that we cannot hope to avoid error by further refinements in the process of selection.' Expressed in terms of the average distribution of secondary school pupils between grammar and modern schools these figures look even more depressing: for it means that of every hundred pupils the twenty or so allocated to grammar schools contain six or seven who have been wrongly placed, and of the eighty or so at modern schools six or seven should have gone to grammar school [33]. It is a central plank of the comprehensive platform that such a margin of error is intolerable, and that selection must therefore be abolished. But before resigning ourselves to this drastic remedy, with mass comprehensivization as its consequence, we should first consider whether, despite the gloomy predictions of the Crowther Report, the tests cannot be improved.

The 11-plus examination proper normally consists of two elements: tests of intelligence or verbal reasoning and attainment tests in English and arithmetic. Primary school records and interviews are also being increasingly used, but as they do not form part of the examination proper consideration of them will be left till later. The tests are secret and actual examples of them cannot be given. But for those not familiar with them an example giving some idea of their nature has been supplied by Mr Tyrrell Burgess [8] and is reprinted as Appendix 2. The result of the intelligence test provides what is known as an intelligence quotient, which is the child's mental age, as calculated from the tests, expressed as a percentage of his actual age. Thus a child of ten whose mental age is twelve has an I.Q. of 120, while a child of ten whose mental age is eight has an I.Q. of 80. Children with I.Q.s of 120 or over usually qualify for grammar school though there is regional variation, for while the average who qualify for grammar school is 20 per cent it may be as low as 10 per cent or as high as 40 per cent [33].

Now all this sounds very scientific and the reader may well wonder why an error as high as 14 per cent occurs. For this there are many reasons and these are given in much more detail than is possible here by Professor Eysenck [122] with that rare combination, the authority of an expert psychologist wedded to a clarity that carries the layman with him. Briefly the difficulties are these. First, though intelligence can be measured with fair accuracy nobody is quite sure what it really is – indeed there is some edge to the epigram that defines intelligence as the quality measured by intelligence tests. This does not invalidate the accuracy of the measurement of intelligence tests any more, as Eysenck points out, than the readings of a thermometer were inaccurate before there was much in the way of a scientific theory about the nature of heat and its measurement. Moreover it has been found that there is a significant correlation between performance in intelligence tests and success in academic studies. All the same if we do not know for certain what intelligence is we cannot be sure that it alone, or even chiefly, is the quality that fits a child for a grammar school type education. Psychologists do identify other traits which, whatever their precise relation to the central concept of intelligence, will be recognized by schoolmasters as having an important part to play in success in this field. Recent research, for instance, suggests that intelligence itself embraces two forms of reasoning, 'convergent', measured by conventional I.Q. tests, and 'divergent', which is not measured by such tests at all – indeed correlation between them is as low as $0 \cdot 2$ or $0 \cdot 3$ (where complete correlation is represented by the figure $1 \cdot 0$) – but by 'open-ended tests'. These demand not a single correct answer but a whole range of suggestions which show the subject's imagination and what is loosely called 'creativity'. The following, for example, is a typical multiple-choice I.Q.-test question:

Shoe is to foot as hat is to — ? Arm, leg, neck, head, ankle. There is only one possible correct answer – 'head'. The open-ended type question, on the other hand, might ask:

How many uses can you think of for a shoe?

and demands a whole list of answers which, from one person actually tested, included suggestions as varied as: put on foot; doll's chamber pot; soak in petrol to start a bonfire. This opens up a whole new field of research and work is in progress on it by Getzels and Jackson in the United States and Liam Hudson in this country [123]. One conclusion that seems to be emerging is that sixth-formers on the arts side are in the main 'divergers' while scientists and mathematicians are 'convergers'. Consequently, since intelligence tests at 11-plus are mainly of the conventional type, it may well be that 'divergers' among primary school pupils are not receiving due recognition except, to some extent, in attainment tests in English.

Again persistence, the willingness to persevere with a problem until it is solved, can be measured, and tests have shown that given equal intelligence persistent people achieve more success at school or university than the non-persistent. Teachers would probably go further, as they think of very able pupils lacking persistence who finished at university with Thirds and others, less endowed with intelligence but possessed of unusual persistence, who achieved Firsts, and say that within certain limits persistence can compensate for the lack of a high degree of intelligence. Indeed correlation between undergraduates' I.Q.s and their degree classes at Cambridge is as low as 0.3 or 0.4 (where completely accurate prediction is represented by a correlation of 1.0) [123]. There is also a 'quality rather like carelessness' [23] which leads a person who has the brains and persistence to solve a problem nevertheless to write down the wrong answer. The teaching profession, who next to 'satisfactory' probably use the word 'careless' most frequently on their reports, would readily concur. Or again, to quote the headmaster of a comprehensive school, 'We've discovered that what distinguishes ability isn't understanding or capacity for abstract thought, it's retention' [103], and though many in the profession would not go all the way with this it is certainly true that blotting-paper mind and photographic memory are valuable assets to the student. Finally there are the allied factors of motivation and anxiety [122]. If a child does not want to learn, or is too worried to concentrate, the other qualities, even perhaps intelligence itself, are atrophied. Conversely a surprisingly low minimum I.Q. is necessary, given motivation, for a high level of accomplishment. Recent research by D. W. MacKinnon in California suggests this minimum 'cut-off point' is somewhere in the region of I.Q. 120, not much higher than the cut-off point for grammar school entry in Britain [123].

It must be emphasized that the fact that these and other traits which are complementary to intelligence in achieving academic success are not measured by intelligence tests proper is not a criticism of those tests (though the new theory we have considered of the dual nature of intelligence does undermine them to some extent). Indeed, as Professor Eysenck points out, in so far as they did measure or take account of these other factors they would be less reliable as a pure test of intelligence, just as one does not reproach a thermometer for failing to measure height or weight. But as a prognostic evidence of probable success in higher education these ancillary qualities cannot be disregarded, and while they are involved to some extent in attainment tests in English and arithmetic, other factors, such as the efficiency of different primary school teachers in these subjects, must also be taken into account. In this respect, therefore, the 11-plus examination gives only a partial and incomplete forecast of a child's prospects at secondary school and beyond.

There is another limitation of intelligence tests. A graph of the growth and decline of mental ability shows a steep rise from birth till twelve years of age or so, then a steadier gradient to a peak around fifteen, then a plateau extending to middle age followed by a decline. Though this somewhat over-simplifies the position, as there are variations between the curves for bright, average and dull intelligences, the lesson for the 11-plus examination is clear. The present age of transfer demands that the test be held before the curve has reached its peak (at age eleven); yet what is really required is a forecast of ability at 15 onwards, when an advanced course at school and university fully stretches the intelligence. But what is an accurate measure of present ability at eleven may not be a good prediction of future ability. There is need, therefore, of predictive tests of this kind and it seems that research that would provide such tests, or refine the present selection tests to make them more predictive, is not being done [122]. Moreover practice or coaching in intelligence tests does improve performance, though only a few hours are needed and beyond that there is no significant increase in scores. Some primary schools give such practice and primary school children have been heard to claim that 'intelligence is their best subject'. Other children are given practice by enthusiastic or anxious parents at home, but there is no uniformity and as a result the tests are not uniformly fair. It would be better if tests were given at regular intervals throughout the primary stage so that no single test carried exaggerated weight. Also there is a strong case for research to make the tests more effectively predictive, and to include other tests of persistence, 'carefulness' and the other qualities which we have seen play their part, along with 'intelligence', in assessing a child's capacity for academic education. The reader may well ask why this is not done:

The reason is a very simple one. If it costs 9d. per child to give one test of intelligence and score it, then it would cost almost 4s. to give five tests. The decision that a child's future happiness is worth only 9d. rather than 3s. 9d. is not made by the psychologist, but by the general public through their elected members of local government bodies. All one can say is that for 9d. the public is getting quite incredibly good value for its money. To have a fairly superficial examination of a car carried out costs several pounds. A reasonably complete health examination costs at least as much. To get a child's intelligence investigated for 9d. can hardly be considered an extravagant expenditure. The degree of accuracy of this measurement, of course, is directly dependent on the amount of money spent on it. The higher the degree of accuracy required, the more money will have to be spent on the examination. During my recent visit to California I was shown a large series of laboratories constructed at a cost of several million dollars for the sole purpose of getting a few thousandths of one degree nearer to absolute zero temperature! Our society is willing to pay large sums of money like this for a slight increase in the accuracy of physical measurement, but it is content with an expenditure of 9d. per child in the measurement of a psychological variable of great importance to both the child and society [124].

Likewise the Crowther Report tells of Ministry statisticians being constantly asked to 'make bricks without straw' and expenditure on educational research which 'can only be described as pitiable' [22]. Thus, while the 11-plus selection tests give no ground for complacency, there seems to be more hope of improvement, given funds for the purpose, than the gloomy conclusion of the Crowther Report or the uncompromising demand for abolition by the comprehensivists might suggest. And it is worth pointing out that the latter, while condemning one system whose failure is due, at least in part, to lack of money, are advocating, in their policy of mass comprehensivization without extra cash, another that seems destined to suffer the same fate for the same reason.

There remains one other aspect of intelligence; the question of whether it is hereditary or acquired, or the 'nature-nurture controversy' as it is sometimes called. The view that environment is all-important has had many adherents since Darwin, including the Marxists, who seem to 'favour the conception of human beings as emerging with perfect uniformity from some conceptual conveyor belt' [124]; and it is becoming increasingly fashionable, for obvious reasons, among those who favour comprehensive reorganization, including the Minister himself [4]. The Russians, on the other hand, or at least some Russian teachers, are beginning to think there may be something in the concept of innate ability after all [125]. So we have the spectacle of a British Minister of Education driving purposefully up a cul-de-sac and facing red-faced reluctant Russians moving tentatively in the opposite direction. For this is a case where political and social wishful thinking flies in the face of scientific evidence. Not all psychologists agree here. The researches of Mrs Jean Floud and Drs Halsey and Vernon stress in particular the fallibility of selection tests and the progressive deterioration in the performance of working-class children, visible even at the primary stage, through lack of intellectual and cultural stimulus in the home. Moreover both Mr Crosland [4] and Sir Edward Boyle (in his Preface to the Newsom Report, *Half Our Future*) influentially beg a difficult question when they speak of 'acquiring intelligence'.* But experiment has produced four pieces of

*It may seem that for the 'nurturist' to say that working-class children are robbed, by an unfavourable home background, of the chance to 'acquire intelligence' and the 'naturist' that largely innate intelligence is atrophied by it merely shows opposite sides of the same coin. But the former encourages the sentimental and misleading hope that anyone can become intelligent given a fair chance, and those with experience of teaching children from 'privileged homes' know that this is just not true. Some figures in Mr Graham Kalton's book on *The Public Schools* (Longmans, 1966) may seem to belie this. A table on p. 102 shows that in a sample of over 900 public school boys who failed the 11-plus 92 per cent gained one or more O-level passes and 15 per cent university places. But there are special factors to explain this: the largely academic syllabus of independent preparatory schools, which rarely practice for or take seriously the 11-plus exam; the small classes and quality of teaching in public schools and their good public relations with universities which helps marginal candidates; and the backing with hard cash and interest of their parents. I do not believe these pupils 'acquire intelligence' – they merely make optimum use of the limited amount they have.

evidence which can be easily explained in hereditary terms but do not admit an environmental explanation. Briefly they are: the phenomenon of regress, which occurs in physical characteristics like height and also in intelligence, so that tall or intelligent parents have children who are taller or more intelligent than the average but not as tall or intelligent as their parents, and so on – in simple terms, all extremes tend back to the average; the fact that identical twins show similar characteristics of intelligence even when brought up in different environments; the converse of this, that orphanage children, though brought up in the same environment, show almost as great a variability of intelligence as normal children brought up in vastly different surroundings; and finally, though less cogent unless we accept intelligence as a biological characteristic not confined to human beings, certain experiments in interbreeding 'bright' with 'bright' and 'dull' with 'dull' animals which showed, after several generations, practically no overlap in performance between the 'bright' and 'dull' strains. These experiments are more fully described by Professor Eysenck [122], who adds that they are supported by other less conclusive experiments and not contradicted by any other evidence.* He concludes that in Western countries at the present time 'about 80 per cent of all factors contributing to individual differences of intelligence are hereditary, 20 per cent environmental; in other words heredity is four times as important as environment', though he stresses that these figures apply only to the Western world at the present time and are averages, not necessarily applicable to every given person. Despite these reservations the evidence for heredity, coupled with the fact that wide differences of ability in a class make, as we have seen, for inefficient teaching (see page 144, and here the practical conclusions of schoolmasters are supported [124] by the results of psychological experiment) strengthens the case, at least on educational grounds, for some form of selection and for perseverance with the refinement of selective tests rather than their complete abolition in favour of the comprehensive principle.

So far we have considered only the 11-plus examination, and

*The new 'convergent–divergent' theory of intelligence also seems to support a hereditary rather than an environmental hypothesis.

chiefly the intelligence test element in it. But few local authorities nowadays rely on this alone, and the importance of primary school records and interviews is increasing. It is all too easy to decry the part that these factors can play in getting selection right. We are told that teachers' judgements are subjective and coloured by groupings already made in the junior school, and that the interview depends on personal impressions of a child's speech, dress and manners and lowers selection to the plane of 'rough inexpert justice' [33]. Here two things must be said. First, while we hear endless exhortations from politicians to 'trust the people' we seldom hear a recommendation to trust the teacher. It is all very well for educationists to belittle their judgement and experience, but if we cannot trust them who can we trust? Indeed, as we shall see in a later chapter, one of the attractions of independent schools, far above the oft-heard and exaggerated reports of higher salaries, is that in so many of them the teachers really are trusted. Here is something that state education can learn from the 'private sector', and give its teachers a feeling that all their training and experience has not been in vain. And need the interview be 'rough inexpert justice'? It is relied upon, among candidates of very similar qualifications, to select for the all-too-few university places, and throughout the world of business, commerce, politics or whatever, for making appointments. Of course its technique needs improvement, in secondary education as well as everywhere else, but it should not just for that reason be butchered to make a comprehensive holiday.

Here the 'Thorne Scheme' of the West Riding, another product of the fertile brain of Sir Alec Clegg, points the way. It is worth recalling that while we deplore the 14 per cent error in the 11-plus selection procedure it still correctly places 13 or 14 out of 20 pupils on average, or over two thirds, in grammar schools, and 73 or 74 out of 80, or over seven eighths of pupils correctly (given the sadly inadequate provision of grammar school places) in secondary modern schools. Anybody with any experience of examining or testing knows that the most difficult and critical decisions are at the margin, with the candidates who narrowly pass or narrowly fail. It is just here, too, that intelligence tests are popularly misunderstood and misapplied. It is a fallacy that these give a sort of horsepower rating of intelligence; they can discriminate fairly accurately over a wide range of ability, but fine grading which places a child with an I.Q. of 120 in a grammar school and one with an I.Q. of 110 in a secondary modern school, though it may suit administrative convenience, in fact makes 'so fine a distinction as to be virtually meaningless' [123]. This the Thorne Scheme frankly faces by allocating junior school pupils to a certain number of grammar school places determined by each junior school's previous record in the 11-plus examination. Each junior school submits its order of merit and only the border-line cases are tested in English and arithmetic and by interview. Time and careful consideration is therefore given where it is most needed, the primary school teachers gain responsibility for which they are well qualified, and therefore self-respect, and all except the marginal children are spared a formal examination. A grammar school headmaster of my acquaintance whose school receives pupils selected in this way is satisfied with its fairness. Admittedly the border-line children are subjected to greater strain than the others, but at least there is more time to get the answer right, and in this imperfect world living on the border is almost bound to be as uncomfortable educationally as it is internationally.

Scepticism about the infallibility of intelligence tests and sympathy for the children is leading local authorities to turn to solutions like the Thorne Scheme or in other ways to modify their selection procedure. In Essex, for instance, a working party has recommended a plan for three verbal reasoning tests to be given at intervals (rather on the lines advocated by Professor Eysenck, though the intervals are somewhat shorter than he visualized) and these averaged, together with primary school assessments, would decide selection after careful attention to border-line cases. Another working party in Surrey urges the abolition of attainment tests in English and arithmetic and complete reliance, for selection, on primary school records and verbal reasoning tests. Meanwhile there is a growing movement to regard such selection, even when correct, as not irrevocable and to develop schemes which make transfer between the grammar and modern streams of secondary education more flexible and easy. The most striking experiment of this kind is at Ifield, in Crawley New Town [126]. Here two schools,

Ifield Grammar School and Sarah Robinson Modern School, are built on a common campus. Facilities and activities are shared – swimming bath, orchestra, dramatic productions and so on. Uniform is common to both, teams can combine and some courses overlap in the two schools. Governors are also shared. Parents do not opt for either of the schools but for the campus as a whole. The two heads allocate children with scrupulous care, consulting the junior school heads, the class teachers, the children's books and 'as a last resort, but informally and at their schools, the children themselves'. Both schools basically correlate their first two years' syllabuses and hold common tests during the first year. Up to the start of G.C.E. courses exchange of pupils between the two schools can be free, and the grammar school sixth form serves pupils from both schools; Sarah Robinson Modern School pupils constitute more than 10 per cent of the total grammar school sixth form and 15 per cent of the lower sixth, while others are able to stay on at the modern school. Thus selection is completely open-ended, and called 'allocation' to avoid overtones of finality. Yet the schools are in two vital senses quite separate. They are a comprehensive campus and not a comprehensive school. First, the approach to subjects differs in the modern and grammar schools in precisely the way, as we shall see later, that suits the needs of the 'modern' and 'grammar' type pupil. And secondly, the modern school pupils attain a responsibility and an identity which is real and meaningful, in the way the Newsom Report advocates, in the context of a smaller community which would be swamped in one large comprehensive. Yet it is doubtful whether this campus would satisfy any of the categories of Circular 10/65, and already there are signs of hostility from local politicians who feel it is not comprehensive enough. Thus a valuable and imaginative educational experiment seems likely to be stifled by the dead hand of politics.*

* Though Ifield enjoys the advantages of a purpose-built campus

*Since these words were written events have borne them out. Ifield Comprehensive Campus has been transformed into a standard pattern comprehensive school and the Headmaster of Ifield Grammar School, rejected in favour of someone more likely to accord with the political requirements of comprehensive orthodoxy, has become head of a more traditional grammar school.

layout, other experiments have developed elsewhere where existing buildings, usually less conveniently sited, must be used. In the London Borough of Harrow a scheme is in operation known as the Collegiate System whereby several secondary modern schools are affiliated to a grammar school with which there is free interchange of pupils where considered advisable, and the grammar school sixth form is shared. In one such grammar school of a collegiate group a former secondary modern boy, having gained a good O-level result, has taken A-levels at the grammar school and been appointed deputy head-boy. The scope for this kind of scheme is endless, and it has a flexibility to suit local requirements and feeling. So the child who is a late developer, or whose early response to the less bookish approach of the secondary modern school enables him later to face the rigours of higher education, can move towards it at his own pace and finish school with A-level qualifications instead of a 'chip on his shoulder'.

At this stage, too, we should take a closer look at Mexborough (see page 88). Though some comprehensivists claim it as their preserve, the plaque at its entrance is firm and unmistakable – 'Mexborough Grammar School' – as is the headmaster's official stationery, and this is significant. It was my privilege to be shown over this school by its head-boy, and his sister, who is in the lower sixth. Both are studying mathematics and physics, and the head-boy goes to Cambridge, as it happens to my own college, in October 1966 to read for an honours degree. A description of the general plan and amenities of this Grammar School and Sixth-Form College has already been given (page 88), but it was from these two young people that I learned the ethos of the place. They left no doubt in my mind that it belongs rather to the grammar school tradition than the comprehensive revolution. Both students came to the College from the Grammar School, to which they gained entry by the 11-plus examination, and both were sure they would not have liked to be in a comprehensive school. They felt that the rigours of a grammar school course had enabled them to welcome in and help the new arrivals from surrounding secondary modern schools far better than if they had been all together at a comprehensive. They could give a lead – and this was said without arrogance, but with the true humility of the student who has come to appreciate study for its own sake – and spread the good news of the worthwhileness of advanced study to those who had joined them without much idea of what it was all about. Both were enthusiastic about the wide range of courses available at Mexborough. Subjects can be studied at four levels: the normal A and O for G.C.E., cultural (C) level, where a broader treatment, entirely free from examinations and their inhibitions, is adopted, and vocational (V) level, leading to professional qualifications or 'just for fun'. Thus the head-boy, while taking Advanced level physics and mathematics, learned to type expertly and drive a car in his 'V' periods. They were also obviously and justly proud of their brightly furnished Common Room, and the fact that their College Society is responsible for running it, with profits derived from the snack-bar enabling them to employ domestic help to serve light refreshments and look after them generally. Again, in the matter of uniform, though it was first retained at the students' own request it has now been abolished, but this concession has not led to a rash of 'outrageous clothing'. But to this, and much else besides, they gave less emphasis than to the point made earlier – that Mexborough owes much to being firmly rooted in a traditional grammar school. From it the Sixth-Form College was an organic growth, and it would not be what it is had it just been planted *in vacuo* as an aggregate of students from a number of schools merely thrown together for the convenience of advanced courses. Some three fifths of the 480 students of the College came from the Grammar School, and though the eventual roll is expected to rise to 600 it is not visualized that more than 40–45 per cent will come from other schools. That this is not merely the view of the students, prejudiced through having been in the Grammar School themselves, is confirmed by the headmaster in his prospectus, though he is diplomatically reticent about the exclusively grammar school ethos of the 'internal students' and the part it plays in making Mexborough the success it is (Dearne Valley, the parliamentary constituency in which Mexborough stands, has a Labour majority of over 30,000):

In the sort of sixth form college that we are developing the majority – say three-fifths – of its members will already have a well developed loyalty to the community. Freedom is likely to be more wisely used in these circumstances. There is, of course, the opposite danger that new incomers will be rejected, but special care is being taken to watch for this and no sign of it has yet been found with those who joined this year. The fact, therefore, that the sixth is already based upon a lower school is vitally important and the links it retains with it are of great consequence.*

Both students had benefited from spending their earlier years in the Grammar School, in an established academic atmosphere, and not at a comprehensive school where there is a tendency, as observed by Miss Lang of Kidbrooke (see page 144) for the academic minority to be influenced by the non-academic majority. There is much talk by comprehensivists about the beneficial 'lead' that the abler pupils give to the less able. Mexborough convinced me that they are better able to do this at the more mature level of the sixth form, with a grammar school discipline behind them, than at the beginning of the secondary stage in a comprehensive school, where they can too easily become depersonalized and seem less likely to give a lead than to be led, or misled. This is not to say that the process, at sixth-form level, is not reciprocal. The incomers, too, have something to contribute, as we shall see. There is also an advantage, both in attracting and keeping staff, especially graduates, in the fact that they are shared between Grammar School and College. As a working sixth-form college Mexborough, at the time of writing, is unique in the country. Those who would follow its lead would do well to probe its deeper lessons that lie beneath the purple exterior décor and glossy amenities – not least the profound message of its nameplate – 'Mexborough Grammar School'.

Another and somewhat different example of how the grammar school can pioneer the spread of higher education is to be found in South Shields. Here the 1,000-strong grammar school is well equipped not only in the wide range of its conventional facilities – including language laboratories and language courses that include Greek, Russian and Chinese – but also in having a fully operational computer making possible a G.C.E. course in computer technology and thus filling a national need. The school's total of sixth-form pupils has risen in twelve years from 40 to 210. But this

*Prospectus of Mexborough Grammar School.

is no preserve of an esoteric élite. At 4 p.m. the school is open to secondary modern school pupils and school leavers who can use the reference libraries, language laboratories, study rooms and sports facilities, including a heated swimming pool. It does not close until nearly 10 p.m. and is staffed by a night shift of teachers. Incidentally much of the success of the school is owed to its teachers, and appreciation of their work is shown by the grant of 100 per cent mortgages by the authority and the provision of council houses for certain people [127]. Thus by its shift system and the dedicated service of its teachers South Shields Grammar School expands in time where Mexborough has expanded in space, each to the benefit of their respective communities.

In such ways the grammar school can play its part in rectifying the errors and effects of selection. Whether through the partnership plan for secondary schools of Ifield and Harrow, or through a mother grammar school adopting, as it were, older children, as at Mexborough, or offering the hospitality of its home to a wider community as at South Shields, imaginative schemes can go far in this way, and seem more likely to succeed than the shot-gun marriages between grammar and secondary modern schools – to name names would only embarrass the victims – with local politicians wielding the blunderbuss and the heavier cannon of Curzon Street deployed menacingly in the rear.

SHOULD THERE BE SELECTION AT ALL?

At this point the reader, though conceding that much is being done and more could be done to get selection right and appreciating the value of plans to right its wrongs, may well ask why selection for secondary education should be necessary at all. He may feel that while psychologists debate and research about intelligence, inherited or acquired, convergent or divergent, the whole business is too indefinite and hazardous to play any part at all in the assessment of schoolchildren. The case of the comprehensivists is that such selection, if essential (and many would dispute this) is better carried out inside the confines of the neighbourhood school. A Ministerial broadcast on the eve of the local elections of May 1966 put it more forcibly. After claiming credit, predictably, for measures to abolish the 11-plus it went on to argue that pupils selected for grammar school had no right to a *superior* education (italics supplied). Now the choice of the word 'superior', though politically adroit, is dialectically devious. For there are two stages in this argument, and by taking them together the intermediate stage is both sidetracked and prejudiced. The first question we have to ask, when considering the educational case for secondary selection, is whether a particular type of pupil or mind should have a *different* kind of education. Whether or not that kind of education is 'superior' to any other, and what the word 'superior' means in educational terms, are follow-up questions to an affirmative answer to the first, not devices to pre-empt a negative one. For instance one might concede that a grammar school type pupil needs a different kind of education but argue that since that kind of education is 'superior' he should be denied it on egalitarian grounds. This would be an ethical or political decision, but the prior question is an educational one and deserves an answer without prejudice. To phrase it more precisely: is there such a thing as a 'grammar school mind' which requires a particular and different kind of education and would suffer from not receiving it? There are cogent witnesses to suggest that there is.

First, a former Chief Education Officer who has since given his name to one government-sponsored inquiry on education and is chairman of another. Sir John Newsom, after a positive warning that 'it is much better to recognise that for many children the grammar school is not the best place, and that a different approach is essential' later makes his point more specifically:

Some children find algebra, French grammar, Latin, physics and chemistry so difficult that they cannot attain more than an elementary standard in them. To put such children in the same school as those who find these mental disciplines relatively easy is to force their particular capacities into a mould they do not fit, and to create a sense of inferiority, frustration and boredom, with the result that their real education is of little value, even if they can say in after life that they went to Barchester Grammar School and wear the old school tie [49].

Secondly, a headmaster affirms that 'the grammar school, whatever its variations, is essentially for those who can learn from books' [129]. And thirdly – for here *maxima debetur puero reverentia* – a child, with rare insight, described grammar schools as 'sit down and think schools' [129].

All these quotations, in their different ways, point to the existence of a particular kind of mind or intelligence – and let us not generate heat here by using the word 'superior' – for which the grammar school strives to cater. It does this in many ways but in two, I believe, especially; first in its approach, and then in its method.

The approach of the grammar school is still, in the main, academic and this, as we have seen in the first chapter, was its historic role. Many of the subjects it teaches, though superficially useless, are of value in training the mind and developing personality. The demand for such trained minds in the adult world is fully established and steadily growing. For example the following is extracted from an advertisement for an intermediate post in a nationalized industry: 'The work requires clear thought, an eye for the relevant point, and the ability to draft quickly, in logical sequence and in plain English. . . .' No mention here of particular knowledge or experience – indeed it is not clear, out of context, which nationalized industry is concerned, and it might well apply to any. Nor could one prescribe any one subject or course of training that would provide the qualities sought. The subject matters less than the approach, and this is, in effect, the academic approach, which broadly means treating a subject of little or no obvious practical value as tremendously important and worthwhile for its own sake. Now one of the hardest tasks of a teacher is to make a child on the threshold of secondary education see this. With some it is well nigh impossible, but it is easier with children of initial reading interest and ability, the prerequisite of which is usually a certain degree of intelligence and the consequence a readiness and desire to think and criticize for its own sake. The approach of the grammar school is therefore literary rather than practical – a 'sit down and think' school for 'sit down and think' children. One consequence of this is its apparently somewhat limited curriculum. Compared with the vast range of subjects offered at a large comprehensive school (see page 70) the grammar school resembles a one-man business competing with an educational supermarket. Yet paradoxically this is its strength.

Offer a boy of eleven or thirteen a choice between commerce and Greek, or let a girl of similar age choose between typing and trigonometry and who can blame each, with their limited vision in a materialist world, for choosing the former option often enough, when they are 'first generation grammar school pupils', with their parents' blessing. For the 'sit down and think' child there is much to be said, on the long view, for such options as commerce and typing just not being available. Though sceptical at the time I personally am glad, in retrospect, that I had no choice but Greek. Both choice of subject and standards of work are involved here. In the words of a grammar school master, 'academically we drive, and only in the later years do the pupils realize why they have been driven'.

If the approach of the grammar school is academic to match the needs of the grammar school mind, its method of teaching is also distinctive. That this should be so is perhaps best seen by considering the different character of teaching in the modern schools. Here the approach is more graphic and often more imaginative and experimental than in grammar schools. Visual and other teaching aids are, or should be, more extensively used and there is need for the teachers to be more concerned with and enterprising in the presentation of their subject. As a comprehensive school headmaster put it (see page 149) 'they can't just preach, they really have to teach'. Now there is nothing wrong with preaching provided that you have an audience more or less prepared to listen, and here is the crux. By and large the grammar school child really does want to learn, though youthful pride would seldom admit it. But with the secondary modern child the teacher first has to persuade his class to want to learn before they can even begin to think about learning. Motivation must precede instruction, and often enough the former is a longer and more frustrating process than the latter. Thus a secondary modern mistress, given the task of imparting some biology to an apathetic class of girls, found that a story about a boy and a girl, with a vast amount of (to the layman) irrelevant detail about the girl's clothes, make-up and hair style, was a necessary preliminary to any initiation into the facts of life. Her grammar school opposite number, with a motivated and receptive class, would probably have completed the subject, neat diagrams in biology notebooks and all, before the modern school teacher had even prepared the ground. Whether or not we confuse the issue by calling the former process 'teaching' and the latter 'preaching' it is quite plain that with the former class elaborate presentation is both necessary and valuable, with the latter time-wasting and, for the pupils, probably tedious. Or again with modern languages. There has been a great deal of discussion lately about the use of the language laboratory, and in a series of television programmes given recently by the B.B.C. one speaker made the point that many sixth-form grammar school pupils, while perfectly capable of writing a lengthy character-study of Racine's Phèdre, would be quite unable to direct the lady in simple French to the psychiatric ward of a hospital. Of course oral fluency in a foreign language is an important objective of its study, but this witty statement of the problem confuses two things: the study of a *foreign language* as a means of communication and the study of *language* in its wider sense as a medium of training the mind and personality. The sixth-form grammar school pupils were studying French and French literature as a training in the humanities, and the object of their study was to learn about human relationships and culture in the widest sense rather than to understudy a porter in a Parisian hospital. If they can do both, so much the better. But, to put the point in its extreme form, one does not learn Latin to direct Aeneas across the Styx or 'have a drink with a dead Roman senator' [130]. Moreover there are differences even where the primary objective is oral fluency. A point raised about the use of language laboratories by the head of the languages department in a comprehensive school was that repetitive exercises in the laboratory, while they were enjoyed by the slower children as they suited their pace and gave them confidence, very soon bored the abler pupils. Thus the difference between the grammar school and non-grammar-school mind, accentuated by their joint presence in a comprehensive school, is again brought out. This difference could be further explored and illustrated by contrasting the more practical approach to mathematics, science and other subjects in the modern school with the more theoretical treatment in grammar schools.

Or we may look at it another way. The following is a random sample of Advanced and Scholarship Level questions in various subjects set by a G.C.E. examining board:

(1) The Bryophytes have been termed 'a blind alley of evolution'. Discuss this statement.

(2) 'Lollardy was first academic, then political, and finally underground and proletarian.' Discuss.

(3) By induction, or otherwise, prove that, for any positive integer n,

$$\sum_{r=1}^{n} r2^r \cos^{r-1} \theta \sin (r+1)\theta = -2 \sin 2\theta + 2^{n+1} \cos \theta (n \sin n\theta - \sin (n-2)\theta)$$

(4) Lordynges, the question thanne wolde I ask now,
Which was the mooste fre, as thynketh yow?

What would be your answer to this question?

(5) '*Une farce nourrie de lyrisme unanimiste*'. Comment on this view of Jules Romain's *Knock*.

(6) Outline modern views on valency using as examples $NaCl$, CCl_4, CO and K_2SO_4.

Discuss the difference between the structure of a single crystal of potassium chloride and that of a diamond. How do these structures account for differences in the physical properties of these substances?

(7) What does the marginal productivity theory of wages tell us about wage differentials?

How many people can honestly say that they were deprived by a perverse educational system of the chance of doing questions of this kind, or that, given the ability, they would have been prepared to face all the hard work and academic drudgery required to equip themselves to cope with them?

It is not suggested that all grammar school pupils could answer questions like these. Some of them move at a slower pace and profit by greater emphasis on practical subjects. The engineering workshop, it will be recalled, originated at Oundle School (see page 48) and some grammar schools have flourishing sixth-form courses in metalwork and similar options. The dividing line between theoretical and practical is sometimes blurred, and it is the existence of pupils who seem to straddle it that lends plausibility to the comprehensive argument. Certainly the education of these marginal children at some selective schools, both grammar and modern, leaves room for improvement. But border-line cases are not a sufficient reason for abolishing borders, and the distinction between an academic and theoretical emphasis and a more practical bias, with 'learning by doing', is still valid. Many a fitter who has a complicated wiring-diagram at his finger-tips would find it hard to write down the formula for Ohm's Law. Nor is this a distinction of social status or earning power. The fitter these days will, as often as not, have his own car, which he takes abroad, and perhaps, in time, his own business; while many a schoolmaster, graduate and non-graduate alike, has his horizons of travel confined to public transport and public library.

But if the grammar school approach to and method of learning is *different*, how far are we justified in suggesting that it is in some way *superior*? This word has two main uses: first, to convey that something is intrinsically better, and secondly, that it carries a higher status. Now things that are 'superior' in the first sense usually cost more, as when we speak of a 'superior quality cloth'. In this sense a grammar school education is often more expensive in two ways. First, most of its staff, and certainly a larger proportion than in a secondary modern school, are graduates, and this means the payment of graduate allowances and usually a more lavish scale of special responsibility posts. Secondly the pupil-teacher ratio in grammar schools is more favourable, on average 17·9 against 20·1 in modern schools [8]. The average size of classes is roughly the same (28·4 and 28·6 respectively) but the larger sixth forms in grammar schools, with their smaller teaching groups, makes the overall ratio more favourable to them. But this is not always so and should not necessarily be so. For one thing, in many areas, as we have seen, it is the secondary modern schools that have the new buildings and equipment, so that in terms of capital expenditure the balance has been redressed. Moreover we have seen that ideally the teaching in modern schools should be more graphic and practical, and here expenditure on workshops, art rooms, language laboratories and even planetaria and computers is justified and should increase. There is a strong case, in equity, for local authorities, pressed by central government, to ensure that expenditure on grammar and secondary modern schools should be roughly equalized,* and the Minister, if he is complaining that grammar school children get a *superior* in the sense of *more expensive* education, is the man to do something about it. But in any case should we necessarily expect precisely the same amount to be spent, in a social service such as education has become under the 1944 Act, on different types of secondary education? Few people, I imagine, who enjoy good health themselves resent the expensive operations and treatment necessary for the physically less fortunate. And in education itself more is spent on the physically and mentally handicapped child – class sizes, for instance, in Special Schools for these children vary from ten to twenty according to the nature of the handicap and amenities are usually superior – than on normal children. Yet we hear no resentment against the negative selection that allocates pupils to these schools, and much charitable and public-spirited effort has gone into their improvement. Sometimes too the physically advanced are given privileged treatment, as when the occasional talented girl is sent at public expense to train with the Bolshoi Ballet in Moscow. Why, when we are so tender towards the physically and mentally backward and even generous to physical talent, should we be ungenerous towards the mentally advanced? First, I suppose, because while the former excite our pity or admiration the latter arouse our envy. Freudian complexes are at work here in what has been called our 'love/hate relationship' [50] towards teachers. Children long for the praise and approval a teacher can give, and because the brighter pupils monopolize, or seem to monopolize it, the less favoured among us carry a resentment, none the less traumatic because it is usually unconscious, against the bestower (the teacher) and the recipient (the abler pupil) of such favour. Secondly there is a feeling, fed by some politicians and teachers who have little experience of them, that the abler pupils can look after themselves – and indeed have a

*In 1955 Hertfordshire, here as in so many ways an exemplary education authority, decided as a matter of policy to bring the general grant for modern school pupils up to that for grammar school pupils of the same age (*The Secondary Modern School*, Hertfordshire Education Committee, 1955).

missionary duty to help the less able as well. Any suggestion, therefore, that the education of able children is costing more can be relied upon to arouse popular resentment.

But even where grammar school education does not cost more it is often regarded as 'superior' in some other sense. To some it may seem it is better absolutely. When we speak of an 'educated man' we usually think of someone who has had a grammar school type education. Yet can we be sure we are right about this? We remember today the educated hands that shaped the mosaics of St Mark's, Venice, or the stained glass of Chartres more than the educated minds that quibbled over how many angels could dance on the point of a needle. Perhaps tomorrow there will be computers that can draft a will, negotiate a contract, research into historical problems or even frame an election-winning party manifesto, but not to build a Coventry Cathedral or a supersonic jet aircraft. In any case the concept of an absolutely superior education shades off imperceptibly into the second meaning of 'superior' – that of 'carrying a higher status'. All too many people want a grammar school education not for what it contains but for the prestige value of the cap, blazer and school and the job it promises when completed. Some are prepared to inflict it on their children merely to impress their neighbours. 'I don't know what Latin or calculus are,' they seem to say, 'but if they are part of a good education my lad (or lass) is going to have them.' A supporter of comprehensive schools, when reproached with sending his children to a grammar school, replied, it is said, that he was not prepared to sacrifice his children to his principles. It is equally true that there are many parents who are determined to sacrifice their children for their ambitions. Nor will comprehensive reorganization change this human trait. The insistence on academic subjects to 'rate' in American high schools and the demand for the 'theoretical stream' in Swedish comprehensives gives ample warning of this. To quote the Deputy Principal of Alviks (comprehensive) School in Stockholm: 'What is so difficult is that those who are not so clever choose the courses they are not suited for, and they are not able to do them. . . . It's not as the authorities hoped it would be, that the clever children would lift up the others' [131]. So even if a grammar school education is 'superior', in whatever sense, it seems unlikely that the abolition of selection will prevent some parents wanting it for their children, or some children choosing it, or even having it thrust upon them.

But it may prevent them getting it as effectively, and lower its quality. This, for Britain, is crucial. Sweden is a wealthy country. An educational journalist, after a recent visit there, came away with the impression of a 'well-stocked larder, expensive to fill and wasteful' [131]. But the Swedes can afford it. They are not short of teachers, and mistakes can be paid for in time and money when all children stay on till 16 and in the next few years 80 per cent will be remaining till 18. So it is with America. But Lord James of Rusholme, after a visit there, gave this warning to Britain:

A relatively poor country, dependent upon technical skill and maximum employment of ability for survival, must rely upon an educational system that by selection and hard work and economical use of its teaching resources reaches a given level of attainment as early as possible.... For perhaps the clearest impression that one derives from the American educational scene is that *the English grammar school is quite simply, in our particular circumstances, one of the greatest hopes for our future national prosperity* [132 – italics supplied].

We have heard a great deal lately about the 'great potentialities of hidden talent in the British people' [61], the pool of ability whose surface is scarcely skimmed, the 'scores of Newtons who never learned to read' of whom H. G. Wells spoke half a century ago [35]. Few would disagree with the arguments for some dredging for educational pearls. But doubts creep in when we are told that the great dredger is to be the comprehensive school. For one thing, to talk hopefully of retrieving talent at secondary school level is rather like commencing dredging operations from a helicopter, and the whole thing becomes a mockery while the size of classes in so many primary schools still exceeds forty. But leaving this aside can we be sure of the effectiveness of the comprehensive dredger and its influence on the clearer waters at the surface of the pool? We have heard so much lately about the 11-plus failures that we have almost forgotten the 11-plus successes. Ifield, Mexborough, Harrow, South Shields, Surrey with its plans for sixth-form courses in all its secondary schools (many of them have them already) and its O- and A-level records bid fair to be just as successful in uncovering submerged talent through equal partnership and cooperation between selective schools as the comprehensives without putting the unquestioned surface treasure at risk. Or, if greater prudence tempers the metaphor, it is all too easy to be too obsessed with scraping the barrel to notice that its more accessible contents have turned sour.

The justification for selection is therefore twofold. First there does exist what may be called a grammar school mind which can be differentiated, is a national asset, and responds best to a grammar school type education. Secondly, appeals to social conscience or envy by calling this *different* education *superior* and therefore demanding the end of separate grammar schools do not really solve the problem. Comprehensive schools still have their 'grammar streams' which many pupils need and more parents demand. Transferring all pupils to the same school merely means that the grammar school type education is given less efficiently, and though the wealthier nations can afford this wasteful inefficiency Britain cannot. 'We cannot afford not to afford it,' dangerous cliché though it so often is, is quite simply true of the separate British grammar school today.

IS THE GRAMMAR SCHOOL A MIDDLE-CLASS INSTITUTION?

That the children of middle-class parents enjoy certain advantages for grammar school education over those of manual workers is a commonplace long familiar to schoolmasters and confirmed, for the sceptical, by the statistics of educationists. As the Crowther Report emphasizes, both parents of two thirds of the pupils in grammar and technical schools left school at 14: these children come from homes 'in which the books children open in their later years at school have remained closed books to their parents. So far as the family is concerned, the greater part of the educational journey the children undertake must be unaccompanied' [22]. For the remaining third, in schools which are 'essentially for those who can learn from books', a home where books, foreign travel and other educative media are taken for granted is an obvious advantage. It is an asset, too, to hear from time to time records other than those which compete for a place in the Top Twenty and discover that 'pictures' can be something other than a cosy synonym for cinema. French logic frankly recognizes this when they call their middle class *les familles éducogènes*. Such children are favoured beside the primary school child who brought home a book from school out of interest only to be sent back by an irate mother with a note saying: 'Books is for school, not home. If you send any more, I'll burn them' [133]. 'We've never had any books in this house,' said another such parent, 'and we're not starting now.'

This is a problem to which the grammar school has long since addressed itself, but the abolition of fees after the war increased its proportions. That it should be blamed for a situation that was none of its making and which it has striven manfully to remedy might seem ungenerous. Yet this, more or less, is the message of *Education and the Working Class* by Brian Jackson and Denis Marsden, published in 1962 [111]. Like many such studies by sociologists the book seeks to make an impact. These people blow in, blow out and blow up. When the dust has settled a dispassionate assessment of their conclusions can be made. The method of the book will be familiar to readers from its more popular form – the 'on the spot' reports of journalists and television reporters. It uses the technique of 'case-study, in which individual circumstances or opinions are collected and drawn upon impressionistically to argue a case' [134]. The theme is the post-war educational development of the northern industrial town where both writers were themselves born and educated, its witnesses the citizens themselves. For instance the following is a statement of his debt to Marburton College for Boys, Huddersfield, by a former pupil who is now a graduate scientist working on advanced problems of aeronautics. His father was a baker's assistant, his mother in domestic service, and both grandparents were farm labourers.

Christ, no, I didn't like Marburton College. Too fast, they just got me there and they crammed my nut from the moment I arrived. That school doesn't turn out human beings, it turns out people to read and write, that's all. Look at the facts they rammed into me. School Cert. in four years. All these facts, Christ, just think of them! All that geography I did period after period, and now I hardly know where

America is, and I've been to the place! Yes, I worked quite hard. I'd be about fifth or sixth in class. You do a day's work at school, go home and you've got two and a half hours' homework because you've got to keep up to schedule, kid, and then you do another two and a half hours. You don't play out any more, and you don't see anybody except on a Friday night. Christ, what a way to grow up! You go back to school next morning, and perhaps some kid hasn't done his homework, perhaps he's been out! What, you'd think he was a bloody Communist the way they carry on. Christ, kid, they don't believe in leisure. Leisure means laziness for them. It means sitting around and loafing with your feet up, that's what leisure means. No time for all those other things like reading serious books (not that I read any serious books, not after having all that crap about Shakespeare and Dickens rammed down my throat. I wouldn't read a word of it now.) But leisure, that's what you need in growing up and Christ, you don't have any leisure.

It is difficult to see exactly what this young man's quarrel with his grammar school is. Is he reproaching it, as Caliban did Prospero, because

> You taught me language; and my profit on't
> Is I know how to curse.

Is he complaining that the institution that could turn the son of a baker's assistant into a research scientist did not, in retrospect, do everything to please him? Or is he, perhaps, pulling the interviewers' legs? In any case the gravamen of the book's charge against the grammar school is that it has 'foundered upon a rock: the working class. . . . The grammar school has now to address itself to a new public; but could it, even if it so wished? . . . Grammar schools are so socially imprisoned that they are most remarkable for the conformity of the minds they train' [111]. The broad conclusion is that the grammar schools have failed the nation by failing the working class, and must give way to the comprehensives.

The first thing to be said about this attack is that it was largely out-of-date before it was published. In order to get the 'follow-up' reactions of former pupils of Marburton already well-established in jobs the period of education reviewed was mainly 1948–52, the time when grammar schools had only recently had fee-paying abolished, when the old group-requirement School and Higher

Certificate was still in process of reform and when the grammar schools were facing the problem of a new kind of clientele. It does not seem, from the evidence of the book, that Marburton was as enterprising or imaginative in dealing with these problems as some other areas, and it has no doubt learned much in the intervening decade. There is a true story of a grammar school boy who went to see his headmaster for leave to attend a university interview. While the headmaster answered his questions and gave him a few tips the boy kept his hands firmly stuck in his pockets, and finally strolled out saying 'Well, cheerio, Sir!' The headmaster called him back and explained that, while not objecting to informality, he advised a modified approach at the actual interview. The boy, so far from being offended, was grateful and said, 'You see, Sir, nobody has ever told me that before' [135]. If this was the grammar school 'foundering upon the rock of the working class' at least it was kindly managed, and no doubt secured the boy his university place. The vast increase in numbers of pupils staying on, including many from the working class, for higher and university education has invalidated much of the complaints of early leaving made by Jackson and Marsden; and the conflict between the standards of home and school, even in such a mundane matter as the bilingual dexterity of some pupils who affect one language for teacher and another for parents, are not peculiar to the grammar schools. Primary and comprehensive schools experience these problems as well.

But the real flaw in Jackson and Marsden's thesis lies in thinking of this issue in terms of the 'class war' at all. For one thing not all 'working-class' parents fit their pattern of dissatisfaction with the grammar school. For those who did not a special sociological category had to be provided, the 'submerged middle class'. And however skilful the processing of the data before conclusions are drawn the validity of those conclusions in the event is inevitably weakened.* But in any case it is doubtful how far the language and

*For similar pre-processing of data before drawing pre-determined conclusions compare Mr Brian Jackson's article on excessive early specialization in grammar and independent schools in *Where?* (March 1966) and its exposure by Dr David Thomson, Master of Sidney Sussex College, Cambridge, in *The Times Educational Supplement* of March 1966.

emotions of the class struggle can make a useful contribution to this educational debate. Britain today is suffering from an acute attack of social hypochondria, fostered by the persuasive bedside manner of some politicians and journalists. We are for ever taking our social temperatures for fear of anything that might be 'divisive'. The favourite whipping boy of the moment is the 'middle class', the anorak that stands between the cloth cap of factory floor and grouse-moor. Albert Doolittle in Bernard Shaw's *Pygmalion* set the fashion of blaming 'middle-class morality' for almost everything, and since then, to give two random examples widely separated in time, their domestic architecture has been pilloried in Osbert Lancaster's *Pillar to Post* [136] and a bishop meant no compliment when he spoke of 'the Church and its whole middle-class ethos' [137]. Small wonder that the schools they attend, first the 'public schools' and then, since rising taxation has put these out of reach of many, the grammar schools, should come in for criticism. The fact that more and more people, according to surveys of public opinion, are coming to regard themselves as middle-class, and that 'the gulf between the generations threatens to become even wider than the gulf between the classes' [138], while even the *New Statesman*, infallibly hyper-sensitive in these matters, detects a 'blurring of class lines which is the most hopeful aspect of modern England' [139] does not deter these critics. Class is their ubiquitous *bête-noire*. They reduce life to a simple equation: 'working-class' is noble, 'middle-class' nasty and 'upper-class' anathema. Moreover the middle-class have a conscience and are gluttons for punishment. The scholarly records of psephological autopsy for the 1966 General Election have yet to be published, but it seems certain that they will show* that increased numbers of the middle class voted with masochistic abandon for a Party that by name and nature scarcely carries their banner. To plunge deeper into the troubled waters of the class struggle would be outside the province of this book. But it is worth pointing out that the concept of class is basically a neutral thing. People of similar interests and backgrounds are not unnaturally drawn together and develop similar tastes. To recognize this is

*One since has been and does. See *The General Election of 1966*, Butler and King, Macmillan, 1966, second table on p. 264.

merely to be realistic. What is unhealthy is the feeling that the habits and values of one class are superior to those of another. One can be class-cognizant without being class-conscious. There is no harm in a Yorkshireman of proudly plebeian origins preferring to take his holidays in the Scillies rather than at Scarborough, or educating his sons at a school which gives 'a full public school education' [140] if that is his choice and he can afford it. Only if it made him feel superior or exclusive would harm be done. Where *Education and the Working Class* appears so wrong-headed in these matters is in taking certain features of an academic education such as its extension of vocabulary, its emphasis on correct speaking (which need not affect or destroy local dialects), its encouragement of cultural tastes and demands for hard study and branding them as 'middle-class' because they seem to conflict with the ethos, real or imagined, of the 'working class'. It is here that the concept in the Crowther Report of the 'first-generation grammar school pupil' is more helpful. The values of the grammar school are classless and inseparable from an academic education, and if the working class want those values, it is for them to come some of the way to meet them. And in honour to them, in spite of Jackson and Marsden's strictures, many of them do. Neither of my own parents had more than a basic elementary education, and my grandparents were respectively a bricklayer and a farm labourer. I could have no help in the home with knowledge or cultural background for my grammar school course. But I did have, like many others, wisdom, understanding and encouragement. There was no resentment or criticism of my grammar school and its values – only an exaggerated and at times embarrassing deference. There is no reason why the 'working class', if we must use that term, should not be something more mobile than a rock in its relationship with the grammar schools – and in any case it is a rock which seems to be steadily disappearing. Why should it prove less capable of assimilating grammar school values than of acquiring a taste for consumer durables and holidays abroad, both hitherto regarded, through economic necessity or social inertia, as the exclusive preserve of the middle and upper classes? To object to or seek to change grammar school values in favour of one class is rather like going to France and objecting to the right-hand rule of the road or *priorité à droite* or feeling resentment because the French speak French. The British working class have enough sense and flexibility to recognize this. In consequence *Education and the Working Class* has become largely obsolete not only through the adaptability of the grammar school but also by the social mobility or erosion of the very class its authors affect to champion.

All the same the shock treatment of this book, while it over-emphasizes the class struggle in education, does remind us of the realities of class difference. Working-class children, as they come halfway to meet grammar school values, bring values of their own, and such class mingling can be reciprocal and fruitful. These working-class values, once disentangled from the sentiment of writers of the Richard Hoggart school, are quite positive and valid. For example one difference between the school at Nottingham where I began teaching and my present one in suburban Hertfordshire is that by and large the Nottingham boys worked harder. This may be partly a regional difference, for it is my belief – I hope not offensive coming from a Southerner – that on the whole people in Britain work harder the further north one goes. But this is not all. The Nottingham school contained a larger proportion of working-class boys, including miners' sons (D. H. Lawrence himself went there). Now the working-class boy, with a father who comes home physically tired and a mother who is over-worked in the home even if not working outside it as well, has a livelier awareness of what eating bread by the sweat of the brow means than the middle- or upper-class boy. The nervous or mental tiredness of the latter's father makes less of an impact on a child's imagination, and the middle- or upper-class mother, though she may be 'harassed', tends to be rather more cushioned and indulgent. The working-class boy, therefore, once he has grasped that studying books can be 'work' as much as going down a mine or to a factory, is often readier to stick at them till he is overcome by the physical exhaustion he has seen in his own father and mother. It is this that makes Jimmy Porter in John Osborne's play *Look Back in Anger*, with his tedious insistence on his working-class background and educational deprivation, seem so bogus; his middle-class wife, with her endless ironing, knows more about working-class values than ever he does. So, in this simple matter of work as in many others, the meeting of working-class and middle-class children can and should be a process of give and take. The working-class boy, having learned from the middle-class boy that work can mean books, can often teach him in return that books mean work.

IS THE GRAMMAR SCHOOL OUT-OF-DATE?

Comprehensivists answer this question with a categorical affirmative. They speak, for instance, of 'remodelling the grammar school to meet modern needs' and replacing it by 'a school which has come into being to meet the needs of twentieth-century society' [141]. Such generalizations, coming from people with an axe to grind, are predictable enough. But more commonly the attack is directed against the content of some subjects in the grammar school curriculum: history, we are told, concentrates too much on the reign of Elizabeth I at the expense of that of Elizabeth II; the approach to subjects like geography or science is too academic; French, despite the growth of language laboratories and audio-visual courses, is still too much preoccupied with *la plume de ma tante*. But the chief butt of such criticism is the continued presence of Latin in the curriculum and *a fortiori*, where it survives, Greek. What we saw in the first chapter to be the chief function of the Elizabethan grammar schools, the teaching of Latin as a *lingua franca* of communication and culture, has today become its Achilles heel. A diatribe by Cassandra of the *Daily Mirror* [130] against the 'scholastic pterodactyls' who keep Latin alive in schools merely advertises the fact that the author was taught Latin badly, or a very long time ago, or possibly both. But we must take more seriously the demand by the schoolmaster authors of *Educating the Intelligent* that the space at present devoted to Latin in the grammar school timetable be devoted to other more pressing purposes. 'Without more ado we must now claim the time allocated to Latin (see Diagram 1) for more worthwhile ends' [21]. Incidentally when we do see Diagram 1, showing the 'Old Type Curriculum' fused for demolition, we find a lucky Latin teacher with six periods a week for each of the four years of the O-level course, but few do as well as that these days. Now while the cutting down to size of the classics was overdue in the twentieth century, their total extinction is another matter. Classical scholars who say this may be cheerfully dismissed as cobblers defending their last to the last; but it gives us pause when we read Lord James of Rusholme, for instance, who took his degree in chemistry, writing thus: 'For a minority of very able people of high linguistic ability ... I do not believe that any educational instrument has ever been devised that is as good as the Greats course at Oxford – and I am not thinking simply of the development of the individual but also of his service to the State' [142]. A full-scale defence of the classics, preserved in proper moderation, is not part of our theme – it would require space urgently needed for other matters and would be an impertinence when expert research on the whole topic is in progress at Cambridge under the auspices of the Nuffield Foundation. But a little more 'ado' there must be. First, there really are some children who actually *like* Latin – and Greek if they have the chance – and loathe mathematics and science. We have shed our dutiful tears (see page 47) for Charles Darwin, mouldering in the alien soil of Butler's Shrewsbury. Let us now spare a few for others. Lord Snow tells this story of one who was 'mathematically blind': 'I recall E. W. Hobson, the pure mathematician, talking of his tribulations in coaching Wallis Budge for the Little-Go. "I used to say to Budge – 'Budge, if 2x equals 1, what does x equal?' and Budge would turn his great wise eyes at me and think, and think, and think, and answer: 'Minus 2'." Budge became an Egyptologist of world repute' [143]. Sir John Newsom was nearly lost from the cause of education, which owes him so much, to the grocery business through his distaste for mathematics. He had already failed it twice in School Certificate, he tells us, and everything hung on the third attempt: 'My father, a just man, had threatened to take me away from school and put me to grocery if I failed again! My whole future life depended on whether I could answer accurately some question about water flowing in or out of a tank, or on the relative speeds of railway trains passing some telegraph pole' [49]. Someone has said that everybody at school should have to master at least one subject he really likes and at least one that he dislikes. Latin provides the former for more people than its opponents care to admit.

Then again we are often told that the claims of Latin to give an unrivalled linguistic training may be met just as well by an intensive study of English itself. This would be splendid if the pundits could agree what the thing called 'English' really is. But some stress mundane matters of spelling and punctuation, others precision in writing, others depth of comprehension, others wealth of literary experience and so on. Nor do the examiners agree: the enterprising headmaster of Otley Grammar School who recently entered his English Language candidates for two different Examining Boards and obtained bewilderingly inconsistent results, with one candidate actually placed in the top grade by one Board and the bottom by the other, provoked a question in the House of Commons [144]. To be fair to the Boards some of these inconsistencies arise, no doubt, from differences in the syllabus or the mark-weighting of the various tests, précis, essay, comprehension and so on. But this only underlines the divisions of opinion as to what 'English' is, and disagreement about what makes a good essay is notorious. Apparently even the specialist study of English is not necessarily the best way to learn to write it to judge by these comments by several examiners of students of English at Oxford:

Lack of range showed itself most clearly in pitiably feeble vocabulary. 'Upset' and 'worried' were often the strongest descriptive terms applied to characters of Sophocles, Shakespeare or Racine in their extremes of passion. Flabby periphrases were substituted for words of strong and definite meaning. From the wide range of sentence-structure open to writers familiar with English books in any variety, a very few were monotonously chosen [145].

Nor does the claim that modern languages can give this linguistic training really stand up to Thring's objection that they can be taught parrot-fashion by a governess; this, after all, is what language laboratories do, and do superlatively well. But learning a language is not necessarily the same as training in language. Meanwhile indignant science teachers wave practical notebooks menacingly at their English colleagues and ask who is supposed to teach their charges to write English. They have a point, and clearly from their tone the task is not for them. Nobody would now claim for Latin the role of central core in the curriculum that Thring gave it a century ago; but it does at least encourage and recognize precision and accuracy in the use of language of the kind which corresponds to getting the right answer in mathematics. Examining Boards agree pretty well over what they want for Latin at O-level; and what they want can still contribute something useful, at least until the English experts make up their minds.

What I have said applies chiefly to Latin at Ordinary Level. Much more could be said about the classics as a more advanced discipline in support of Lord James's observations quoted earlier, but this must be left to expert research at Cambridge. One more thing needs to be said. We have seen (page 43) that grammar and glamour are etymologically akin; so are classics and class. A few famous schools have kept their classical sides intact (Eton without Greek, for instance, is said to be almost as difficult a proposition as Plato's Academy was without geometry) and are likely to continue to do so. It would be a pity if too many other grammar or comprehensive schools were persuaded by plausible arguments like those advanced in *Educating the Intelligent** to leave these schools with a monopoly. A classical education had been in danger of being a preserve of one class for centuries through the exclusiveness of some of its champions; it is now in similar danger through the intolerance of its opponents. When I was a schoolboy a well-meaning old lady warned me that a boy from a little-known grammar school could not hope to win a classical scholarship to Cambridge. Thirty years ago she was proved wrong; thirty years hence, or even sooner, she could be right.

This is not to say that we should set our face resolutely against change. Grammar schools are not static institutions. On the contrary they have shown themselves springboards for new ideas and experiments. The 'New Mathematics', with its emphasis on ideas rather than mere numerical manipulation, the Nuffield Science Project, with its 'open-ended experiments' both owe much of their momentum to grammar schools – many of them independent grammar schools at that. Field work and expeditions play an

---

*Though critical on this point I strongly support many of the arguments in this book; in particular it contains more sound sense on the structure of teachers' salaries than most of what has been said or written about the matter for a long time.

increasing part in grammar school geographical studies. 'Literary evaluation' in the Dr Leavis tradition is overflowing from English studies into the approach to the literature of foreign languages and even the classics. It would be quite wrong to think of grammar schools as islands of resistance to change. They are rather vessels which, though anchored in an academic tradition, are moving with the tide and are at times even ready to up-anchor and launch out into the deep under their own power. The right balance between tradition and innovation is one of the most difficult of educational problems, and curricular inertia is a formidable obstacle. All the same it is well to remember, in days when modernization has become a fetish, that what is modern today can become out-of-date tomorrow, while things that have stood the test of time last a little longer. The fact that even Latin has a case to be heard should make us cautious of the current demand for up-to-date schools geared to the needs of the twentieth century; change may be our ally, but there is little to be said for a curriculum as susceptible to the vagaries of fashion as the styling of an automobile or the length of a lady's skirt.

POSITIVE MERITS OF THE GRAMMAR SCHOOL

It may seem that the argument of this chapter so far has been somewhat negative. We have considered various objections to the grammar school and attempted to answer them. In one sense this is enough; for the theme of many of the opponents of grammar school education is not that it is bad, but that so few people can have it that everybody must have something else. Still, something perhaps more positive may be said by way of analogy. The coining of educational analogies is a popular and sometimes misleading pursuit these days. For instance education in England has been compared to a 400-metre running-track with three lanes but without a staggered start. The inside lane is for children from fee-paying preparatory and 'public' or direct-grant schools, the middle lane for those who gain places at maintained grammar schools and the outside lane for the vast majority in the secondary modern schools [33]. This, it is admitted, is an over-simplified picture. What is more to the point, it has little to do with education at all. 'They that run in a race run all, but one receives the prize.' But education is not an athletics meeting. The prizes are many, and not only he who runs may read. It is not really a race at all, rat- or human-, but a journey whose pace is infinitely varied and destinations far more complex than a single finishing tape. Even the analogy of a journey is somewhat misleading, for so many journeys these days are routine return affairs that leave the traveller weary but unchanged, and generally they imply a fairly clear idea of a destination. Education is not like that, and it is more instructive to consider the derivation of the word itself than pluck analogies out of the air. Some European countries use a different word altogether – the Germans, for instance, with *Bildung* and *Erziehung* and the Russians with *Obrazovanye* suggest a process of 'moulding', 'shaping' or 'bringing up' to a preconceived pattern, and this is reflected in the educational practices of these countries. But more commonly the word for 'education' traces back to the Latin *educare*, which in its earliest and most precise sense means to nourish or feed – what a nurse does, for instance, for an infant (*educat nutrix* [146] in the words of Varro, an early writer on the precise use of the Latin language). It was later applied to the process of nourishing the mind. Now mental appetites vary as greatly as do physical ones. Some minds thrive on a plain diet of books, others have a more delicate palate that needs to be tempted and cosseted by visual aids, interest projects and so on before they will feed at all. Some tough mental constitutions even benefit from a diet that is quite unpleasant. For instance, I sometimes cheer rather bored pupils through the less spell-binding stages of a Latin course by telling them that plants profit from manure, and a good gardener must dig it in. Of course this analogy is not strictly fair as plants, if they have any taste, may like the flavour – but usually I manage to get away with this piece of 'hidden persuasion'. All the same the analogy by derivation of 'mental feeding' is helpful, and does strengthen the case for selection. It is obviously better, in schools as in catering establishments, not to have too many menus running at once. Those who require a plain, simple mental diet can be more easily served under one roof by cooks who specialize in that sphere; others who require more elaborate menus, and food that needs to be carefully prepared to make it tempting and appetizing, can be better served elsewhere:

New methods of education, individual learning in mixed ability groups, group projects, discovery, activity and experience ... team teaching, programmed learning in books and on teaching machines; language laboratories, tapes, television, radio, correspondence courses – all these are providing the opportunities for a flexible school environment where far more is chosen by the pupil than is determined by the teacher [147].

But such an educational menu, served indiscriminately, is expensive and wasteful. There are plenty who can thrive on simpler fare – even if it is made to sound unappetizing by calling it 'the old "chalk and talk" rote of learning facts to be memorised, regurgitated and later forgotten' [147]. This latter is the diet of the educationally 'privileged' in maintained, direct-grant and independent grammar schools, while the more elaborate fare above is, or should be available for the 'deprived'. It is this that makes nonsense of these terms. There is nothing 'privileged' about the grim Victorian buildings of Strand Grammar School, sw2, or 'deprived' about the splendid amenities available to the nongrammar streams at Tulse Hill Comprehensive School which towers in magnificent nine-storey splendour above it. The Americans, who have taught us so much about multi-storey construction, have valuable advice to offer too from their experience in education:

If I had time and opportunity to say one thing to Britain, it would be this: My dear fellow, get your priorities right and stop sweating so much about where snobs and rich men send their sons to school, and where many not so rich and not so snobbish, and even Labour lords, send their sons to school. Stop fighting the best of your maintained schools. Stop shooting at the direct grant schools. Stop quarrelling with educational excellence as though it were a reprehensible thing or simply because everybody can't have it.*

A NOTE ON SECONDARY MODERN SCHOOLS

Though the secondary modern school is not our direct concern, a brief reference to it must be made here, for the case for the

*Appendix 1, page 261.

grammar school implies the coexistence and welcomes the partnership between both kinds of school. Three things need to be said. First, these schools have been subjected to sensational press reports over the years, and books of fiction or quasi-fiction of the *Blackboard Jungle* school have mushroomed in which aspiring young writers have used a brief sojourn on their staffs as a launching-pad for a literary or other non-teaching career [148]. A recent such book, typically, is described on the dust-jacket as 'a deeply disturbing Anatomy of the Secondary Modern School' [149]. No doubt there is some truth in these reports, particularly of schools in difficult areas, but the general public have been 'deeply disturbed' for so long that they are coming to believe that all these schools are as bad as the worst.

Secondly, we have seen in the previous chapter that these schools are beginning to record successes in G.C.E. O- and A-level, but even this has been given less than due recognition, and there are still some who maintain that examinations are none of their business. As we recall how, until recently, secondary modern schools were discouraged from taking external examinations at all, and consider the difficulties they still face in entering candidates for them, we are reminded of Dr Johnson's observation about women preachers: 'Sir, a woman's preaching is like a dog's walking on his hind legs. It is not done well; but you are surprised to find it done at all' [150]. All things considered the performance of the secondary moderns in the G.C.E. *is* something done well, and it is only fair to say so loud and clear.

Finally, while the literary birds of prey swoop on these schools for carrion, we should remember the gifted and devoted teachers who give their lives to them. Their service merits greater appreciation than it has so far received. We have heard much lately of the growth of voluntary service schemes in grammar and independent schools; but few realize that similar schemes have been in operation in the secondary modern schools of Manchester, for instance, long before more prestigious institutions ever thought of them. We need to hear more of these and other achievements of these schools not from first novels and journalists, nor from educationists who often enough vilify them to advance the cause of the comprehensives, but from people who stay to do a lifetime's dedicated work in them – a headmaster, perhaps, or senior master who, like a good Cromwellian, 'knows what he fights for and loves what he knows'. Such reliable informants would not deny that their schools need and are capable of a great deal of improvement, but they have the knowledge to show the way, and disabuse us of the popular notion that they are past redemption.

SUMMARY

The case for the grammar school, then, crystallizes into a case for educational efficiency. Selection, for all its mistakes, is capable of improvement given research and the money for it, and imaginative experiments are in progress to redeem its errors. There is such a thing as the 'grammar school mind' which the nation needs and other nations covet, and selection, for all the propaganda against it, is the best way so far devised to identify such minds and give them the kind of education that will develop their full potential. To call that education 'superior', though politically specious, is misleading; and to claim that the ethos of the grammar school conflicts with that of the working class is to make an out-of-date and class-obsessed generalization that is unfair both to the schools and to the working class itself. The traditional values and approach of the grammar school, despite plausible demands for modernization, are still relevant to the world of today. And, paradoxically, to preserve a system that appears to be socially divisive is the best road to educational efficiency, while social engineering through reorganization invites stagnation or decline. It is a disagreeable dilemma, especially for social reformers, but it needs to be squarely faced; and living in a dream world in which all secondary modern schools are sinks and all comprehensive schools are giant grammar schools is no solution.

CHAPTER SIX

THE DIRECT-GRANT AND INDEPENDENT GRAMMAR SCHOOLS

EDUCATION AND INDEPENDENCE

So far this book, apart from its first chapter, has concerned itself almost exclusively with the state system of secondary education. It is important, therefore, to recall from that first chapter that this system is scarcely a century old, and that governments during that century, from a policy of *laissez-faire*, only gradually and reluctantly involved themselves in secondary education and were all too grateful for such private and independent provision as already existed. It is easy to be so bemused by the Welfare State, with its post-Beveridge furniture of an all-providing 'public sector' and a fast-shrinking 'private sector' towards which the public sector stretches its predatory if well-intentioned tentacles, as to forget how recent a growth all this is, in education no less than in other social services. On the other hand the expanding schemes for private medical insurance and pensions, the undiminished registrations for independent schools and the general atmosphere of impatience and disillusion with state welfare services are symptoms that cannot be lightly dismissed.

On whom, then, should the responsibility for children's education fall? Clearly they are not mature enough to decide for themselves, and must be regarded as a trust. But whose trust? Their parents' or the State's? The classic extremes in this dilemma are presented by John Stuart Mill and Matthew Arnold. Mill, while conceding that the law should make education compulsory, would limit its function to 'public examinations, extending to all children': 'A general state education is a mere contrivance for moulding people to be exactly like one another: and as the mould in which it casts them is that which pleases the predominant power in the government . . . in proportion as it is efficient and successful, it establishes a despotism over the mind, leading by natural tendency to one over the body' [151]. Matthew Arnold, by instinct and through his position as a Board of Education Inspector and from what he saw of state education on his official travels in Europe, became a powerful advocate of far-reaching state action to provide education, especially for those who are unable or unlikely to provide it for themselves:

The aristocratic classes in England may, perhaps, be well content to rest satisfied with their Eton and Harrow. The State is not likely to do better for them. Nay, the superior confidence, spirit, and style, engendered by a training in the great public schools, constitute for these classes a real privilege, a real engine of command, which they might, if they were selfish, be sorry to lose by the establishment of schools great enough to beget a like spirit in the classes below them. But the middle classes in England have every reason not to rest content with their private schools; the State can do a great deal better for them [152].

In the half-century or more since Arnold wrote these words the pendulum has swung more and more towards him and away from Mill. Indeed, could Arnold, who insisted that state initiative in education should be tempered with economy, see some of the exorbitant school building of today, peruse the much-maligned Burnham Scale and hear the current demands that independent schools should be integrated within an all-embracing state system he might feel it had swung too far. Nor is this the work of any one political party. The 1944 Education Act was an all-party affair and the present tax structure, in its attitude to children, is unchallenged. This, by child tax allowance and family allowances, recognizes the responsibility of parents to feed and clothe their children; but by its refusal to recognize, in further tax allowances, those who 'contract out' of the state system by sending their children to private schools, implies that it is the responsibility and business of the State to educate them at least to the end of the secondary stage. There are some who believe that state control of education has gone too far. It has been suggested, for instance, that instead of free schooling parents should be issued with selective vouchers, to be used in state or private schools as they wish [153]. More striking is the recent book by Dr E. G. West, *Education and the State* [58], to which we have already referred (page 96). His theme is twofold. First, that since the State, in the Forster Education Act of 1870, assumed wide responsibilities for providing education, that provision has been little better than, if as good as, that made hitherto by the parents themselves. Secondly, that universal free education robs parents of choice and responsibility, and even where state provision is made it should not be free; state vouchers, on the lines suggested above, should be provided for use, at parents' choice, at maintained or private schools and supplemented, on a graded scale, from their own resources. To his second thesis we shall return in the next chapter. Of the first, though no doubt it contains much truth and is well documented by historical evidence, it is only fair to point out that it applies chiefly to primary education. As for the secondary stage, the vast mass of the British public before 1870 needed persuasion to seek it at all, and it is doubtful whether, left to individual initiative without the powerful advocacy and measures of Matthew Arnold and others, including Lord Butler himself, it would have made the vast strides it has in the last hundred years.

But now that 'secondary education for all' has become a commonplace, and the school leaving age is to be raised to 16 in 1970, the question of state or parental responsibility takes a different form. No doubt there is truth in the epigram that parents are the last people who ought to have children; we all know the advantages of a 'good home' for children's education, and can even sympathize with those, like Sir Alec Clegg, who argue that parents are not fit to choose in educational matters, or the writer who sees education as a corrective to family circumstances: 'The family remains a tremendous influence on the life and prospects of the young. Our educational institutions have the duty to minimise and not enhance it' [154]. Yet what is the alternative? If the State assumes full responsibility for education there are dangers no less formidable. Politicians may be wise, benevolent and impartial. They may even, in a democratic society, be the best watchdogs of liberty. But Juvenal's sixty-four thousand dollar question remains: *Quis custodiet ipsos custodes?* – Who will watch the watchdogs? What if the politicians turn sour, or authoritarian (for which an economic crisis can be excuse enough) or doctrinaire? While politics remain normal, checks and balances operate to ensure that educational policy, at national and local level, goes more or less hand in hand with public pressure, whatever the exact extent of state authority over education. If a State becomes totalitarian, then all education, public and private alike, is at its mercy as it was in Nazi Germany. (It is worth recalling that Gordonstoun School was a pre-war migrant to this country from Germany under its headmaster, Kurt Hahn, for this very reason.) But there is an intermediate stage, through which this country seems to be passing at the moment, where a government, while remaining sensitive to public opinion, has a doctrinaire education policy which, on the evidence of opinion polls reinforced by a certain amount of wishful thinking, it believes coincides with the popular will. There is a parallel here in the demand for the return of hanging, especially strong, as revealed in *News of the World* opinion polls, after the recent police murders. Nobody in the Government suggests that Mr Sidney Silverman's Bill should be rescinded because of this, and no reasonable person would expect it. But there is an inconsistency in dismissing the demand for the return of hanging as mass hysteria while accepting the demand for comprehensivization as being a groundswell of opinion.* The problem of capital punishment is much more difficult because, as has been pointed out, once you have hung a murderer you cannot 'unhang' him after second thoughts. But in education there is more room to manoeuvre. The objection to comprehensive education comes from a minority, but a vociferous and well-informed one that really cares about education. That is why some respect for these parents' wishes is vital, however inconvenient, if the doctrinaire is not to become tantamount to the totalitarian. Parents, for all their shortcomings, are only doctrinaire about their children's virtues, rarely about how they should be used. And nowhere are the dangers of a doctrinaire approach to education by politicians better illustrated than in the recent treatment of a type of school which has genuinely tried, over the years, to serve as a bridge between state and independent education – the direct-grant grammar school. To this we shall now turn our attention.

*In this context the experience of a canvasser for signatures to a pro-comprehensive petition in anti-comprehensive Surrey is illuminating. 'There's another for you,' announced one man who had already signed himself, 'I told my wife it was to bring back hanging and she signed without reading it' (*The Times Educational Supplement*, 2 September 1966).

THE DIRECT-GRANT GRAMMAR SCHOOL

For reasons which will become apparent later it must be emphasized at the outset that what are called direct-grant grammar schools are, in origin, *independent* grammar schools, usually old foundations, with their own endowments and trusts, and independent Board of Governors, and revenues derived in origin entirely, and still partly, from fees. The exact status of these schools is hard to define: some would call them semi-independent, hybrid or 'poised somewhere between independence and the State' [8]. But the following statement of their origin, written by a group of headmasters with long experience of working in them, stresses that their independence is in no sense compromised:

The history of the Direct Grant system is largely the history of State recognition of three main channels of educational endeavour: the desire of long-established and highly successful city schools to continue to serve all strata of the society of their city by providing an education of proven worth: the desire of religious denominations to provide an education for their members' children (and others too) in accordance with the particular emphasis of their Christian faith: the desire of some (previously independent) schools to work in association with the developing theory and practice of national education and thus to serve national education *while at the same time retaining their independence* [155 – italics supplied].

Briefly the arrangement is this: There are 179 such schools, 83 for boys, 94 for girls and 2 mixed. Nearly one third are denominational schools, 57 Roman Catholic. 57 headmasters of such schools are members of the Headmasters' Conference which, by one definition, ranks them as 'public schools'. Some are boarding schools, a large number town or city grammar schools serving a wider area than the local maintained schools. Manchester Grammar School, for instance, actually has some 'commuters' from the other side of the Pennines. Though academic standards are generally high, the denominational schools recruit from a wider range of ability. Their relationship with the State, which began in the 1920s, is now governed by Direct Grant School Regulations, 1959. Under these they have a statutory obligation to reserve not less than 25 per cent of the previous year's admission as *Free Places* to children who have attended a grant-aided primary school for at least two years. These may be offered by the Governors as 'scholarships' or through one or more local authorities. Further *Reserved Places* up to a total of 50 per cent may be taken up by the local authorities under certain conditions, and these are not restricted to children from grant-aided primary schools. All these places are normally awarded on the local authorities' own examinations. The remaining places, known as *Residuary Places*, are awarded on the school's own examination, but although these are normally known as 'fee-payers' there is a scale of fees graded according to parental income so that there is no financial bar to entry of day-children (boarders must pay the full cost of boarding), the Ministry of Education making up the difference between 'scale-fee' and full fee. It is theoretically possible, in the unlikely event of *all* fee-paying parents being too poor to pay any part of the fees, for all pupils in a direct-grant school to be paid for by central or local authorities. In return for this the school receives a capitation grant from the Ministry of Education – £45 per annum for each child over eleven and a further £84 for each pupil in the Sixth Form under 20 but over 17, or intending to take at least two G.C.E. Advanced Level subjects in that or the following year. Direct-grant schools thus have the following sources of income:

(1) Endowment income.

(2) Fees paid by parents (supplemented, if need be, by the Ministry).

(3) Fees paid by the local education authority for *Free* or *Reserved* places.

(4) Capitation grant from the Ministry.

The Governors are entirely responsible for buildings, and at least one third of them must be nominated by the local education authority, or the majority of them must be 'representative', as defined by paragraph 7 of Grant Regulations, 1959.

Without going into further detail we may thus accept this definition of a direct-grant school: 'an independent secondary grammar school which is required to award a number of free places each year to suitably qualified pupils' [155]. To this definition we shall return, but first a number of points about these schools should be mentioned. First, they have an academic reputation second to none. They have a higher percentage of sixth-form pupils than in maintained grammar schools: 27·32 per cent in direct-grant schools on the Headmasters' Conference, 21 per cent in all direct-grant schools, and 15·72 per cent in maintained grammar schools. 43 per cent of their pupils go on to further full-time education, the vast majority to universities. They do proportionately better than maintained or other independent schools in G.C.E. O- and A-levels [8], and they do this economically. Their weighted staffing ratio (counting each sixth-form pupil as two) is the same as for maintained schools (1-20·7) and while the average tuition fee in a direct-grant school represented on the Headmasters' Conference is £90 per annum, the amount paid by one local authority to another for an 'out-county' place in a maintained school is £107 per annum for pupils up to age 15 and £188 per annum for pupils over that age [155]. Moreover, unlike some nationalized industries, they balance their budgets. In the six year period 1958/9 to 1963/4 there was only once an excess of expenditure over income of £157, and this was offset by a cumulative balance the other way of £816.*

Secondly they show wider social mixing than in maintained schools, for their non-local character ensures that they are not so closely conditioned by their immediate neighbourhood. To quote a headmaster of one of these schools: 'There can be few schools in the western world where the sons of a Bishop, an M.P. and a Vice-Chancellor can mix on terms of complete equality with the sons of a fitter, a cotton operative and an invalid widow on public assistance' [155]. The gratitude a pupil of the latter kind feels to such a school is well illustrated by these words of Sir Ernest Barker, the miner's son from Manchester Grammar School who became Professor of Political Economy at Cambridge: 'What a mother it was! It gave me a great drill and a stirring stimulus. . . . It taught me to work, to read, and to think. It gave me great friendships. It filled me entirely and utterly for nearly the space of seven years. Outside the cottage I had nothing but school, but having school I had everything' [31]. A leading light in the Musical Society at North London Collegiate School, until she left recently, was a coloured girl; so is the captain of my daughter's rounders team.

*Statistics of Education 1964, I, p. 74, H.M.S.O., 1965.

This is not to say that social mixing in direct-grant schools is as wide as one could wish. There appears to be only one piece of research on this question, originally published in *Where?*, July 1966 [147]. Table 6 shows the social class composition, according to the Registrar General's main classifications, in Bristol Grammar School compared with that of Bristol residents as a whole:

Table 6: Social Class Composition in Bristol

Social Class	Bristol	Bristol GS
	%	%
1. professional	3·8	23·0
2. managerial	8·0	38·5
3. white collar,	20·4 ⎫	34·0
skilled manual	39·4 ⎭	
4. partly skilled manual	16·6	1·5
5. unskilled manual	11·8	–
6. unclassified	–	3·0

These findings are open to four objections. First, since direct-grant schools are academically selective – though less so in denominational ones, Roman Catholic and other, where a religious common denominator produces a wider ability band – we should expect their social composition to correspond broadly to the I.Q. ratings of the various social strata and this, if we compare Table 7 [122] is very much what we do find, even though their classifications do not exactly coincide:

Table 7: I.Q.s of Groups in Eight Different Social Strata

	I.Q.	
professional group	parents	children
1. higher professional and administrative	153	120
2. lower professional; technical and executive	132	115
3. highly skilled; clerical	117	110
4. skilled	109	105
5. semi-skilled	98	97
6. unskilled	87	92
7. casual	82	89
8. institutional	57	67

In the light of this table (which, incidentally, well illustrates the phenomenon of 'regress', see page 173) what is surprising about direct-grant schools is not that social mixing in them is not extensive, but that it occurs at all. Secondly the survey was carried out by the boys of Bristol Grammar School sociological society and is therefore an amateur affair. For instance it is partial in coverage and response, being based on questionnaires distributed to only two 'years' of the school from which only 63·4 per cent replies were received. Thirdly, the fact that 'white-collar' and 'skilled-manual' are undifferentiated is a serious omission. How the 34·1 per cent in this group divided is a crucial question. Finally Bristol is something of a special case. Two thirds of the city is already provided for in comprehensive schools, there has been a long political campaign against selection there, and the declared policy to terminate local authority places at the City's direct-grant schools would discourage parents, except those who could afford the fees in the event of those schools becoming independent, from putting their children's future at risk. The statement of Lord James of Rusholme that 10 per cent of the boys at Manchester Grammar School, by tradition one of the most academically selective institutions in the country, are the sons of manual workers [1] seems to me more reliable and significant than this juvenile exercise in sociology.*

*Since these words were written a book by Mr Graham Kalton, of the London School of Economics (*The Public Schools*, Longmans, 1966) takes us a good deal further. In a table (p. 35) showing an analysis of entrants to Head Masters' Conference direct-grant day schools on the basis of the Registrar General's five classes, Class III parents *are* subdivided into manual and non-manual, and we find that 13 per cent of these parents were skilled manual workers and 3 per cent partly skilled manual – a total of 16 per cent. Furthermore, as the headmaster of Bristol Grammar School points out (*The Times Educational Supplement*, 18 November 1966) roughly a quarter of all direct-grant schools are Roman Catholic foundations, many of which are not Head Masters' Conference schools and therefore excluded from Mr Kalton's table. Yet these, as the authors of the Fabian pamphlet [147] admit, contain a larger proportion of working-class children. Thus the direct-grant schools as a whole must contain more working-class children than Mr Kalton's figure (for Head Masters' Conference boys' schools only) of 16 per cent – perhaps, according to the headmaster of Bristol Grammar School, as much as 20 per cent or even 25 per cent. When we set this against the words of the Fabian pamphlet about the Bristol figures 'the only hard

Thirdly, the atmosphere and ethos of direct-grant schools, for all their social diversity, shows little difference from a fully independent school. I can speak with some knowledge here, having begun my teaching career and having a daughter now at one of the former and having taught for many years at one of the latter. In both kinds of school there is the same feeling of independence, the same sense of partnership between parents and staff (something more natural and spontaneous than the rather artificial collaboration generated by formal Parent-Teachers' Associations), the same dedicated teachers who remain long years at the same school, the same absence of bureaucratic interference. Dame Kitty Anderson, who recently retired from long service as headmistress of North London Collegiate School, said something at her farewell meeting with parents which is not easily forgotten: 'Thank you for letting us share your children.' When we compare this with the words quoted by Professor John Vaizey (no friend of independent schools) as an example of what he calls the 'Poor Law attitude to education' of some local authorities – an extract from a leaflet purporting to explain the selection procedure which runs 'You may want to know how the committee chooses a school for your child . . .' [9] – it seems that we are in different worlds.

For those who find this picture of the direct-grant ethos too utopian the seamier side is presented in the Fabian pamphlet on the subject to which we have already referred [147]. Its main objection is that they are academically and therefore socially selective, and this we shall consider in a moment. But it also argues that only a few are as good as the best, which is no doubt true: not all direct-grant schools can match Manchester Grammar

----

evidence of working-class parents [in Bristol Grammar School] is the 1·5 per cent in Class IV', it becomes all too apparent, in the light of Mr Kalton's subsequent figures, how dangerous it is to draw tendentious and wishful conclusions from incomplete evidence. Yet these same Fabian authors, from their assumed but thus exploded posture of statistical expertise, are quite content (*The Times Educational Supplement*, 18 November 1966) patronizingly to dismiss the evidence of another correspondent as being 'disarmingly innocent of the approved methods of social science'!

School or North London Collegiate School any more than all comprehensive schools can equal Tulse Hill or Holland Park. This truism damns neither kind of school. And finally – that infallible weapon of condemnation – they are 'pale imitations of the public schools' with 'an emphasis on uniform, rules, organised games, corporal punishment (by masters and boys), combined cadet force and religion'. But all these things I found at Tulse Hill Comprehensive School (except that corporal punishment is permitted only by housemasters, not boys, but this, in a state school, is unusual, and enlightened or retrograde according to one's view) and believe it to be all the better school for that.* This seems to me an example of Fabian confusion of thought – to object to certain distinctive features of a 'public school' and yet to object because some who believe in them can buy them while others cannot.

By and large, therefore, despite Fabian strictures, these direct-grant schools are good schools, described by the master-planner of the London comprehensives as 'the scaffolding on which a good state system of secondary education is slowly being built' [35], and they play a valuable part in 'making and keeping available for pupils from all kinds of homes, irrespective of parents' income, access to established independent schools' [155]. The reader may well feel they should be left to get on with their worthwhile job unmolested.

But there is a complication. These schools are frankly and unashamedly selective. Not socially, for they can, as we have seen, turn a miner's son into a professor, but academically. To the comprehensivists they are an abomination, for while the grammar schools 'cream', direct-grant schools take the *crème de la crème*. Dame Kitty Anderson, in the farewell address just mentioned, was clearly thinking in 'direct-grant terms' when she listed as one of the ingredients of a good school 'enough academic types to stimulate each other'. Defenders of the direct-grant schools point out that whenever any choice is given in education 'creaming' takes place. An alternative zoning, as we have seen, creates its own problems. 'At university level, for example, zoning would pre-

---

*The Tulse Hill Magazine for 1966 even has on its first page a splendid Etonian-looking picture of the School Rowing Eight.

sumably restrict Oxford and Cambridge to candidates from the Home Counties' [155]. But such arguments, in a climate of comprehensive orthodoxy, make little impact. The direct-grant schools are 'anomalies' – something about which, as 'progressive' educationists say, something must be done.

Nor are suggestions lacking. Professor Boris Ford, for instance, has urged that the direct grant be made conditional upon the schools turning themselves into centres of genuine educational experiment:

The range of possible experiments is enormous, extending from organisational experiments to curriculum studies, from the education of special categories of children (the outstandingly bright or the very weak, the potential professional musicians or the very deprived, and so on) to the education of quite 'normal' children from exceptional backgrounds or in special settings. There are problems of learning and motivation to be explored, as well as problems of method and orientation, and there are a variety of experiments to be undertaken in relation to the training and supply of teachers, or to the use of auxiliaries or married women [57].

The spectacle of Manchester Grammar School, permanent head of the Oxbridge Scholarship League, attempting, perhaps, to turn out professional musicians with the aid of teaching auxiliaries is intriguing; but centres of experiment outlive their usefulness and are not easily adaptable to new functions – and what kind of staff would such a school attract? Or there is the suggestion of Mrs Shirley Williams, a Labour Junior Minister, again for Manchester Grammar School (why cannot they leave good schools alone, and concentrate on making the less good better?): 'Direct grant schools are a very hard case. You might try to use them as schools which specialise in classics and humanities, the things they are best at, so that they become like German *academische Hochschule*. For example, Manchester Grammar School could concentrate on classics and maths' [156]. But can Britain – or America for that matter – do without the steady stream of outstanding physicists, chemists, biologists and so on that roll off the M.G.S. conveyor-belt with impeccable precision?

While the lesser physicians produce their nostrums for a healthy patient the Minister himself reaches for the surgeon's knife. In

Circular 10/65 hopes are thus expressed with ministerial menace:

The Secretary of State looks to both local education authorities and the governors of direct grant schools to consider ways of maintaining and developing this co-operation in the new context of comprehensive education. He hopes that authorities will study ways in which the schools might be associated with their plans, and that governing bodies will be ready to consider changes, for instance in curriculum and in method and age of entry, which will enable them to participate fully in the local scheme [47].*

The Chairman of the Headmasters' Conference and Lord Fisher of Lambeth may plead in vain that the fate of the direct-grant schools should be considered by the Public Schools Commission [157]. The Minister is adamant in his determination to divide and rule. Nor is an appeal to Regulation 17 of Direct Grant Regulations, 1959, which requires these schools to be academically selective, of any avail: 'I want to make it clear that I do not – repeat not – regard the regulations as a genuine obstacle to co-operation in schemes of secondary reorganisation. . . . If, however, there is any real doubt on this subject, I shall not hesitate to amend the regulations in a way which would leave no room for any doubt at all' [158].† Yet if the direct-grant schools are not academically selective they are nothing. They become neighbourhood schools, lose their non-local and socially classless character and might just as well be administered in name, as well as in fact, by local education authorities.

Rather than do this, those who can will go completely independent. One of their headmasters thus makes it clear in a desperate appeal to the Minister to 'think again': 'Here we must nail our colours to the mast. . . . It is the question of selection that will be crucial. Of course, if it came to the crunch, I know that I could

*His arm is being jogged, though it scarcely needs it, by the Fabian pamphlet to which we have already referred [147], which describes the direct-grant school as a 'privileged predator on the publicly maintained system of secondary education'. This, as an illustration of the kind of 'hidden persuasion' discussed in Chapter 4, could scarcely be bettered.

†One direct-grant school headmaster, not surprisingly, has confessed to a 'nightmarish feeling of playing poker for high stakes with someone entitled to change the rules as he goes along' (*Conference*, Journal of the Headmasters' Conference, December 1966).

recommend my Governors either to give their own free places or, if that resort were closed to us (as I surmise may well happen), *to go completely independent'* ([159] – italics supplied). Here is a grisly warning to those schools which still enjoy complete independence, as we shall see. For, by definition, a direct-grant school is 'an independent secondary grammar school which is required to award a number of free places each year to suitably qualified pupils' (see page 211). A lawyer would rule their independence qualified only in this latter respect; any other requirement, that they be comprehensive for instance, would be tantamount to a breach of contract. It is, of course, a corollary of this independence of the direct-grant schools to educate their children as they choose that the fee-paying local authority should also have the right to decide whether or not to avail itself of these schools, and to alter or amend that choice at any time. But this right to contract out of the agreement to send pupils to these schools is very different from the right, implicit in the Minister's attitude, to change the character of the schools or dictate the kind of education they give. So much for those schools who put their independence at risk by financial flirtation with the State. The bridge that these independent schools have sought to erect between the 'public' and 'private' sectors has been perfidiously blown in the name of 'the public', and when the day of reckoning comes this unobtrusive breach of contract by threat of legislation will deserve no mean place in the annals of 'democratic' tyranny. Meanwhile Mr Crosland, who knows his Juvenal and can garnish an election address (in the appropriate place) with an apt quotation from him [160] stands challenged at the bar of history by Juvenal's question: *Quis custodiet ipsos custodes?* The electorate have several years to wait and, as Plato has warned us, are not very good as watchdogs anyway.

INDEPENDENT GRAMMAR SCHOOLS

It is estimated that Britain has some 1,755 independent fee-paying schools, but of these only a comparatively small proportion cater mainly or exclusively for children of secondary age. Of these our concern will be chiefly with those 110 fully independent, wholly or partly boarding schools which are represented on the

Headmasters' Conference – what are commonly called the 'public schools' and, for reasons we have considered in the first chapter, ought not to be. The mere mention of the 'public schools' seldom fails to inflame passions. The blind devotion of their champions is matched by the journalistic contortions of their detractors, of which the following is a collector's piece: 'At its worst the English class-obsession creates an endless social *coitus interruptus* between ambition and fear. And nothing so much contributes to – and expresses – the judgement of quality by accent, to the promotion of mediocrity by connexion, as the public schools' [161]. Having the knowledge that comes from long experience of teaching in one of these schools without the prejudice, for or against, that seems to be a consequence of having been educated in one, I hope I can view them objectively. Any full treatment of these independent schools requires, and usually – perhaps too often – commands a book to itself. For this I have neither the space nor the inclination. The reader will look in vain, for instance, for any mention of that hoary trinity of 'public school' literature, fagging, flogging and fornication (or its substitutes). I shall confine myself to three topics that seem to me to make these schools relevant to our theme of the grammar school in its wider national aspect. First, the question of boarding, which has lately become a live issue through the enterprising research of Dr Royston Lambert, of King's College, Cambridge [162]. Secondly, the question of their independence – an issue far more important, to my mind, than whether or not they are 'public', whatever that may mean. And finally, for reasons that need no amplification, the explosive issue of 'integration'.

BOARDING

We have seen in the first chapter that boarding education was largely a creation of Dr Thomas Arnold of Rugby and the Victorian railways. That it should have outlived both, despite the supersession of the latter by the motor-car, is the measure of the evangelical power of the former. That its popularity often continues for the wrong reasons can give him little posthumous pleasure. For it must be frankly admitted that for many, a boarding education, like their style of car and house or choice of holiday, is a status symbol that reflects little consideration for the feelings or welfare of its recipients, the children. I can think of parents, for instance, who provide ideal homes and live within easy reach of a good independent day school who have insisted on packing off their boys to boarding school and often enough come back, at the end, reproachful that the Oxbridge 'place' that the day school could certainly have assured was not forthcoming. For my own part, even if I could afford 'Miss Beale' for my daughter, I would still opt for 'Miss Buss'. But before the reader dismisses me as a hopelessly biased witness, day school educated and day school (predominantly) employed, let me be more explicit.

The boarding school has many and substantial advantages. It has the child for twenty-four hours of every day, without the distraction of travel or (unless strictly controlled) television. It has opportunities for leisure activities which no ordinary home or day school – usually though perhaps inexplicably closed after 5 p.m. – can offer. The rural setting of many of them is conducive to quiet study or healthy outdoor exercise. The staff are more or less on duty all day and sometimes part of the night. The child has the advantage of living half the year in the company of contemporaries with a wide range of choice for friends. It would be interesting to know more about the comparative benefits of a child spending school days entirely within an age-peer group in a boarding school as against dividing them between age-peers and an age microcosm (the family) in a day school. This is a topic on which research is needed. Experience suggests that much depends on the individual child, and that boys and girls are vastly different in this respect. There is much misleading generalization on the subject, for misplaced and frustrated boarders often become angry and articulate young men and women. But the child for whom boarding is the right choice has much to gain from it. He (or she) learns perforce to live in a community and be a 'good mixer' who must accept discipline, or some equivalent if the school is a progressive one. He must be public-spirited or perish. All this I freely admit, and for those who believe in it and buy it for their children with their eyes open I have the utmost respect.

Nevertheless it is, and should be seen to be, a piece of calculated parental abdication. The acid test for parents with children at boarding schools is this. Do they, in conversation with the legendary Jones family, say 'My child is at boarding school' or 'My son is at . . . (some school name to conjure with)'? Or do they simply say 'I have sent my child away to school because I cannot cope so well myself (for reasons supplied if need be)'? The second kind of parent has probably done the right thing but with the first it is more doubtful. Having said this we must not assume that boarding schools are mainly for children with peripatetic or separated parents, bad homes or other domestic problems. There are reasons in plenty why a boarding education may be right for a child. That indefatigable legislator C. Northcote Parkinson has recently framed a new 'law' in this field: 'beyond a certain point in prosperity the home's suitability for children is in inverse ratio to the family's income' [163]. Those with wealthy privileged homes, top business executives, for instance, or Labour Cabinet Ministers, do well to bear this in mind. That is why Lord Snow was right, though for the wrong socio-snobbish reasons, in sending his son to Eton. For these high-powered homes are no places for children to grow up in and, as Parkinson warns, 'as for father being a Good Influence, he is absent for half the time and preoccupied the rest'. While agreeing with those who say that the criterion for boarding education should be need, not status, we should note that this criterion of need does not necessarily exclude the rich.

But if there is irrational prejudice in favour of boarding education among wealthy people there is an equally powerful prejudice against it among the working class, where even more cogent reasons make it desirable for some homes. Indeed in Dr Royston Lambert's surveys [162] the parents who did not want boarding were predominantly of this class. Their reasons were various: partly the strength of family feeling, partly anxiety about possible expense, partly 'prejudice or fear'. It is also clear from his findings that there is room, among those interested in boarding, for a much more varied pattern than is available at present. Weekly boarding, for instance, which is a commonplace in Russian schools but comparatively rare (Westminster School, for instance, has it) in this country, had a strong appeal that could well be further explored and developed. It is to be hoped that this important research will be followed up, and carefully considered by the Public Schools Commission and also by local authorities. There are many who look to the Public Schools Commission chiefly to find a suitably ingenious and vindictive way to 'ditch' the independent schools. If, instead, it can find a means of using the boarding facilities of those schools to meet genuine need, in its widest and most rational and human interpretation, it will have achieved something far more constructive and permanent.

INDEPENDENCE

The appointment of a Public Schools Commission to integrate these schools into the national system has inevitably raised the wider issue of whether independent education should continue to exist at all. There is an atmosphere of 'jitters' running through headmasters and schools as the Commissioners set to work; nervous and tight-lipped letters and articles begin to appear in the newspapers; no doubt the heavy artillery of the Headmasters' Conference and the Governing Bodies Association is quietly massing; there is a sense of deadly calm before a barrage. It is with some trepidation, therefore, that one sets forth into this educational no man's land to attempt a cool, objective appraisal. Yet there is no other way. It is all very well to conjure governors on speech-day platforms not to stand idly by while independence is eroded. Such fighting words will draw their applause from the already converted, with the highest decibel-rating from under those 'emphatic hats' whose wearers elsewhere, no doubt, demand the return of the birch and hangman's noose. But there will not be the suspicion of a cheer from the ranks of Tuscany.

Let us turn, however, to the Lars Porsenna of the comprehensivists, Mr Robin Pedley himself. In discussing the shortcomings of conventional rewards and punishments in schools and the need for reform he says:

The lead has in fact been given by independent 'progressive' schools such as Summerhill and Dartington Hall, and this is one reason good enough in itself to make us beware of ever creating a purely State-controlled educational monolith ... [some pages later] ... Had independent schools been prohibited in 1923, would Neill ever have been allowed to do, unhindered, what he needed to do? Freedom in education is a first requirement for the establishment and maintenance of a free society. It must be preserved [33].

Here is the crux. In a democratic society Mr A. S. Neill must indeed be given his freedom to run a school on such doctrines as 'all sin is sickness' and 'education should concern itself with the emotions and leave the intellect to look after itself' [164]. But the corollary of freedom to be eccentric is freedom to be traditional; the right of Mr Neill never to punish carries with it the right of the headmaster of Eton to punish – if he thinks fit, even to use the cane. The thing about an independent school is quite simply that it is independent. And who can say, justice apart, whether today's heresy may not be tomorrow's orthodoxy and vice versa.

This the 'progressives' are prepared to concede in principle; but there is a practical snag. Whereas 'progressive' schools are moderately successful, traditional independent schools are embarrassingly so. The reasons for this are as varied as the variety of the schools themselves, and need not concern us here. One point, however, is worth making. The decision to send a child to a fee-paying school requires plans for registration and finance well in advance, sometimes even at birth. Many parents are conservative in these matters and like to know in advance what they are buying. And, as C. Northcote Parkinson reminds us, the best guarantee of this is in the 'private sector':

Differing from each other, and so offering a choice, the schools remain more or less the same. By contrast state schools are liable to change in character at every general election – indeed with every alteration in the party strength on the borough council. Should the far-seeing parent decide to live near Whatsit Grammar School, that institution may have ceased to exist before little Billy can even compete for a place. It can be Comprehensive next year, Incomprehensible the year after, and may be turned, subsequently, into offices for the Board of Trade [163].

Realizing this, and jealous of their success, the opponents of traditional independent schools shift their attack to fee-paying itself. Education, they say, should not be bought and sold, and thus become a matter of wealth and privilege. They conveniently forget that Summerhill and Dartington Hall charge fees no less than Eton and Winchester, and to proscribe the latter is to proscribe the former as well. Some of them accept that the abolition of fee-paying is impracticable. As Mr Crosland himself recognizes it would be an 'intolerable restriction on private liberty', and nothing could prevent new fee-paying schools being established elsewhere, perhaps in Southern Ireland. 'The right headmaster could set up a new high-prestige Public School in ten years' [4]. Moreover to make fee-paying schools illegal would, as has been pointed out, put them on a par with pornographic literature, dangerous drugs and certain forms of gambling [165].

But if this line of attack on fee-paying is not very profitable, it has recently been given a new twist. We are told that independent schools seduce valuable graduate teachers from the maintained schools and thus steal an unfair advantage. Thus Professor John Vaizey (himself a member of the Public Schools Commission) complains that 'the public schools have unscrupulously taken more than their fair share of the most able mathematics and physics teachers by offering them more favourable conditions and salaries, while the maintained schools have been starved of these specialists' [9]. And Robin Pedley, with a similar complaint that independent schools 'steal the cream of talent by the chink of money alone', would legislate to make all independent schools conform to the same pupil-teacher ratio as the maintained schools and pay salaries only according to the Burnham Scale, with deductions for benefits (presumably including dormitory duties) such as residence [33].

Now this attack does require an answer and seldom receives one. It is twofold. First, the alleged higher salaries paid to teachers in independent schools are exaggerated, as those who know the facts can confirm. Where a salary is substantially above Burnham it usually carries corresponding extra responsibilities, such as those of running a boarding house, where the extra money is hard-earned – just how hard only those with real experience of it know, and some teachers in maintained day schools would be horrified if they saw what happens to their sacrosanct Saturday and Sunday in a boarding school. The gap is even further narrowed when we compare the slightly higher salaries of independent schoolmasters not with their alleged opposite numbers in maintained schools, but with the salaries some of them, with their qualifications, could command elsewhere – heads of departments, senior posts in educational administration or Her Majesty's Inspectors (a sizeable number of whom are outstanding schoolmasters 'creamed off' from the independent schools never, alas, to teach again), to mention only the educational field. That many of them stay at their posts in independent schools for a marginally higher salary – and many independent schools pay only Burnham Scale anyway – is a tribute to their dedication to their job, not a concession to the 'chink of money'. And this brings us to the second point. Why do they stay? The answer lies, I believe, in their love of their independence. Decisions on matters of school policy in independent schools are mostly made by the schoolmasters themselves in consultation with the headmaster, who respects and values their advice as experts in their job; and the governors, even in matters where they do not leave him a free hand, are usually ready to be guided by, or at least to listen to the headmaster. In the maintained system, though there is much variation between areas, there is a vast superstructure of education officers, technical and subject advisers, inspectors (local and Her Majesty's), local councillors and so on, all of whom expect some say, smaller or larger, in school policy. Some of them may protest that their function is purely advisory; but they know, and the teachers know that their advice had better be listened to. Many of them, too, receive higher salaries than the teachers and are known to do so. Edward Thring, long before the bureaucratic empire of educational administrators and fringe non-teachers reached its present proportions, had this to say:

It is a strange spectacle everywhere seen, though no one sees it; the spectacle of the nation putting their best hopes, their children, under the charge of men whom they do not trust to do their work, and so put them in turn under the charge of others. And those others enjoy the singular advantage of not knowing the work – with the additional recommendation of very often having been hopelessly left behind by the very men whom they now control [15].

To parody George Bernard Shaw, 'Those who can, do; those who can't, teach; those who can't teach, supervise teachers', would be unfair. Yet a former headmaster warns us what can happen:

Occasionally one finds councillors (who are possibly not Governors of schools) who look upon the schools in much the same way as they look upon public parks or swimming baths, as places which belong to the community, and where the councillor has a duty to carry out occasional inspections to see that the community is getting its money's worth. Nothing, of course, could be worse for the self-respect of teachers than to be treated as though they were the kind of employees who needed constant watching [128].

Schoolmasters who have once experienced the atmosphere of an independent school resent being controlled and directed by officials who may not, as teachers, have seen the inside of a classroom for years and councillors, some of whom, to judge by their utterances, never at all.

So those who talk glibly of transferring the teaching resources of independent schools to the state sector by edict are in for a rude shock. It has been said of Winchester that it 'attracts into teaching adolescents the sort of men who in Paris, say, or Boston would be teaching post-graduates' [166]. A headmaster of a well-known independent school, when asked why he chose teaching, replied that he did not. He was offered a post at a famous school whose traditions, scholarship and independence appealed to him, and accepted it. Otherwise he might well never have taught at all. Robbed of their chosen way of life – teaching in a context of independence – many of these schoolmasters could and would leave the profession altogether. Mr Crosland himself has confessed that he recognizes this [4], and the number of staff leaving Manchester Grammar School at the mere suggestion of a threat to direct-grant independence (page 154) rather confirms it. It is an illusion to imagine that legislating about the staffing ratio or salary scales of independent schools would automatically add a captive bonus to the staffs of maintained schools. It might net a few reluctant classicists, historians and other arts graduates, but as for the mathematicians, scientists and economists, industry with its insatiable maw of laboratories and computers could and would comfortably swallow them. And what is probable while maintained grammar schools still exist becomes a certainty if the only option is a comprehensive.

Finally there is an argument for the abolition of independent schools whose mere statement is its refutation. If everybody were forced to use the maintained schools, we are told, they would automatically become better than they are: 'Without a doubt, the most valid and powerful argument for bringing all independent schools into the State system is that it would bring the young Macmillans, Hailshams, Gaitskells and Bonham-Carters into the local classrooms. The chance of early vigorous action to wipe out the black spots in national education would be transformed overnight' [33]. Just in case the transparent fallacy of this reasoning needs spelling out, one has only to think of the National Health Service or nationalized transport. Though originally intended to serve everybody, their inadequacies have forced alternatives on many of those who can escape the net – private medical insurance and the exorbitant use of the private car. The imposition of a monolithic comprehensive state monopoly in education seems scarcely likely to fare any better.*

INTEGRATION

To describe the major brief of the Public Schools Commission as 'integration' was bad logic but good politics. Bad logic in that to 'integrate' is to 'make a whole by combining its parts or elements', but as the *independent* schools were never, by definition, part of the *state* system they do not help to form the *whole* of that state system. One might as well speak of integrating a pendulum into a watch. Integration, it is true, has a wider 'usage' sense in that independent schools form part of society's whole educational resources. Here the schools themselves are anxious to play a fuller part, but not at the price of their independence. A pendulum cannot be bent into an escapement wheel. But it was good politics, for it suggests to the gullible that they do form part of the state system and to idealists that they ought to. The Commission have an unenviable task. To leave the independent schools more or less as they are, with perhaps a few state bursaries, would not satisfy many members of the present Government. The other extreme of

*It may be, of course, that in the long run there will be a popular demand for some kind of ban on the private motor-car, private medical insurance or private education. But this has not happened yet and, on balance, the first seems the most likely.

complete take-over would cost money – an estimated figure of £15 million [167] – which, though it sounds modest enough beside the £13 million spent in 1964 on gambling with 'one-armed bandits' (or 'fruit machines') alone, will not be readily acceptable to the ordinary citizen who cannot get a mortgage and pays more and more in rates and taxes as the years go by. Faced with the intrinsic difficulties of steering some middle course, the Commission have two further obstacles to contend with. The first is defeatism, of which the following assessment is typical :

All that will happen, in fact, is that the educational Commission will deliberate for a couple of years and carry out some useful pilot surveys. And when it reports the situation will remain much the same as now, except, perhaps, that the private sector will be rather larger because some Direct Grant Schools will have gone independent. There may well be an attempt to cut down their staffing standards and prevent them from employing more than their share of scarce teachers. But education costs are rising rapidly – far faster than the gross national product, and twice as fast as the Treasury's limit on Government expenditure as a whole. Hard cash, if nothing else, will rule out any large-scale transfer of the costs of private education to the Exchequer [168].

While agreeing with what is said here about the direct-grant schools and disagreeing about staffing ratios, for reasons elaborated above, I cannot feel that this is an inspiration to the Commission in their work. The second obstacle is ignorance. Of this an article in the *New Statesman* [169], whose author seemed to fancy himself as a progressive pathfinder for the Commission, will serve as an example. In it he laments that few public school boys will read his article, conditioned as they are by the limitations of their parents and teachers. After reading the article, in my proper place in the queue of colleagues, in our own (independent school) Common Room copy of the journal and then looking at it again in the well-thumbed school library copy, I formed the conclusion that a journalist who is so unflatteringly pessimistic about the circulation of his own journal scarcely deserved a reading. There was little in the article to change my mind.*
Fortunately the Commission is not likely to allow itself to be deluded or starved of the true facts. Indeed, its composition gives

*In fairness, his summary of Dr Royston Lambert's work on boarding education is substantially correct.

one heart. The Chairman, Sir John Newsom, has already been shown from his views (see page 163) to be a realist with no illusions about the amount of money at his disposal. Dame Kitty Anderson, from what she has said (see page 216), is unlikely to swallow the bait that these independent schools can become comprehensive. The High Master of St Paul's had this to say at an independent school speech day: 'Some of the most inflammatory and strident voices in education today have never confronted a class of real live children in their lives – and wouldn't survive ten minutes if they did without a rescue operation being mounted by the headmaster' [170]. His intention was to persuade his fellow Commissioners that there is more in such schools worth preserving than needs reforming, and he can be relied upon to curb the wilder excesses of some of his more theorist colleagues. Over the Master of Marlborough there are more grounds for anxiety. In a recent book he urged the extension of the direct-grant principle as the main vehicle for integration of the independent schools [171]. It is only fair to point out that the book was written before the present Minister of Education had spoken and behaved towards the direct-grant schools as he has since done. Some of us could have warned Mr Dancy of the dangers inherent in his thesis. He can now read for himself the writing on the wall. Whatever the views of the rest of the Commission – and some of them look predictable enough – this leaven of classroom experience should at least give some prospect of a fair and realistic solution – or a weighty minority report.

Just in case any of the Commission happen to read these words I would mention two themes for consideration – one a matter of principle, the other of experience. The first is axiomatic to anyone with an open mind. If the independent schools are to be integrated and not destroyed, their essential independence must be preserved. The experience of the direct-grant schools should be a warning against any arrangement to saddle them, however attractive it may sound, with any direct subvention of public money. This would reduce them to the status of the recruit who has taken the Queen's Shilling. If local authorities send pupils to them they should do so by paying fees, thus remaining *in loco parentis*; any form of capitation or other grant from rates or taxes places the State, as the direct-grant schools know to their cost, *in loco domini*. There are two other essential ingredients of independence. First, the right to choose and (just as important) get rid of, if need be, their staff and pupils. Anything that violates this ultimate right – though of course local authorities or central government would make recommendations about pupils which, in normal cases, would be accepted – means the end of independence. Equally there must be independence in matters of religion. It has been said that if you want a child taught Christianity or atheism you have to pay fees, and this is largely true. Most of the best-known independent schools owe a great deal to the frankly denominational (Church of England, Roman Catholic or whatever) religion that they teach and, helped particularly by their chaplains, strive to practise. They must be preserved at all costs from the anaemic compromise of the Agreed Syllabus.

From principle we turn to experience. We have shown (page 30) that in intention and in fact Merchant Taylors' School in its early days provided education for a complete cross-section of society, from knight's to labourer's son. Over the years its range narrowed, as with all the old grammar schools, especially boarding schools, though less than most, partly through its central London site and partly through a substantial subvention from the Merchant Taylors' Company which kept the fees low. All the same the Governors were not happy about the social range of entry to the School, and there was a strong feeling that the proposals of the Fleming Report, adapted to the particular conditions of the School, should be operated immediately after the war. Lord Clauson, who had been a boy at the School and became a High Court Judge, thus addressed the Court of the Company: 'Our predecessors made an educational ladder on which boys could climb to the university, whatever their circumstances. The ladder is still here, but a rung is missing and we must put it back' [10]. The idealism of the Governors was met, as rarely happened elsewhere when the Fleming Report was considered, by enlightened and imaginative local education authorities. As a result of a conference between the Merchant Taylors' School Committee and the Chairman and Directors of Education for Middlesex and Hertfordshire the Governors decided to offer ten places to Middlesex and five to Hertfordshire for boys aged eleven attending maintained primary schools. The Education Committees accepted the offer and agreed to pay the fees and other charges and the agreement, made in 1945, was for ten years in the first instance. Since then Hertfordshire have given up their places, largely because the original area from which their boys were recruited was limited, and a new grammar school at Rickmansworth now served it. But Middlesex accepted the extra five places readily, this time for 'assisted' rather than 'free' scholars, and so the scheme has continued to the present day. Its success is truly inspiring to any schoolmaster who has worked closely with it. The boys fit naturally into the School life, have had a distinguished record of university successes and have played their full part in games and positions of responsibility. To go into further detail would sound like a school prospectus – not the bogus kind burlesqued by one critic of the 'public schools' [172] – and this is not the place for it. The effect of the plan is that the School now has on its strength a steady figure of about 100 free or assisted scholars, about one sixth of its total, without changing its character, and thus accords more closely with the intention of its founders 400 years ago. In effect the arrangement is similar to that in the direct-grant schools – though their percentage of such scholars, between 25 and 50 per cent, is larger – but with one vital difference. The School's independence has not been compromised in any way; the local authorities who send their boys remain firmly *in loco parentis* – there is no subsidy from local or central government funds to put the School at the mercy of an authoritarian Minister of Education of Mr Crosland's persuasion. Here is integration at its best, leaving the School's independence secure. Of course it is vulnerable, like any other institution, to take-over by legislation, but at least, unlike the direct-grant schools, it cannot be taken over by administrative sleight of hand.

One argument that is sometimes heard against this and other 'Fleming type schemes' is that thereby the independent schools 'cream' the local maintained schools. Those who thus oppose them are trying to have it both ways. At one moment they complain that the independent schools confer privilege open only to fee-payers; at another, when those privileges are extended to include non-fee-payers by some form of integration, they object again. Either these independent schools offer something better than the maintained schools – and it is worth remembering that they represent a huge capital investment built up over the years in buildings, playing fields and other equipment, not to mention the 'goodwill' of their staff, as well as, in the case of schools run by City Livery Companies and some others, an annual subsidy, this relatively reduced by taxation, but still substantial, so that the Middlesex scholars at Merchant Taylors' are receiving an education at public expense considerably subsidized by private enterprise – or they do not, in which case they are unexceptionable, and all the complaints about 'privilege' and 'buying education' are beside the point. Both propositions cannot be true at the same time.

The mechanics of integration, if agreement in principle could be reached, should not prove too difficult. Many independent schools have charters originally granted by the Crown, or negotiated with the (then) Board of Education, and these could be reviewed. In them the schools could define their educational aims and the State, if it found them acceptable, could pay for a proportion of the pupils sent to them, subject to the terms of the charters being fulfilled and to their being reviewed from time to time in the light of new educational practices and ideas. But any compromise of independence, apart from the terms of the mutually agreed charter, must be avoided, and above all the schools should beware of the Trojan Horse of a direct grant.

There we must leave the future of the independent schools with their Commission. Sir John Newsom has no easy task. I remember, however, when I was a candidate for a headmastership in Hertfordshire while he was still Director there, that he told me that if I was appointed he would pay an annual cheque to the school which I could spend on Bibles or footballs (if I recall his illustration correctly) as I pleased. With a former Director of Education who managed to introduce that degree of freedom into the maintained schools under his care the independence of the independent schools should be in safe hands.

CHAPTER SEVEN

TOWARDS REAL PARENTAL CHOICE

A SOCIAL historian of Britain in the sixties might call this the Age of the Consumer. The ever-increasing range of what are significantly called 'consumer goods', the cloying ingenuity of advertising through print and television; the growth of consumer councils and consumer journals all conspire to inflate the self-importance of the consumer and his inseparable attribute, choice. What is true of commerce applies also, in theory, to education by both national and international profession. The 1944 Education Act, Section 76, charges local authorities to 'have regard to the principle that, so far as is compatible with the provision of efficient instruction and training and the avoidance of unreasonable public expenditure, pupils are to be educated in accordance with the wishes of their parents'. The Universal Declaration of Human Rights, which the United Kingdom played a large part in drafting, prescribes in Article 26(3) that 'Parents have a prior right to choose the kind of education that shall be given to their children.'

So much for theory; but the facts are somewhat different. If pre-war secondary education was largely 'rationed by the purse' there was little choice either in the post-war tripartite system. Only those who qualified for grammar school could go there and the few who, though qualified, nevertheless chose a secondary modern school generally did so for the wrong reasons. Some children in Manchester for instance, and no doubt elsewhere, discovering that a grammar school meant hard work and separation from their 'mates' who had not qualified, would persuade feckless parents to let them go to a secondary modern – and often they were willing enough, if they gave it any thought, for it meant earlier leaving and a younger breadwinner. Such choice, being in effect the children's own, was immature and misguided, and for the rest it was the 11-plus that did the choosing. Yet now, under a system of comprehensive neighbourhood schools, with their 'Berlin Wall of zoning', we have the prospect of 'moving from a system which permitted hardly any choice of secondary school to another that appears to offer none at all' [173].

Supporters of the comprehensive principle may object to this on two grounds. First, since the schools are large and cater for *all* children in their neighbourhood they offer a built-in choice of the widest possible kind. But this overlooks the essential quality of a school, which is not a sort of supermarket but a living institution with a personality and ethos of its own. The parent who seeks education for his children in a single-sex school, a school teaching religion of a particular denomination, a school with a predominantly academic character, or simply a small school where the pace, quick or slow, suits the child and by the presence of a majority of others of similar needs helps him to feel at home and not an odd man out, will not find precisely these things in a large neighbourhood comprehensive. And what of the parent who, from motives of snobbery or inverted snobbery or, more reputably, from a desire for wider social mixing prefers his child to be educated, not necessarily as a boarder, in a school differing in atmosphere from the immediate neighbourhood where he lives? We may disapprove of such choices, but by judging them we are denying them, and though the neighbourhood comprehensive may claim to educate choice this is not the same as granting it.

Secondly it may be argued that the comprehensive school is the People's Choice since they gave a mandate to a Government whose policy it is. This appears to be the view of Mr Crosland. When asked in the House of Commons what evidence there was of public reaction to comprehensive reorganization, he replied that it was to be found in the result of the General Election and a 50 per cent favourable verdict in the latest Gallup Poll, with only 18 per cent against and the rest either 'don't-knows' or 'not-heard-ofs'. But the wish of the majority is not the same as choice. We do well to heed the warning about 'the deplorable and lazy modern cult of majority wishes and majority opinion' and remember that there is no 'moral sanction whatever behind the votes and wishes of a majority' [174]. Choice means respect for the wishes of a minority, and democracy is not government by Gallup Poll.

Of course choice within the maintained system must be limited to the administratively feasible. There is the classic case of Mrs Joy Baker, who claimed a right as a parent to educate her children at home. Only after a ten-year legal battle has she established that right [175], and now that she has moved her home to the province of another education authority she seems likely to have to fight the same battle all over again. Mrs Baker's struggle has been difficult enough though it involved only the right to contract out of school altogether. To reconcile choice with participation in the maintained system is even more difficult. This is recognized in the triple limitation of parental choice in the passage from the 1944 Act we have already quoted. First, it is only a principle, to be weighed against other principles that may override it, and the behaviour of the present Government suggests that they regard the comprehensive principle as precisely of this kind; secondly, the choice must be compatible with the provision of efficient instruction and training, and it was chiefly on this ground that Mrs Baker had to justify her 'choice' in the Courts; thirdly, it must avoid unreasonable public expenditure, a qualification which arises, for instance, when a parent expresses a choice to send a child to an independent school.

Choice, therefore, within the maintained system is something much more limited than a superficial reading of the 1944 Act suggests; a fact which the Ealing Parents' Committee found to their cost (an estimated £2,000 or more) when they sought in vain an injunction restraining the Greater London Borough of Ealing from introducing comprehensive education. A bitter comment from one parent after the hearing seemed to concede victory to Mr Crosland's attitude to choice we have just noted: 'What has come out of the case is that there is no way, apart from the ballot-box, in which parents in this democratic country of ours can have a real choice of education' [176]. A legal expert, in an interesting article, takes the different view that there are many other ways of challenging comprehensive reorganization, and that this test case is not the end, only the beginning [177]. But test cases are expensive, and the ordinary citizen will be forced to the conclusion that the only way for parents to achieve a real choice is by paying fees and, at the end of the day, when the fate of direct-grant and independent schools is finally decided, perhaps not even then.

In the matter of choice we should be quite clear how uncompromising the comprehensive position is. The Minister's own definition of comprehensiveness is absolute and exclusive: 'A comprehensive school cannot be comprehensive as long as there are selective schools in its area' [178]. Circular 10/65, though it offers a series of acceptable forms of comprehensive organization, directs that some two-tier arrangements like the Leicestershire Plan are to be regarded only as interim measures, for they are not fully comprehensive as they involve 'the separation of children of differing aims and aptitudes into different schools at the age of 13 or 14' [47]. Two-tier schemes must be comprehensive, ultimately, at each tier. 'The French can keep their *lycées*, the Germans their *Gymnasien*, and even the Americans can have selective high schools like the Bronx in New York, Lowell in San Francisco, and selective independent schools like Groton and Andover' [179]. But in Britain you can have a pound of comprehensive education or two separate half-pounds, and that is all. Even this choice depends on where you live. Thus the Greater London Borough of Hillingdon proposes for its area nineteen all-through comprehensive schools and parents may choose any one of them. Parents' choice is therefore limited to deciding the distance the child will have to travel to school.*

Perhaps an analogy will help here. I happen to possess a car of popular make fitted with front-wheel drive. I am a fanatic about this arrangement. Cars of this design are safe, economical, corner well and hold the road in icy conditions when conventional rear-wheel-drive models are slipping all over the place. A spot check of traffic on any busy road shows that there is a groundswell of opinion in favour of front-wheel-drive cars. They even abolish selection, for though the cars come with a variety of names and in three different sizes it is still basically the same car. If I were Minister of Transport I would introduce legislation to reorganize road transport on front-transmission lines. But I would be quite

*Incidentally there are in the Borough at the time of writing only nine 'good-honours' graduate teachers of mathematics and nine capable of teaching Latin to a standard required by many universities to read for an Arts degree. These teachers, it seems, can expect a fairly mobile future.

wrong: first, because for all the arrogant certainty of my conviction I could just conceivably be mistaken, and secondly because I would be denying drivers' choice.

Is there no alternative, in secondary education, to this prospect of dull uniformity and total denial of parental choice? I believe there is, given a little flexibility, a slight revision of the comprehensive creed. 'Comprehensive', in the relevant sense, is thus defined in the Oxford English Dictionary: 'comprising much; of large content or scope' [180]. In a spirit of give-and-take we will concede the comprehensivists their extension to 'comprising *everything*', but ask, as a counter-concession, that they do not insist on '*everybody*' as well. If they would cede this one piece of occupied territory the present gloomy prospect for parental choice could be transformed at a stroke.

A PLAN FOR PARENTS' CHOICE

Briefly the proposal is this. Let us forget the neighbourhood secondary school altogether – it has little enough to commend it as we have seen (pages 157–60). Instead there would be flexible groups of secondary schools each consisting of a purpose-built comprehensive and one or more grammar schools and secondary modern schools. Parents with children in maintained primary schools would, towards the end of that stage of schooling, be asked to make a choice. *Either* their children could proceed, without any 11-plus or selection procedure whatever, to a comprehensive school *or* they could opt for some form of selection after which their children would go to a grammar school or a secondary modern school. Each type of school would offer G.C.E. courses to O- and A-level and, where appropriate, for C.S.E. and other examinations, and there would be, for those who opted for selection, flexible transfer, on the imaginative lines already developed by some authorities (see Chapter 5), at any suitable stage and in particular at sixth-form level for 'late developers'. There might even be a case for transfer the other way for what have been called 'late deteriorators' [54]. What could *not* happen is that parents who opted for selection, if their children failed to secure a grammar school place, should then expect a place at a comprehensive school, for this would be quite unfair to the comprehensive. Those who go to the comprehensive school *must* go there because they believe in it and reject selection, not as a sort of second-best. Such a plan, well-suited to populous urban areas, would have to be modified in scattered rural districts. Here very often to opt for selection would be to opt also for boarding education, and extended boarding facilities, including perhaps the practice of weekly boarding mentioned in the last chapter, would be needed. But everywhere the overriding aim would be to give the maximum degree of parents' choice. Such a plan would have a number of advantages :

(1) Those parents who join the politicians in denouncing the evils of selection could demonstrate the strength of their convictions by exercising genuine choice, leaving others to do the same.

(2) The secondary school building programme would be dramatically cut. There would be a need for new comprehensives in areas that do not possess them already. But existing 'tripartite building' would still serve the purpose for which it was originally intended (including the splendid secondary modern buildings to be found, for instance, in one-time Middlesex and my native Canterbury) and the present comprehensive hotch-potch of 'all-through' plans, two-tier plans and non-plans with scattered buildings could be superseded. Where new grammar and secondary modern schools were required they could be built on the campus layout, as at Ifield (see page 176), thus satisfying the demand of Circular 10/66 that all *new* building must be for comprehensive organization. Then, if eventually selective schools went out of fashion in favour of all-through comprehensives, these complexes of campus schools could be amalgamated into orthodox comprehensives as has already happened at Ifield, but this time through the operation of parental choice instead of political pressure. Building would thus be pragmatic rather than dogmatic.

(3) There would be variety, always desirable in education. The large comprehensive, the smaller school with academic or practical bias, perhaps even, according to local tradition, the single-sex school of either type – though not with the comprehensive, for to my mind a single-sex comprehensive school is a contradiction in terms – would all be available *for parents to choose.*

(4) There would be choice for the teachers – a thing we hear little of these days and something that might attract more recruits. The choice they have in the present period of transition from selective to comprehensive schools would be preserved, with the added advantage that pupils would be in the school of their parents' choice, whereas the eventual prospect when re-organization is complete would be comprehensive or nothing.*

(5) There would be, for the first time, real and healthy competition within the maintained system. The comprehensives would have a chance to prove themselves on their merits without what some of their teachers regard as the embarrassing advocacy of doctrinaire politicians; and the grammar and secondary modern schools, particularly the latter, could show their paces secure in the knowledge that politicians will think twice about damning schools which the parents, their voters, have chosen.

(6) The fact that the pupils were in these schools because they and their parents, by the exercise of choice, had demonstrated their belief in them, would improve standards all round. There would be no room for excuses, but rather an incentive to get on with the business of education instead of bleating about the inadequacies of this or that system. Parents, like parents who choose

*Teachers' views on secondary reorganization deserve more attention than they have so far received. Some attempt to assess them unofficially has been made in *A Verdict on Comprehensives* by P. Biggin, C. R. Coast and J. M. Stansfield, available from Wheelright's Grammar School for Boys, Dewsbury, Yorkshire, 1966. This studies the answers to a questionnaire of some 400 teachers of all ages and positions, and from all parts of the country. Of these teachers 74 per cent were against a completely comprehensive system. Of the remaining 26 per cent only 15 per cent favoured the conversion of existing schools to comprehensives; 51 per cent preferred a gradual changeover as purpose-built schools become available. In reply to a question about the existing bipartite system of grammar and modern schools only 6 per cent favoured it. 38 per cent preferred an improved bipartite system with easier transfer, while 56 per cent wanted a mixed system, with some purpose-built comprehensives and the best of existing schools. On this evidence, partial admittedly but at least enjoying the frankness of anonymity on the teachers' part (for critical views expressed on official working parties or elsewhere cannot entirely escape a veiled threat, real or imagined, to their security of employment) it would seem that the thesis of this chapter has more support among my fellow-teachers than has Government policy.

an independent school, would have made their decision and might fairly be expected to live with it. In making that decision they would, of course, have available advice from primary schools, local authorities and other well-informed sources, but the final decision would be their own.

One other advantage of this proposal calls for a paragraph to itself. Britain is, by temperament, a nation of gamblers. In 1965 the estimated turnover in gambling was £1,000 million, over two thirds of the total budget for education in the previous year.* The revenue this year from a quite modest betting tax actually surprised the Chancellor of the Exchequer into not increasing it; and the gambling itch has even invaded politics, so that nowadays at general election times there is greater interest in polls than policies and more concern about who will win than who deserves to win. Now to suggest that the choice of a child's secondary school is a gamble would be quite wrong. Certain elements in it, it is true, are largely fortuitous: the ability and character of the child, the secondary schools available in the place of residence, the economic circumstances of the parents; for the range of choice is much wider if funds are sufficient to contemplate fee-paying, or the nature of the father's job makes possible a move to an area where state secondary education is better provided for. But other factors call for a mixture of informed judgement and, at worst, calculated risk-taking: an objective appraisal of the child's strengths and weaknesses and a shrewd assessment of the schools available which is not satisfied with a superficial status grading but examines their intrinsic merits – the quality of the teaching, the nature and range of the courses and, above all, how these fit the individual child's talents and personality. Now the parents who carefully consider all these things usually secure the best education for their children, whether or not they can afford to pay fees; and because many of them happen to belong to the middle-class they and their children are often envied and accused of being 'privileged'. Others are content merely to accept passively whatever is first offered. Yet these, not infrequently, are the very parents who take gambling seriously. They are prepared to study and research on the 'form' of a horse or football team, whose success or failure

* £1,437 million, as given by *Statistics of Education 1964*, I, H.M.S.O., 1965.

depends to a large extent on pure chance, while they leave to chance the educational arrangements for their children, for whom a little parental homework could make all the difference. Such irrational behaviour is not easy to explain; an important factor, no doubt, is that with the horse or football team the backer's own money is involved, whereas with his child, whose education is provided by the State from rates and taxes, it does not appear to be. This aspect of the matter will be considered later in the chapter.

But the plan we have suggested, with its positive choice between offering a child some sort of selection and accepting a place at a comprehensive without it, has a double advantage. For the conscientious parents, who are prepared to take time and trouble over the choice of a secondary school for their children, the range of that choice is increased. For the apathetic parents who 'take what comes' a choice is forced upon them, a choice which could seem to have something of the flavour of a gamble. It is not this, but, paradoxically, it is better for them and the child that it should seem to be. For only then will they exercise the sort of judgement and calculation which the matter requires, and which they normally reserve for their gambling activities. The fact that there is a decision to be made between selection and non-selection will at least provoke a little thought, and if they give the matter as much attention as they do the relative merits of horses, football teams or whatever, something worthwhile is gained. Thinking about one's children in terms of odds, however shocking and misguided it may appear, is at least better than not thinking about them at all. Moreover the knowledge that one has made a decision, one way or the other, offers some prospect of a more active interest in its results. Perhaps this is not a very respectable dynamic for educational interest, but any dynamic is better than the present mixture of apathy and dissatisfaction. Parents in the independent schools, who back with hard cash Bryanston rather than Eton, or Sedbergh rather than St Paul's, usually become deeply involved in what happens at their 'fancy'. The same could be true in the maintained schools.

This plan lays no claim to originality. Something of the sort was put forward by Professor Boris Ford [57], though as I understand him he would have selection only for grammar schools – perhaps even allowing those schools to do their own selection – and those who were rejected, or did not wish to undergo the selection procedure, would go to a comprehensive. But such a plan would be unjust to the comprehensive school, which should be for those who oppose selection, not those who accept it, whatever the result. Also, as Professor Ford admits, it would provide a choice only for the bright children of grammar school calibre; whereas the plan we have suggested gives a choice also to the child who would not qualify for grammar school – either a comprehensive without selection or a secondary modern after it. The plan is in fact in operation to some extent in London, not from policy but because direct-grant and voluntary grammar schools coexist with the comprehensives until they can be dislodged by legislation. But the effect of this is that many children are in the London comprehensives from parents' choice,* and this contributes to their success in no small measure. A similar plan was also tried in the Church-fields comprehensive school district of West Bromwich [33]. In the event over 90 per cent of the parents chose the comprehensive school and no 11-plus. In 1961 Labour lost control of the Council and its successor, quite wrongly, modified the system to enable those who took the 11-plus to fall back on Churchfields as a second choice. But equally wrong is the comprehensivist argument that because 90 per cent opted for Churchfields and no 11-plus the selection procedure should be abolished. There might be an administrative problem here, but the principle is important. A system of choice where 90 per cent opt for the comprehensive school is one thing; the imposition of a comprehensive system that rides roughshod over the remaining 10 per cent, which might be more in a different area, is quite another.

Two objections to any coexistence of selective and comprehensive schools must be considered. First, that under it comprehensive schools would be 'glorified secondary modern schools'. This, surely, is something of a confession of the weakness of their case by the comprehensivists if they believe the only way they can attract children of grammar school calibre is by conscription. One would

*Holland Park, for instance, Woodberry Down and Forest Hill (*London Comprehensive Schools 1966*, Inner London Education Authority Report, p. 26).

have thought parents who support the comprehensive school would choose it when given a chance to practise what they preach. Moreover there is nothing wrong with a secondary modern school that really is 'glorified', as in Surrey for instance, instead of being maligned. This objection is, in effect, a product of the sort of 'hidden persuasion' we have analysed in an earlier chapter, which would condemn secondary modern schools to a sort of witch-hunt and propagate the Divine Right of Comprehensives.

The second objection is a more serious one: that it would be an administrative nightmare. If parents exercised choice, not only might there be bewildering regional variations in the popularity of comprehensive and selective schools, but also the rolls of the schools would fluctuate from year to year with the vagaries of parental choice. Administrators love a simple, tidy solution and could well argue that the system was uneconomic if they could point to some schools half-empty, others over-full from time to time. But this is the perennial challenge to administration, enshrined in the old Army slogan, 'We can do the impossible, but miracles take a little longer'; and educational administration is there to serve the children, not the other way round. * It is the price of choice, and not insuperable, especially if new building of selective schools were on the campus lines suggested above. There is a parallel in the sphere of transport. After a Beeching to close uneconomic lines we have a Barbara Castle to reopen them on social grounds, with the cost to be met from local resources. In secondary education we might have a sort of Barbara Beeching to combine both processes in an administrative Judgement of Solomon. Here is a real challenge, with its prize something of the choice in state education that parents who can afford fee-paying schools already enjoy.

A sort of optional extra would further extend consumer choice in state education. In the last chapter we mentioned the suggestion

*In the metropolitan area, where we have seen that parental choice operates under a reluctant Authority, the distribution of secondary pupils, which make up 38·9 per cent of the school population, is as follows: Modern, 12·7; Grammar, 10·5; Comprehensive, 11·5; Technical, 0·3; other, 3·9 (*Statistics of Education 1964*, I, H.M.S.O., 1965). This balance suggests, *prima facie*, that parental choice on the lines suggested in this chapter would not present insuperable administrative problems.

of the Master of Marlborough of integrating independent schools by giving them direct-grant status, and rejected it in view of the cavalier treatment of direct-grant independence by the Minister. But there is no reason why it should not be extended to schools which are less, not more independent – the voluntary grammar schools. These schools, unlike the entirely state-controlled county grammar schools, still have a measure of independence greater or less according to whether they are 'voluntary aided' or 'voluntary controlled' (see page 37), and cannot therefore be comprehensivized quite so easily as the county schools, merely by local authority edict. Many are schools with a long and distinguished academic tradition, and in some cases only became 'aided' rather than direct-grant by an accident of history. To give these schools direct-grant status in areas where there is no adequate direct-grant provision would have a number of advantages. First, as with the direct-grant schools themselves, it would recognize their academic ethos and enable them to concentrate on the faster pace suited to academic high-flyers. The Watford grammar schools, for instance, are (to me) a local example of schools which, with their firm Oxbridge connections and strong sixth forms, built up the hard way through merit, would serve their local community much better as direct-grant schools than in the miscellaneous comprehensive roles so far suggested for them. Also, if this happened on a considerable scale, it would have the advantage of shifting the cost of education from local rates partly, via the direct-grant, to the Exchequer and partly, with the 50 per cent or more 'residuary places' (see page 211), to the pockets of parents. The latter point raises the question of fee-paying in maintained secondary schools, to be considered later in this chapter. But for our immediate theme of parents' choice it would extend to parents of children who qualify two further options:

(1) The chance of a faster academic pace than is usual in ordinary maintained grammar schools and, in some cases, the choice of a single-sex school where the normal grammar school provision is coeducational.

(2) The opportunity to parents who could not afford to pay the higher fees of fully independent schools nevertheless to pay moderate fees, on a graded scale, which many of them would

welcome, to judge by the popularity of direct-grant schools, as a more tangible gesture of involvement in their children's education. This is surely better than the farce of an established grammar school like Wilson's, Camberwell, soon to move to Surrey, voting with its feet to escape comprehensivization.

One last suggestion – not indeed an extension of parental choice, rather a calculated limitation of it, but designed in the long term to strengthen that choice. If comprehensive and selective schools, by the operation of parental choice we have suggested, could be freed from the cut and thrust of party politics, there would be a demand for reliable information towards making that choice. Something on the lines of the Stockholm experiment (see page 145), whose conclusions we found misleading owing to the different conditions in Sweden and this country, would be invaluable for deciding the comprehensive issue on fact rather than prejudice. There could be, for instance, a comparative study of the comprehensive and selective systems at Crawley New Town, with the Ifield Campus, resurrected from its suppression by local politics, operating side by side with one of the successful Crawley comprehensives like Thomas Bennett School. An expert analysis of the performance, in academic, social and other spheres, of children from similar home backgrounds educated under the two systems would furnish, over a decade, guidance to parents not necessarily about which system is better – for these matters are rarely as simple as that – but which catered better for particular needs. Again there is a strong case, in the interests of research, for the Government providing the money to complete the remaining nine comprehensive schools for inner Bristol so that it could become a guinea-pig city of fully comprehensive experiment. Both at Bristol and Crawley it might be desirable that there be no special provision for academic high-flyers as suggested in the last paragraph, thus anticipating comprehensivist objections that these experimental schools had been creamed or deprived of able children. It may seem that this is unfair to the children living in 'guinea-pig areas', but it is the price of experiment everywhere, just as new drugs are tested against a control-group which is not inoculated.

The suggestions put forward in this chapter to give parents real choice in secondary education may perhaps be clearer from the diagrammatic summary in Table 8. They make no claim to finality, or to being blueprints for immediate application, and may well be open to objections more serious than those we have considered. But at least they are an attempt to rescue state secondary education from the lurch into *dirigisme* that now threatens it and would reassert the importance of a parent's wishes in shaping a child's educational future. Sir Winston Churchill is credited with having said that democracy is the worst form of government except for all the others. Something like this is true of parental choice in education, and it needs to be safeguarded and extended.

THE COST OF CHOICE

'He who pays the piper calls the tune.'

'You pays your money and you takes your choice.'

When proverbial wisdom thus coincides with the earthy common sense of a cockney we do well to heed the message. It is certainly true in education, where 'the most distinctive difference in practice between people who pay privately and people who don't is that people who pay choose' [8]. Now a major provision of the 1944 Education Act, with its unassailable aura of bipartisan respectability, was the abolition of fee-paying in all maintained secondary schools. It is a daring man who questions that provision, if only to suggest that what was right in 1944 could conceivably be wrong in 1964 and after. But the Act was drafted against the background of the thirties, when many children were not getting enough food, let alone education, and a blanket guarantee that no child should be robbed of proper education through its parents' inability to pay was understandable. Times have changed. In the thirties, while citizens queued for the dole, Britain still possessed an Empire and reserves undrained by a second world war, and was rightly rebuked for not doing enough for them. Now it is the other way round. While the ordinary citizen, with a few shameful exceptions, finds himself better and better off, it is the Government that queues for the dole – or rather high-interest loans – from America and Zurich, and it seems to have no Jarrow hunger-marchers to capture the public

Table 8: A Plan for Secondary Education in an Urban Situation* offering Parents' Choice

Catchment Area A ⎫ Catchment Area B ⎬ (notional total of 3,500 children of secondary age)	Group of Secondary Schools (Each offering G.C.E. courses to O- and A-level and, except grammar schools, C.S.E. and other qualifications)	Notes
Parents' choice EITHER (a) with NO selection	Comprehensive 1,500	Mixed, purpose-built, with wide range of courses at all levels.
OR (b) after selection	Grammar 500	Mixed, or could be single-sex, according to local tradition. They would also serve two more areas, one providing boys' school, the other girls'.
	Secondary Modern 500 / Secondary Modern 500	Could be mixed, with different, practical bias for parents' choice, or single-sex, one with practical bias to suit boys (engineering, etc.), the other girls (commercial, etc.).
OR (c) after selection, for academic high-flyers, Free and Residuary Places	Direct-grant or Voluntary Grammar school with direct-grant status. Boys 500 / Girls 500 (or larger mixed school if locally preferred)	Schools with strong academic tradition and fast academic pace. + 250 boys and 250 girls from two or more other catchment areas.

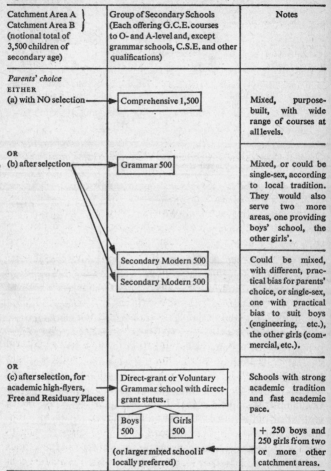

*In scattered rural areas some of these schools would be partly for boarding, terminal or weekly according to need, and might include some places in 'integrated' independent schools.

B. Areas of Comprehensive Experiment

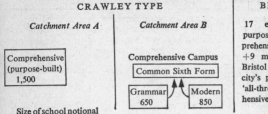

CRAWLEY TYPE		BRISTOL
Catchment Area A	*Catchment Area B*	17 existing zoned purpose – built comprehensives.
Comprehensive (purpose-built) 1,500	Comprehensive Campus	+9 more for inner Bristol to complete the city's provision of 26 'all-through' comprehensives.
Size of school notional	Common Sixth Form / Grammar 650 / Modern 850	

imagination. Nor does it help itself when it dispenses free medical prescriptions with empty-handed generosity regardless of need and postures expensively in an impotent big-power role east of Suez while the Europe that could keep the wolf from the door stands only half-heeded at its doorstep. Post-war British governments of both parties alike have extended a nursemaid's care to citizens long since weaned from poverty, and an exaggerated retrospective conscience about the thirties, anachronistically tender towards an increasingly affluent society, has been at least a contributory cause of the economic crises of the fifties and sixties. Against this background it is perhaps not blasphemous to question the wisdom of universal free secondary education.

Four practical advantages, apart from the larger question of the national interest, would flow from the restoration of some form of fee-paying in state education. First, paradoxically, it could cost some parents less. Dr E. G. West, in his book *Education and the State* [58], quotes some striking figures published by the Central Statistical Office [181]. In a sample survey, cash benefits, in the form of family allowances and pensions and also the estimated money value of state education and the National Health Service, including subsidies given to school meals, welfare foods and housing subsidies for each family, are measured against contributions in income tax, rates, national insurance and also indirect taxation (purchase tax, duties on drink, tobacco, motor vehicles, etc.). Table 9 shows the results for a family with two children in 1962.

Table 9: Family with two Children, 1962

Original Income	Value of benefits received	Amount paid in taxes, etc.	Net gain(+) or loss(—)
£	£	£	£
559 – 676	219	176	+ 43
676 – 816	192	213	– 21
816 – 988	181	249	– 68
988 – 1,196	218	298	– 80
1,196 – 1,448	201	330	– 129
1,448 – 1,752	206	437	– 231
Above £1,752	210	490	– 280

As the most typical income range was £676 – £816 (the average weekly earnings of male manual workers in 1962 amounted to £15 11s.) most families, as Dr West points out, just about break even in their payments and receipts and even the lowest income bracket shown pays £176 to receive £219. If we also bear in mind the administrative cost of these 'free' services it is clear that the Welfare State is something of an illusion, an organization for robbing Peter to pay Paul and, to a considerable extent, merely to pay Peter back again. Perhaps, therefore, there would be little direct saving to the State if services like education were paid for direct rather than distributed 'free' from taxation. But there is a difference. For increased rates and taxes to meet the rising cost of education and other services are regarded as part of the cost of living and often merely spark off wage inflation. But if taxation were reduced and the services paid for direct there might be a stronger incentive to regard their cost as part of a family man's responsibility for which he works harder when they cost more. Indeed there are not a few mothers who go out to work to help meet the fees of independent schools.

The second point is this. It is often argued that in view of the meteoric rise in rates the cost of education should be shifted from rates to taxes, where the burden is more equitably shared and less resented, for 'people pay their taxes in sorrow but their rates in anger'.* But a great deal of the local cost of education is already met by the central government (see page 39) and excessive centralization of finance could threaten local concern with and control of schools. Whether the cost of education is met by County Hall or Whitehall the financial involvement is still remote from the parents, and the risk remains of the Welfare State becoming the Master State. Against this parents have less protection through P.A.Y.E. or rate demand than through their personal cheque-book.

The third advantage of some form of fee-paying is more positive. We have already referred to the gambling instinct of the British people and suggested how it might be canalized, for some parents, into a more vigorous interest in education. People care more about what they pay for directly, or 'invest in'. Those who 'invest in' the Football Pools – and £61 million was 'invested' last year with one promoter alone – show deep and obvious concern in the 'dividends'. The same could be true if they 'invested in' their children's education instead of receiving it 'free' from rates and taxes. A local grammar school headmaster confessed to me that he envied the way parents who already pay fees in independent schools willingly subscribe further when there are appeal funds while parents with children in maintained schools often resent even giving a book or two to the school library because they expect everything to be free. The charging of modest fees in maintained schools could well be beneficial here and help to stimulate, in the apathetic, an interest in what touched their pockets directly. Even an inattentive pupil, given the task of working out as a fraction of terminal fees the cost in hard cash of a wasted lesson, can sometimes be surprised into a determination to have his money's worth. Mr Crosland met a recent demand for higher teacher's salaries and more money for education generally by a counter-demand that the teachers themselves should galvanize the general public into greater interest in educational

*The urgent need to reform rates, called not unfairly 'extraction without anaesthetic', was scarcely helped by the last Conservative Government's device of revaluation. Though it avoided the bad impression given by rates in excess of 20s. in the £, it was one of the more cynical applications of the French adage *Reculer pour mieux sauter*.

matters. This could be done overnight if the next rise in teachers' salaries came from the parents' own pockets.

Finally the return of fees would have a beneficial effect on teachers and educational administrators. The Italian poet Alfieri was once reproached because having attacked tyranny he then attacked the French Revolutionaries. He replied that he was being perfectly consistent, for first he had attacked the big tyrants and then the little ones. We have referred already to what has been called (page 215) the Poor Law attitude to education of some local authorities, and the caption to an article in *Where?* tells the same story: 'Are parents a nuisance? You might think so if you read some of the material local authorities send out to parents. How rarely parents find themselves regarded as equal partners in the educational process!' [187]. Readers may recall, by way of contrast, the headmistress of a direct-grant school who thanked the parents for letting the school share their children (see page 215). The same is true, to some extent, of teachers. As a housemaster in an independent school it is my duty from time to time to interview parents about boys in my house; the realization at the back of my mind that these parents are customers, who are paying for education is, I am sure, good for me. Of course it is unfair to generalize, but there must be a temptation to some teachers in the maintained system to regard themselves as donors of state educational bounty, for the concept of parent as pay-master through rates and taxes is too nebulous to have much impact. There is a Chinese proverb which says: 'When I came close to him, I found he was my brother.' The parent as ratepayer and taxpayer is remote enough to be regarded with comparative indifference, though good teachers and administrators make the effort to overcome it; the man who pays your salary cheque, be you teacher or administrator, whether you regard him as customer or brother, comes close enough to help you to care.

These advantages of the return of some form of fee paying are offset by formidable difficulties in the mechanics of it, and many mistakes of pre-1944 days to be avoided. Fees would have to be charged in all secondary schools to avoid the suggestion that some schools were better than others. They would be partial and sub-sidized, and there would be generous provision for need. This could be done by reduction or remission according to parents' income much as occurs now with the Residuary Places at direct-grant schools. This raises the vexed question of a 'means test', and anything of the kind still provokes unpleasant memories from the thirties, as the last general election campaign showed when the cry 'means-test state' against one's opponents proved a sure vote-winner. Yet all that is needed is some form of cert-ificate supplied confidentially from the local Tax Office, who have to know the facts anyway.* An exaggerated conspiracy of silence about one's earnings has always seemed strange to me, and can be a bar to social progress as well as a cause of dis-harmony and even disaster between husband and wife. Assistance in meeting fees might be given by increased family allowances or child allowances against income tax. But the important thing, if the advantages explained above are to be secured, is that the parent should pay directly at least part of the cost of the child's education, and be seen to do so by teachers, educational ad-ministrators and all concerned.

The real dilemma about fee-paying is this. On the one hand an element of compulsion is essential if we are to avoid what seems to be a Bow Group fallacy, reflected to some extent in Dr West's argument, that when a social class achieves the larger income previously possessed only by a different class it will automatically assume the values and priorities of that class as well. More pre-cisely, in educational terms, it is fallacious to assume that those whose rising incomes now permit them to pay school fees will not spend their money on something else instead. And this applies with even greater force to education beyond the statutory school

---

*The answer to this problem could lie with a computer. This, the Automatic Unit for National Taxation and Insurance, or 'Auntie' for short, is described by Mrs Hilary Sewell in a Conservative Political Centre pamphlet (1966). It is estimated that a feasibility study would cost a mere (in these matters) £250,000, and if successful the computer would carry out for an outlay of between £20 and £30 million, work which at present costs the Ministries of Social Security and Health and the Inland Revenue at least £200 million a year and requires some 120,000 civil servants. If its impersonality could also cure the British means-test neurosis, which even thwarts the benign purpose of the Ministry of Social Security, 'Auntie' might well perform a national service far greater than 'Ernie'.

leaving age. If fee-paying were restored, compulsion would be necessary for some parents to ensure that children were educated up to the school leaving age, and strong pressure, with the extension of maintenance grants, would be required to secure any staying on at school beyond it. The Gilbertian picture in *The Rise of the Meritocracy* [54] of a grammar school weekly pay day, with a 'learning wage on a sliding scale 60 per cent above industrial earnings' shows here, as in so much else, the satirical shrewdness of that book. Yet once compulsion is introduced much of the feeling of personal involvement and 'gambling dynamic' we have sought to transfer to education evaporates. Order a man to back a horse, and three quarters of the fun of it has gone. It could well be the same if you ordered him to back his child. I believe something would be gained by the enforced payment being direct to the school rather than disappearing less identifiably 'down the drain' in rates and taxes, but would this be enough? Yet the prospect, as things are, of the rise in legitimate educational costs pushing up rates and taxes to the point of revolt, or alternatively pushing them up only as far as discretion dares and thereby having both marginal resentment and an inefficient and inadequate educational service, is even less pleasant to contemplate. It is this which makes it worthwhile, side-issue though it is to the main theme of this book, to take a fresh look at the question of school fees – a question too easily dismissed these days as having been finally and irrevocably settled in 1944.

Even if the difficulties in the reintroduction of some form of fee-paying proved insuperable there is a much stronger case for the withdrawal, or scaling-down of some of the more questionable fringe benefits of state education, except in cases of established need. The expenditure on free milk and school meal subsidies while university spending has been cut back has already been criticized by Sir Edward Boyle in a plea to 'get our posteriorities right'. One wonders, too, whether free travel is necessary on the present scale. There are two other apparent extravagances. First, even if we regard the free preparation of a pupil for examinations as part of the State's educational responsibility, need the examination fees themselves be met by ratepayer or taxpayer, again except in cases of proven need? Local authorities vary in their policy here. Some do not pay the fees except for candidates whose prospect of success is certified by the school; nor do they meet the fees when a pupil enters for more than one Examining Board to improve his chances. Even so, long experience as a G.C.E. examiner leaves me far from happy as a ratepayer. Untidiness, illegibility and marginal literacy in some of the candidates in whom the ratepayer 'invests' are irritating enough. Others who see in an examination the anonymity of the confessional or regard the examiner as a fit target for abuse are perhaps part of the hazards of the profession. But the last straw is the candidate who wastes ratepayers' money with ostentatious satisfaction, like the one who was required to take four subjects in order to get extra time for revision of his History, about which he really cared. So there he was wasting ratepayers' money (he quoted the exact amount) taking Russian, Additional Maths and Latin, about which he knew nothing (and how right he was about the Latin!) just to secure extra revision time for History. There is surely a case for the parent rather than the ratepayer footing this sort of bill. Secondly there is the cost of books, furniture and equipment of various kinds. When these are damaged, sometimes wantonly, it would seem fair that the cost should fall on the culprit rather than the public. But one informant in a maintained school told me that when he tried to do this he was met with every kind of difficulty, even the introduction of a psychologist, and in the end found it easier to concede that the pupil was 'accident prone' and let the ratepayer pay. This sort of thing, multiplied over the country, not only increases the national bill for education but also encourages the practice of wrecking a railway carriage or telephone kiosk 'for a giggle'.

Much of this chapter is controversial, and even propositions that gain acceptance involve difficulties formidable enough to excuse inaction. But while politicians pontificate about priorities and time-scales and organization it is well to remember that education has a good deal in common with the housekeeping of an ordinary family – a matter of making choices and paying for them and sometimes saying, quite simply, 'we cannot afford it'.

CHAPTER EIGHT

PROSPECTS

THE role of prophet is always invidious, and especially after the last chapter which unashamedly argues a case. It is so easy to give the impression of propagating what ought to be by the menace of what will be. Prophecy is therefore better left to others, and it so happens that two prophets with superlative credentials have spoken.

In the Introduction I suggested that the best person to survey the contemporary scene in secondary education would be one of Her Majesty's Inspectors of Schools, were it not that, in their official position, their lips are sealed. Even after retirement, when they can speak more freely, the habit of discretion usually inhibits them from rushing madly into print. When, therefore, the latest Senior Chief Inspector of Schools to retire speaks publicly and unequivocally about the consequences of secondary reorganization, knowledge that has overcome the habit of official silence commands attention:

On ideological grounds, I would say no more than this: that if Circular 10/65 had claimed that in the interests of social justice the most highly qualified and experienced teachers ought to be shared equally amongst all secondary school pupils of all grades of intelligence, regardless of a predictable steep fall in the attainment of those going on to higher education, I could have accepted the argument as logical. I would not have agreed with the premise – I think social justice is a much more drastic, expensive and radical matter than this. And I would have deplored, as I think all would and will, the fall in standards as they occur. The argument would, however, have made consistent doctrine. But the circular and the arguments with which it has been publicly supported want it both ways. They want social justice of a limited and questionable kind, but will not concede that a price must be paid. Indeed Humpty Dumpty has been invoked to have us believe that such will be the release of talent from the 'underprivileged' that the dispersal of highly qualified teachers, already in short supply, over an impossibly wide area of assorted levels of work, will leave standards as they are, or actually improve them. * I can find no argument in nature, experience, or logic that lends any support to this extraordinary claim. It has taken other countries at least two or three generations of comprehensive or multilateral education to reach pre-college standards that are still, on those other countries' own admission, at least a year below ours. And such countries have, mostly, four or five year college courses and a larger superstructure of post-graduate education than we have, with which to redress the balance [183].

The message here is the message of this book. Comprehensive reorganization, which claims to further social justice without sacrifice of academic standards, is not radical enough to achieve the former – indeed it is doubtful if any educational reform ever could, for systems of education are rather a reflection of social conditions than an instrument to reshape them – but too radical not to upset the latter.

But our second prophet takes the different view that it will never happen. The author of *The Rise of the Meritocracy* [54] forecasts the rejection of the comprehensive school by the Labour Government for reasons that carry conviction. The book purports to have been written in A.D. 2033, and starting from the formula 'Intelligence and effort together make up merit $(I + E = M)$' tells of the growth of a society ruled by meritocrats much as Plato's Republic was to be ruled by philosopher kings. It has been much praised as a satirical essay, and it is easy for those who do not like its message to describe it as a 'nightmare of the future' [1] or deprecate those 'dreaded meritocrats' [4] and then dismiss it as a literary *jeu d'esprit* which could never happen. But I believe the author deserves the compliment of being taken much more seriously. His description of the socialist volte-face on the comprehensives, which I have reluctantly compressed for lack of space, has the plausibility of historical hindsight:

'Had there been nothing to the [comprehensivist] movement except wishy-washy idealism, then of course it would have evaporated harmlessly in a hundred summer schools. As it was, the leaders actually had

*For a similar view of the effects of dispersing highly-qualified teachers, also by a recently retired member of Her Majesty's Inspectorate, see David Ayerst, *Understanding Schools*, Penguin Books, 1967, p. 234.

followers. The idealists were backed by the discontented, people who had suffered from the judgement of educational selection, and were just intelligent enough to be able to focus their resentment on some limited grievance, the streaming of infant schools, the eleven plus exam, the smaller classes in grammar schools, or whatever it might happen to be. They were backed by parents whose children were allotted, in all fairness in everyone's eyes except their own, to secondary modern schools; and by frustrated adults who blamed their own schooling for later disappointments, and wanted to deprive others too of the chances which they felt they themselves had missed. It was a motley band, yet as always when intellectual idealism chimes with lumpen frustration, it was formidable . . . .

Opposition from parents, teachers, and children – from the whole grammar stream of society – was the main reason for the failure of the comprehensive schools. These were not conceived as an entirely new kind of school – when it came to detailed planning the American model was fortunately forgotten. Their advocates realized well enough that some children were brighter than others. Yet at the same time they wanted children of grammar-school ability to walk beside their inferiors in a deceit of equality. For the full success of their plans they needed to combine grammar schools with secondary modern. About the latter there was no problem; their status could only be raised by unification. Grammar schools were in a quite different state: they had nothing to gain, and almost everything to lose, by the change. This hard fact daunted the most resolute of Labour Education Committees, and some of them were certainly determined. But they were up against grammar-school masters who knew that Labour aspirations were simply impractical, and, to the country's undying credit, this has usually been sufficient to condemn anything. . . .

Once general opinion, even in the Labour Party, turned against comprehensive schools, it became possible to concentrate upon the most fundamental of reforms, that is, upon the all-round improvement of grammar schools. . . . From the moment that Sir Anthony Crosland [sic] was persuaded that the battle for national survival would be won or lost in the 'A' streams all the way from nursery to grammar school, the money began to flow [54].

It will of course be protested that such a reversal of Government educational policy could never happen. But a revolt of parents, teachers and children is a daunting prospect to a Government sensitive to public opinion and a Prime Minister for whom the political correspondent of the *New Statesman* [184] coined, though never quite used, the title Gannex Macchiavelli, would have little difficulty in seeing it through. Nor need we necessarily assume that a meritocracy would be an unmitigated disaster. It is interesting to ask why, after its Rise, the meritocracy suffered a Decline and Fall; and though the book itself makes some suggestions. I believe an important reason is overlooked. The meritocrats, in their educational reforms, quite rightly saw that the private schools (what we should call the 'public schools') gave 'too much attention to Athens and too little to the atom' and 'overvalued the past, Rome and Athens as well as their own history'. But in 'replacing Gibbon by Galton' they threw away not only the past but its lessons as well. The baby went out with the bath-water. Education of the future, even where it discards Greek and Latin, can still learn, perhaps from the Penguin Classics, lessons writ plainly in Homer, Aeschylus and Herodotus, and in particular the dangers of arrogance and the value of humility. The man of whose execution Pontius Pilate washed his hands taught his disciples to wash each others' feet. It is here that the movement of voluntary social service – it is not extravagant to call it a revolution as it sweeps through schools from the secondary moderns of Manchester to Friends Anonymous of Harvey Grammar School Folkestone, Sevenoaks, Merchant Taylors' and Eton – offers the brightest hope for the future. Arrogance that stands on soap-boxes to declaim can be humiliated, in the best sense, by learning to chop them up as firewood for old-age pensioners, and the 'élitist' education that studies Plato in the original can be cut down to size by a day devoted to cleaning up the back-street home of a solitary widow returning from hospital or using expensively acquired musical talents to provide a concert in a school for the blind. And the taunt that this is charity misses the mark when what is given is not easily afforded money but something more costly to rich and poor alike : time.

The weakness of the case for unadulterated meritocracy is not, then, that it involves an embarrassing reversal of policy for the Government, nor that it need sow the seeds of its own destruction through its arrogance. Rather is it that it involves a return to naked tripartitism in secondary education, a putting back of the clock from 1965 to 1945. This would be to reject out of hand the comprehensive experiment, and it deserves a better fate. Twice since the war a radical government has sought to impose a system of secondary education on the British people and each time it has been mistaken. Governments, in this respect, reflect the disease of so much recent educational thinking, that of lurching between extremes. Because selection at 11-plus makes mistakes, we must get rid of the 11-plus. Because the classics dominated secondary education for too long, they must be banished from the curriculum altogether. Because grammar schools are selective and class-orientated, grammar schools must be abolished. Because some secondary modern schools are bad, all secondary modern schools must go. Because independent schools are not all they should be, they must lose their independence. Above all, because selective schools are unsatisfactory, they must be replaced by the still insufficiently tested comprehensives. Yet both have their faults. If selection is too narrowly educational a solution, comprehension overstresses social engineering. The former invites meritocracy, the latter mediocrity, and so on. It is tempting to look for some Aristotelian solution in a mean between extremes – to steer, as it were, a middle course between the Scylla of selection and the Charybdis of comprehension. But this is an over-simplification that merely dazzles by its rhetoric. For some children selection is no Scylla but their salvation, for others the comprehensive is best. We are forced back on the question posed in the last chapter – Who is to choose? Twice in twenty years the government has claimed to make that choice, and got it wrong. There is a case for salvaging or completing the essential machinery for both systems and this time letting the parents choose. Who knows? This time *they* may get it right, and for the quite surprisingly simple reason that it is *they* who have chosen.

APPENDIX 1

AN AMERICAN VIEW OF
THE COMPREHENSIVE DEBATE*

THE COMPREHENSIVE FALLACY
BY JAMES D. KOERNER

Dr Koerner, formerly of the Massachusetts Institute of Technology, has been studying the educational system of Britain for the American Council for Basic Education.

FOR the past 18 months I have had the enviable job of travelling around the United Kingdom visiting all kinds of educational institutions and talking with many hundreds of people in and out of the education service. My purpose has been to look for ideas that we can use in America, but inevitably I have been caught up in the controversies that fill the educational air – especially the whole tormented question of the comprehensive school.

Frankly, I have been disheartened at your failure, if I may address my readers with a collective 'you', to look abroad to see what might be learned from other people about comprehensive schools.

The United States has probably had more experience with such schools than any nation in the world, and you could do a lot worse than make a detailed study of that experience. If you did, you might then reconsider your decision to 'go comprehensive', or at the very least you might avoid some of our mistakes.

Faith and doctrine have badly out-stripped knowledge in your present policies. Looking at English education in the light of American experience, I would say that you are going to pay a stiff price for changing your present system to one that is wholly comprehensive.

The main problem is that you expect so much of something called a comprehensive school. You expect it somehow to correct all of the deficiencies that you have for years refused to correct in the present system.

*Reprinted, by kind permission, from the *Daily Telegraph*, 26 February 1966.

APPENDIX 1

SWEEPING CLAIMS

The comprehensive school will rescue, you say, those children who would otherwise have been misjudged at 11-plus; it will make for fluid movement within and among streams; it will equalise and extend educational opportunity for all children; it will allow good students to move ahead as well as they would in a grammar school and at the same time encourage the less able by their example; it will develop everybody's capacity for intelligence and make the most of Britain's 'pool of ability'; it will allow economies in buildings and equipment; it will make the services of the best teachers available to all instead of to a narrow band of top students. Most of all, it will overcome social barriers and snobbery and inequality, and put an end to the social divisiveness of the present system.

But the comprehensive school, I regret to say will not necessarily do any of these things, certainly will not do all of them and probably can never do some of them. Moreover, none of them really has much to do with how schools are organised and administered. Most of the things that need doing in British education *could* be done through the existing school system. For example, the mistakes inevitably made at 11-plus, which you should long ago have done something about, could be corrected just as well, perhaps better, in the present system as in a comprehensive one, if you would bend yourselves to the task.

The pool of ability could be plumbed just as deeply, perhaps more so, in separate as in comprehensive schools, if that is what you want to do. The 'Newsom children' could be educated just as well, perhaps better, in secondary modern as in comprehensive schools, especially if a number of your educationists, sociologists and politicians would stop telling the modern schools how awful they are and get busy trying to make all of them as good as the best of them.

All this, however, is unrelated to what I take to be the main reason for going comprehensive. Whatever the educational arguments, it is clear to me after listening to the discussion for 18 months that the idea of social equality is what the fighting is mostly about. In my view this is the weakest and least tenable ground on which to base the comprehensive movement in Britain, for two reasons.

First, comprehensive schools, because they are comprehensive, serve relatively small catchment areas precisely in those parts of the country where problems of inequality are greatest – in and around cities. Here the comprehensive school becomes indeed a neighbourhood school. This obviously means that the quality of a given school is often dictated by housing patterns. And housing patterns are becoming more, not less, homogeneous with middle-class parents fleeing the cities to the desirable suburbs and lower-class families concentrating more than ever in undesirable areas of cities.

The result, as can be seen in a thousand cities of America, is socially homogeneous schools that are called comprehensive. They can be very impressive in, say, an affluent Chicago suburb that may spend £500 a year on each child, and they can be appalling 15 miles away in a down-town slum.

The social effect of such schools is to reinforce rather than combat class consciousness.

One can debate the causes and cures for this condition, but the immediate point is that neighbourliness between classes is not a function of the comprehensive school where neighbourhoods are themselves homogeneous.

Second, it is very doubtful that schools, no matter how they are organised or what the housing patterns are, can create such a thing as social equality. They can strengthen it, but only if the driving force comes first from the community at large, as it has in the United States. To be sure, there is a wide gap between the theory of American society and the practices we all know about; but equality is still a major characteristic of American life.

THE SOCIAL PATTERN

The egalitarian impulse of American society, its dislike of artificial barriers and unearned privileges, gave rise to the kind of schools that would reinforce these same convictions. But it probably does not work the other way around. If there is no real consensus in British society in support of the equality of classes, you can hardly expect organisations so closely related to homes as are schools to do the job. People, not institutions, decide what a community will be.

All this does not argue against comprehensive schools. I am myself a graduate of a quite typical comprehensive school in a quite typical city of the American Middle West, and my instincts are with this kind of school. Although we still have serious problems to solve in our comprehensive schools, I would oppose any movement to reorganise our educational system in some other way. I am sure we must solve our problems without the cataclysmic effects of converting to a different system.

But our situation is not yours. For Britain I would argue against what I can only call the ill-considered, head-long rush into a monolithic system of comprehensive schools that is now being encouraged, indeed commanded, by the Government.

There is a strong case to be made in Britain for maintaining multiplicity'in types of schools, for avoiding massive standardisation, for leaving room for heterodoxy and choice and dissent, even within the State system. And surely there is an even stronger case to be made for the survival of those many schools, both independent and maintained, that have earned over many years a reputation for excellence, some of them the envy of half the world.

By all means have comprehensive schools, and don't wait for research to tell you how to do it – educational research is primitive and eminently unreliable. But why assume that one type of school, one with which you have had little experience, is so superior that it must be made to prevail at all cost throughout the country? Why are you not content to build comprehensive schools (as we did in America) in new towns, or in places where for special financial or geographical reasons they offer clear and concrete advantages, or in places where existing institutions of established quality do not have to be sacrificed?

TRIUMPH OF DOGMA

Instead you seem perversely bent on dismantling the whole system you have been building these many years. Your comprehensive spokesmen seem to be saying that the wisdom of going completely comprehensive in as short a time as possible is so self-evident and incontestable that no reasonable man can disagree. The certitude of your comprehensive zealots awes me.

The greatest problem of the American comprehensive school has been to escape mediocrity – to avoid having the standards and the ethos of the school established by the average instead of the best. Thus it is both bizarre and tragic to me to see Britain now attacking and threatening to destroy its best schools in the name of comprehension. I was shocked and saddened, for example, by Mr Crosland's recent cannonade against those unique institutions, the direct grant schools.

Academically these schools must be among the best to be found anywhere, and socially they are fully as mixed and democratic as thousands of schools in America. For the English people now, with forethought and deliberation, to set about destroying the flower of their educational system seems to me, if I may put it candidly, sheer masochism. It is the triumph of purblind political dogma over educational common sense.

So I hope Britain will think again and perhaps redirect its welcome sense of urgency in education. If I had time and opportunity to say only one thing to Britain, it would be this: My dear fellow, get your priorities right and stop sweating so much about where snobs and rich men send their sons to school, and where many not so rich and not so snobbish, and even Labour lords, send their sons to school. Stop fighting the best of your maintained schools. Stop shooting at the direct grant schools. Stop quarrelling with educational excellence as though it were a reprehensible thing or simply because everybody can't have it.

In short, take the revolver from your own head and save yourself for the greatest of all the educational problems that confront you: *How to get and keep first-rate teachers, in decent classrooms, with classes of reasonable size – throughout the country – for the extended schooling of all children.* This is the supreme problem of English education for a long time in the future, no matter how you organise secondary schools.

APPENDIX 2

THE 11–PLUS EXAMINATION*

THE TESTS

Many of the standardized tests used by local authorities are supplied either by the National Foundation for Educational Research in London or by Moray House College of Education at Edinburgh. The tests are secret and actual examples of them may not be given. The following will give an idea of the kind of tests used in English, arithmetic, and verbal reasoning. The children are given half- or three-quarters of an hour for each paper, which may contain 50 or 100 short questions.

English

1–3 One word in each sentence below is left unfinished. Write this word in full in the bracket at the side, taking care to spell it carefully.

    1. A person who can't hear is d——   (........)

    2. Windsor C—— is the home of the Queen (........)

    3. Mary took her raincoat in c—— it rained (........)

4–9 In each line below a sentence has been started for you. Write some more words to finish each sentence. The first one has been done for you.

    4. Although he disliked *running, he entered every race.*

    5. Because of ....

    6. Since hearing from ....

    7. Crying with ....

    8. To the astonishment of ....

    9. After waiting for more than ....

10–15 Put the necessary punctuation marks in the sentence below. Mark the word which should begin with capital letters like this – friday

    In each case the marks will be one of these , . " " ?

    Where is john that naughty boy demanded the teacher

16–17 Change these sentences to the past, by writing ONE word in each empty space.

    16. Today I sing in my bath because I feel happy.

        Yesterday I ...... in my bath because I ...... happy.

*Reprinted from Tyrrell Burgess, *A Guide to English Schools*, Penguin Books, 1964, with the author's and publishers' kind permission.

17. Later on I shall go out and spend my pocket money.
   Earlier today I ...... out and ...... my pocket money.

18–25 Read through this passage and answer the questions below.

A year ago, a large red-faced farmer went to Shrewsbury market on his old grey mare. Behind him rode his comely daughter. As they approached a crossroads a large black raven who had concealed himself in the foliage of a tree suddenly cried 'Croak!' The aged mare was so terrified that she fell down and broke her leg, and the farmer was thrown to the ground and struck his head on a stone. The raven flew off, quite content with the trouble he had caused.

In Numbers 18 to 25 underline the one correct answer in brackets.

18. This story is about
   (Shrewsbury/a wicked raven/a journey/birds/mares).
19. The farmer was
   (rich/old/big/frightened/lost).
20. The raven was
   (invisible/mischievous/noisy/helpful/walking).
21. The raven hid
   (behind a bush/by the roadside/all the time/among the leaves of a tree/with a friend).
22. All this happened
   (today/yesterday/some years ago/twelve months ago/never).
23. Write one word from the passage which means 'beautiful'.
24. Write one word from the passage which means 'very frightened'.
25. Write one word from the passage which means 'satisfied'.

Arithmetic

1. Add
   28
   15
   36
   —

2. Subtract
   £ s d
   15 0 5
    8 3 6

3. Multiply
   Yds ft ins
   74   3 6
            5

4. Divide
   Stones lbs ozs
   9) 29   9   2

5. Take 19 from 37 and divide the answer by 6.
6. Write in figures two thousand and twelve.
7. If oranges are 3 for 10d., how many oranges shall I get for 3s. 4d.?

8. Our family uses 16 pints of milk a week. How many *gallons* do we use in a year?
9. In which of the following numbers does 7 represent the largest quantity?   675   487   1578   710
10. If there are 1760 yds to a mile, how many *feet* are there in a quarter of a mile?

Verbal Reasoning

1. Underline the right answer in the brackets.
   In is to out as up is to (top/bottom/down/through/hole)
2. Underline the TWO words which mean something different from the rest.
   daisy/weed/chrysanthemum/flower/tulip/daffodil
3. Write ONE letter in the brackets to finish the first word and start the last.
   REN(..)FA
4. Fill in the missing number below.
   36, 27, (..), 9.
5. If 29384791 means STRENGTH, what does 184 mean?
6. Underline the TWO words in the brackets which ALWAYS go with the word outside:
   TREE (park/leaves/birds/bushes/branches)
7. Underline the TWO words which must change places to make this sentence sensible:
   The cows milks the farmer
8. Write TWO letters in the brackets to continue the series:
   A Z Y A X W A V U (..) (..)
9. Write a word in the empty brackets so that the three things on the right go together like the three things on the left:
   girl (two) feet :: horse (......) hooves
10. Underline TWO words, one from each bracket, that mean most nearly the OPPOSITE of each other
    (leave, run, start) (walk, finish, go)

REFERENCES

1. Anthony Sampson, *Anatomy of Britain Today*, Hodder & Stoughton, 1965.
2. David Thomson, *England in the Twentieth Century*, Penguin Books, 1965.
3. Vivian Ogilvie, *The English Public School*, Batsford, 1957.
4. C. A. R. Crosland, *The Conservative Enemy*, Jonathan Cape, 1962.
5. Reported in *The Times Educational Supplement*, March 1965.
6. *Guardian*, May 1965.
7. Foster Watson, *The Old Grammar Schools*, Cambridge University Press, 1916.
8. Tyrrell Burgess, *A Guide to English Schools*, Penguin Books, 1964.
9. John Vaizey, *Britain in the Sixties: Education for Tomorrow*, Penguin Books, 1962, revised edn, 1966.
10. F. W. M. Draper, *Four Centuries of Merchant Taylors' School*, Oxford University Press, 1962 (copyright vested in the Merchant Taylors' Company).
11. Merchant Taylors' School Register compiled by William Dugard (Headmaster 1644–61), now preserved in the Company's Muniment Room at 30 Threadneedle Street, London EC2.
12. Norman Wymer, *Arnold of Rugby*, Robert Hale Ltd, 1953.
13. C. Norwood and A. Hope, *Higher Education for Boys in England*, John Murray, 1909.
14. W. G. Hughes and M. Sweeney, *Watford Grammar Schools for Boys and Girls, 1704–1954*, By order of the Governors of Watford Grammar Schools, 1954.
15. A. D. C. Peterson, *A Hundred Years of Education*, Duckworth, 1952.
16. *Observer*, August 1965.
17. Roy Lewis and Angus Maude, *The English Middle Classes*, Penguin Books, 1953.
18. Sir John Newsom, *The Education of Girls*, Faber, 1948.
19. Sir Winston Churchill, *My Early Life*, Odhams Press, 1934.
20. Bernard Darwin, *The English Public School*, Longmans, Green, 1929
21. Michael Hutchinson and Christopher Young, *Educating the Intelligent*, Penguin Books, 1962.

REFERENCES

22. *15 to 18*, *Report of the Central Advisory Council for Education* (*England*), H.M.S.O., 1959 (the Crowther Report).

23. H. J. Eysenck, *Uses and Abuses of Psychology*, Penguin Books, 1953.

24. *New Statesman*, September 1954.

25. Science Masters' Association and Association of Women Science Teachers' policy statement, *Science and Education*, 1961.

26. *Journal of Education*, March 1953.

27. Oxford University Department of Education, *Arts and Science Sides in the Sixth Form*, 1960.

28. *The Teaching of Russian*, H.M.S.O., 1962 (the Annan Report).

29. e.g. *The Times*, April 1965; *Observer Colour Supplement*, April 1965.

30. R. H. Tawney (ed.), *Secondary Education for All*, published for the Labour Party by George Allen & Unwin (around 1925 – exact date not given).

31. Quoted by W. O. Lester Smith in *Education, An Introductory Survey*, Penguin Books, 1957.

32. Quoted by H. A. Rée in *The Essential Grammar School*, Harrap, 1956.

33. Robin Pedley, *The Comprehensive School*, Penguin Books, 1964.

34. *New Statesman*, September 1965.

35. *The Comprehensives – A Closer Look*, *The Times*, April 1965.

36. Dr Robert Birley, letter in *The Times*, 19 February 1965; *New Statesman*, May 1966.

37. *Spectator*, 4 June 1965.

38. *Observer*, September 1964.

39. *The Times Educational Supplement*, 27 February 1965.

40. *Board of Education Pamphlet 56*, H.M.S.O., 1928.

41. *The Times Educational Supplement*, 3 December 1965, where the L.C.C. Report is quoted in full.

42. *Daily Telegraph*, 3 January 1966.

43. Stewart C. Mason, *The Leicestershire Experiment and Plan*, Council and Education Press Ltd (revised edn, 1964).

44. '*A Look at Leicestershire*' in *The Times Educational Supplement* of 12 February 1965.

45. *Higher Education*, Cmd 2154, H.M.S.O., October 1963 (the Robbins Report).

46. Letter in *The Times Educational Supplement* of 12 March 1965.

47. *The Organisation of Secondary Education*, Circular 10/65, H.M.S.O., 1965.

48. *Vision of a Sixth-Form College*, obtainable free (at time of writing) from the headmaster of Luton Secondary Technical College, Barnfield Avenue, Luton, Bedfordshire.

49. Sir John Newsom, *The Child at School*, Penguin Books, 1950.

50. Speech to the Assistant Masters' Association at Swansea, January 1966, quoted in their journal (*The A.M.A.*) for that month. The figures given above are also his.

51. Angus Wilson, reviewing books on Winchester, Westminster and Manchester Grammar Schools in the *Observer*, November 1965.

52. Kingsley Martin, *Father Figures: A Volume of Autobiography*, Hutchinson, 1966.

53. *New Statesman*, September 1965.

54. Michael Young, *The Rise of the Meritocracy*, Thames & Hudson, 1956, Penguin Books, 1961.

55. Sir Desmond Lee, Introduction to a translation of Plato's *Republic*, Penguin Books, 1955.

56. *Children in Primary Schools*, H.M.S.O., January 1967 (the Plowden Report).

57. *Ford Report*, commissioned by and published with the *Bristol Evening Post* of 22 June 1965.

58. E. G. West, *Education and the State*, Institute of Economic Affairs, 1965.

59. C. A. R. Crosland, *The Future of Socialism*, Jonathan Cape, 1956.

60. *The Times Educational Supplement*, March 1966.

61. *Signposts for the Sixties*, Transport House, 1961.

62. *The Times Educational Supplement*, October 1965.

63. Anthony Lejeune in *The Weekly World*, 10 September 1965.

64. *Putting Britain Right Ahead*, Conservative Central Office, 1965.

65. Quoted in *The Times Educational Supplement*, January 1966.

66. *Observer*, March 1966.

67. e.g. Alan Watkins in the *Spectator*, 25 March 1966, and Robert Blake in the *Illustrated London News*, 26 March 1966.

68. *The Times Educational Supplement*, September 1965.

69. *The Times Educational Supplement*, January 1966.

70. *The Times Educational Supplement*, March 1966.

71. *Daily Telegraph*, February 1965.

72. *Education*, October 1965.

73. *Sunday Times*, November 1965.

74. *Sunday Times*, October 1965.

75. *The Times Educational Supplement*, March 1966.

76. *Daily Telegraph*, February 1966.

77. *Guardian*, November 1965.
78. W. O. Lester Smith, *Government of Education*, Penguin Books, 1965.
79. *Daily Telegraph*, June 1965.
80. Vance Packard, *The Hidden Persuaders*, Penguin Books, 1960.
81. R. H. S. Crossman, *Plato Today*, George Allen & Unwin, 1937 (revised 2nd edn, 1959).
82. Letter in *The Times*, May 1965.
83. Quoted by Sir Arthur Bryant, *Illustrated London News*, March 1966.
84. *The Times Educational Supplement*, June 1965.
85. Letter in *The Times Educational Supplement*, October 1965.
86. *The Times Educational Supplement*, May 1965.
87. *The Times Educational Supplement*, November 1965.
88. *Where?*, September 1965.
89. Statistics published by University of London University Entrance and School Examinations Council, 1959/62/65.
90. Interim Report of the Northwood Grammar Schools Association, January 1966.
91. *Where?*, November 1965.
92. *Observer*, November 1965.
93. *The Times*, January 1965.
94. Quoted by A. D. C. Peterson in *A Hundred Years of Education*, Duckworth, 1952 and cf. Professor Richard Hofstadter, *Anti-Intellectualism in American Life*, Part 5, *Education in a Democracy*, Jonathan Cape 1964.
95. Quoted by Lord Butler in the Noel Buxton Lecture at Essex University, reported in *The Times Educational Supplement*, May 1965.
96. *Daily Telegraph*, May 1965.
97. *The Times Educational Supplement*, November 1965.
98. Jonas Orring, *Comprehensive Schools and Continuation Schools in Sweden*, Stockholm, 1962, and Herman Ruge, *Educational Systems in Scandinavia*, Norwegian Universities Press, 1962.
99. Vance Packard, *The Status Seekers*, Penguin Books, 1961.
100. *The Times Educational Supplement*, January 1966, reviewing Willis Dixon, *Society, Schools and Progress in Scandinavia*, Pergamon Press, 1962.
101. Much of the information here is derived from reliable Swedish sources whose request to remain anonymous must be respected. The official view, of which we hear so much, gives only one

facet of the truth. Compare also 'The Swedish Example' in *The Times Educational Supplement*, May 1966.

102. *Economist*, November 1964.

103. *Observer Colour Supplement*, April 1965.

104. *The Times Educational Supplement*, November 1966.

105. W. O. Lester Smith, *Education*, Penguin Books, 1957.

106. Letter in *The Times Educational Supplement*, December 1965.

107. The McNair Committee Report, *Teachers and Youth Leaders*, H.M.S.O., 1944.

108. *Daily Telegraph*, September 1965.

109. *The Times Educational Supplement*, January 1966.

110. *The Times Educational Supplement*, December 1965.

111. B. Jackson and D. Marsden, *Education and The Working Class*, Routledge & Kegan Paul, 1962, Penguin Books, 1966.

112. Article in *Town and Country Planning* reported in the *Daily Telegraph*, January 1966.

113. J. Tucker, *Honourable Estates*, Victor Gollancz, 1966.

114. David Henschel, 'Ifield Comprehensive Campus', *The Times Educational Supplement*, March 1965.

115. *The Times Educational Supplement*, February 1965.

116. *Sunday Telegraph*, April 1965.

117. *Sunday Times*, March 1966.

118. *The Times Educational Supplement*, January 1965.

119. *The Times Educational Supplement*, November 1965.

120. *Daily Telegraph*, January 1964.

121. *Trends in Education*, H.M.S.O., January 1966.

122. H. J. Eysenck, introduction to *Know Your Own IQ*, Penguin Books, 1962.

123. Liam Hudson, *Intelligence: Convergent and Divergent*, in Penguin Science Survey 1965 B, Penguin Books, 1965. Also *Contrary Imaginations*, Methuen, 1966.

124. H. J. Eysenck, *Sense and Nonsense in Psychology*, Penguin Books, 1957.

125. Nigel Grant, *Soviet Education*, University of London Press, 1965, Penguin Books, 1966.

126. David Henschel, 'Ifield Comprehensive Campus', *The Times Educational Supplement*, March 1965.

127. *Sunday Times*, April 1966.

128. H. A. Rée, *The Essential Grammar School*, Harrap, 1956.

129. Frances Stevens, *The Living Tradition*, Hutchinson, 1961.

130. Cassandra in the *Daily Mirror*, March 1966.

131. *The Times Educational Supplement*, May 1966.

132. *The Times Educational Supplement*, November 1957.

133. *The Times Educational Supplement*, 'No Comment' – exact reference not traced.

134. David Thomson (Master of Sidney Sussex College, Cambridge) in *The Times Educational Supplement*, April 1966.

135. Harry Davies, *Culture and The Grammar School*, Routledge & Kegan Paul, 1965. To this book I owe some of the points made in reply to *Education and The Working Class* in this section.

136. 'By-pass Variegated' in Osbert Lancaster, *Pillar to Post*, John Murray, 1948 edn.

137. John A. T. Robinson, Bishop of Woolwich, *Honest to God*, S.C.M. Paperback, 1963.

138. *Spectator*, May 1966.

139. *New Statesman*, June 1966.

140. *Public Schools Year Book*, 1966, under University College School, Hampstead.

141. Margaret Miles, *And Gladly Teach*, Educational Explorers: My Life and Work Series, 1966.

142. *Sunday Times*, March 1954.

143. *Sunday Times*, March 1957.

144. *Sunday Times Colour Supplement*, July 1965.

145. *The Times Educational Supplement*, May 1959.

146. Quoted in Lewis and Short, *A Latin Dictionary*, Oxford University Press, 1958, under *educare*.

147. Elizabeth Allsopp and David Grugeon, *Direct Grant Grammar Schools*, Fabian Society, 1966.

148. For a full analysis of Press reports and books of this kind see W. Taylor, *The Secondary Modern School*, Faber, 1963.

149. John Partridge, *Middle School*, Gollancz, 1966.

150. Boswell, *Life of Dr Johnson*, Everyman Library, I, 1906.

151. J. S. Mill, *On Liberty*, Fontana edn, 1962.

152. Matthew Arnold, 'Democracy', in *Mixed Essays*, Smith, Elder, 1903.

153. *Choice in Welfare, 1965*, Institute of Economic Affairs, 1965.

154. F. S. Musgrove, *The Family, Education and Society*, Routledge & Kegan Paul, 1966.

155. *The Direct Grant School*, Headmasters' Conference pamphlet, 1964.

156. *Sunday Times Colour Supplement*, April 1966.

157. Letters to *The Times*, 2 and 4 December 1965.

158. Speech to the North of England Education Conference, reported in *The Times Educational Supplement*, January 1966.

REFERENCES

159. J. M. Cobban, Headmaster of Abingdon School, in the *Spectator*, January 1966.
160. *Occidit miseros crambe repetita magistros* in *The Times Educational Supplement*, March 1966.
161. John Morgan in the *Sunday Times*, January 1966.
162. Royston Lambert, *The State and Boarding Education*, Methuen, 1966, and *The Demand for Boarding Education*, published by King's College Research Centre, Cambridge, 1966.
163. C. Northcote Parkinson, *Illustrated London News*, July 1966.
164. A. S. Neill in *The Times Educational Supplement*, June 1966.
165. By the former headmaster of Eton, Dr Robert Birley, who kindly reminded me of this in a recent conversation I had with him.
166. Godfrey Hodgson in the *Sunday Times Colour Supplement*, March 1966.
167. *Daily Telegraph*, July 1965.
168. *Observer*, April 1965.
169 Mervyn Jones in the *New Statesman*, May 1966.
170. At Berkhamsted School, as reported in the *Watford Observer*, June 1966.
171. John Dancy, *The Public Schools and the Future*, Faber, 1963.
172. John Wilson, *Public Schools and Private Practice*, George Allen & Unwin, 1962.
173. *The Times Educational Supplement*, October 1965.
174. Lord Radcliffe in the *Spectator*, May 1966.
175. J. Baker, *Children in Chancery*, Hutchinson, 1964.
176. *The Times Educational Supplement*, July 1966.
177. *The Times Educational Supplement*, July 1966.
178. Answering a question in Parliament, reported in *The Times Educational Supplement*, August 1966.
179. *The Times Educational Supplement*, March 1966.
180. *Shorter Oxford English Dictionary*, Oxford University Press, 1947.
181. *Economic Trends*, February 1964, H.M.S.O., for Central Statistical Office.
182. *Where?*, Summer 1964.
183. *The A.M.A.* (Journal of the Incorporated Association of Assistant Masters), May 1966, reprinted from *The Teachers' World*, April 1966.
184. *New Statesman*, June 1966.

BOOKS FOR FURTHER READING

A. GENERAL

Among the many non-specialist books for parents and others that discuss the grammar school in the wider educational context the following are especially useful: David Ayerst, *Understanding Schools*, Penguin Books, 1967; Walter James, *A Middle-Class Parents' Guide to Education*, Hodder & Stoughton, 1964; W. O. Lester Smith, *Education*, Penguin Books, 1957; G. A. N. Lowndes, *The English Educational System*, Hutchinson, 1960; Tyrrell Burgess, *A Guide to English Schools*, Penguin Books, 1964. The last gives much factual information in a concise form and also provides a valuable, short and on the whole impartial discussion of important educational controversies affecting both primary and secondary education.

B. PARTICULAR ASPECTS

For those who wish to pursue further the historical development of the grammar-school tradition the following cover most aspects of the subject and have bibliographies to guide further research: V. Ogilvie, *The English Public School*, Batsford, 1957; Foster Watson, *The Old Grammar Schools*, Cambridge University Press, 1916; R. L. Archer, *Secondary Education in the Nineteenth Century*, Cambridge University Press, 1921; H. C. Barnard, *A Short History of English Education 1760 – 1944*, University of London Press, 1947; A. D. C. Peterson, *A Hundred Years of Education*, Duckworth, 1952. The last is of particular interest for those who wish to compare developments in British education with those in the rest of Europe.

The best popular book on the comprehensive schools, despite its partisan intensity and political bias, is still Robin Pedley, *The Comprehensive School*, Penguin Books, 1964. Also of interest, though somewhat subject to the same limitations, is the symposium by several heads of comprehensive schools, *Inside the Comprehensive School*, Schoolmaster Publishing Co. Ltd, 1958. As a corrective the following, though more limited in scope, provide much useful information and a more objective approach: *The Comprehensives – A Closer Look*, *The Times*, April 1965; The Incorporated Association of Assistant Masters Second Report, *Teaching In Comprehensive Schools*, Cambridge University Press, 1967. Though there are dangers in pressing comparisons with other countries too far, R. Hofstadter, *Anti-Intellectualism in American Life* (Part 5 – *Education in a Democracy*), Jonathan Cape, 1964, is well worth reading for his detailed study of the slow deterioration of the American high school as the ultimate logic of comprehensiveness was applied to it. An interesting, if somewhat idealized recent study of Scandinavian comprehensives appears in Willis Dixon, *Society, Schools and Progress in Scandinavia*, Pergamon Press, 1966.

For fuller consideration of the impact of politics on education, the educational creed of Mr C. A. R. Crosland is set forth in the appropriate chapters of *The Future of Socialism*, Jonathan Cape, 1956, and *The Conservative Enemy*, Jonathan Cape, 1962. The Labour Party line on education is also expounded in F. T. Willey, *Education Today and Tomorrow*, Michael Joseph, 1964. There is a notable lack of a similar statement in depth of Conservative educational philosophy (though Bow Group pamphlets flutter disconcertingly on the surface from time to time) which somebody, perhaps Sir Edward Boyle, might be persuaded to fill. Other information on politics in education at national and local level is fragmented over countless manifestos and journals and not easily assimilated. But the *Ford Report* of the *Bristol Evening Post* of 22 June 1965 on the Bristol comprehensives is well worth reading and a shining example of how local journalism at its best deserves national stature.

An important facet of the grammar-school case is the problem of selection, intelligence and the tantalizing 'nature–nurture' controversy. The naturist emphasis is well presented, in eminently readable form, in Professor H. J. Eysenck's Pelican books, in particular the introduction to *Know Your Own I.Q.*, Penguin Books, 1962, and the relevant chapters of *Uses and Abuses of Psychology*, Penguin Books, 1953, and *Sense and Nonsense in Psychology*, Penguin Books, 1957. The nurturist view appears in J. W. B. Douglas, *The Home and the School*, Macgibbon & Kee, 1964; J. Floud, A. H. Halsey and F. M. Martin, *Social Class and Educational Opportunity*, Heinemann, 1956; and P. E. Vernon, *Secondary School Selection*, Methuen, 1957. Other aspects of grammar school education are discussed at greater length and from various points of view in H. A. Rée, *The Essential Grammar School*, Harrap, 1956; F. Stevens, *The Living Tradition*, Hutchinson, 1961; H. Davies, *Culture and the Grammar School*, Routledge & Kegan Paul, 1965; B. Jackson and D. Marsden, *Education and the Working Class*, Routledge & Kegan Paul, 1962, Penguin Books, 1966; M. Hutchinson and C. Young, *Educating the Intelligent*, Penguin Books, 1962.

Apart from histories of individual schools there is, as far as I know, no book dealing specifically with the direct-grant grammar schools, but the following pamphlets are both stimulating and diametrically opposed and between them provide most of the evidence for an objective judgement: Headmasters' Conference pamphlet, *The Direct Grant School*, 1964; Elizabeth Allsopp and David Grugeon, *Direct Grant Grammar Schools*, Fabian Research Series 256, 1966. Of books on the independent grammar schools or 'public schools', however, there is an *embarras de richesse*. The most useful and up-to-date are A. N. Gilkes, *In Defence of Independent Education*, Gollancz, 1957, which achieves its declared purpose in a well-reasoned and persuasive manner, and J. Dancy, *The Public Schools and the Future*, Faber, 1963, and J. Wilson, *Public Schools and Private Practice*, George Allen & Unwin, both of which offer some solutions to the problem of 'integration'. The question of boarding education is admirably discussed and analysed in Dr Royston Lambert's *The State and Boarding Education*, Methuen, 1966, and *The Demand for Boarding Education*, King's College Research Centre, Cambridge, 1966. As a mine of factual information on the 'public schools', impartially presented, Graham Kalton's *The Public Schools*, Longmans, 1966, is indispensable. The allied topics of parents' choice and fee-paying are stimulatingly discussed, with interesting documentary evidence and a full bibliography, in Dr E. G. West's *Education and the State*, Institute of Economic Affairs, 1965.

C. OFFICIAL PUBLICATIONS

The philosophy behind the tripartite organization of secondary education is set forth in the Report of the Consultative Committee *Secondary Education* (The Spens Report), H.M.S.O., 1938. The most important Reports of the Central Advisory Council for Education (England) dealing with secondary education are *Early Leaving*, H.M.S.O., 1954, *15 to 18* (The Crowther Report), H.M.S.O., 1959, and *Half Our Future* (The Newsom Report), H.M.S.O., 1963. Also relevant in their respective concern with what takes place at the pre-and post-secondary stage are *Children and Their Primary Schools* (The Plowden Report), H.M.S.O., 1967, and *Higher Education* (The Robbins Report), H.M.S.O., 1963. Tentative and so far largely abortive proposals for a measure of 'integration' of the 'public schools' appear in *The Public Schools and the General Educational System* (The Fleming Report), H.M.S.O., 1944. On educational matters generally a vast amount of information is available in the Annual Reports and Statistics of the Department of Education and Science, also published by H.M.S.O.

Many interesting facts and opinions on the London comprehensive schools appear in the Inner London Education Authority Report, *London Comprehensive Schools*, 1966, but its conclusions should be treated with some reserve. A well-timed appearance shortly before the

Greater London Council Elections of 1966 arouses suspicions which, at least in the matter of G.C.E. results, adroitly selective statistics tend to confirm.

D.

Finally, in a class by itself and strongly recommended to anyone interested in the future of secondary education, Michael Young, *The Rise of the Meritocracy*, Thames & Hudson, 1956, Penguin Books, 1961.

INDEX

INDEX